Volume 25

No.
3. Representative American Speeches: 1952-1953. A. C. Baird. $1.75.

Volume 24

No.
1. Political Ethics and the Voter. T. A. Rousse. $1.75.

3. Representative American Speeches: 1951-1952. A. C. Baird. $1.75.

No.
6. Latin America in the Cold War. W. M. Daniels. $1.75.

Volume 23

No.
2. Representative American Speeches: 1950-1951. A. C. Baird. $1.75

Volume 22

No.
3. Representative American Speeches: 1949-1950. A. C. Baird. $1.75.

Volume 20

No.
5. Federal World Government. J. E. Johnsen. $1.50.

Volume 18

No.
3. Representative American Speeches: 1944-1945. A. C. Baird. $1.25.

No.
6. Palestine: Jewish Homeland? J. E. Johnsen. $1.25.

THE REFERENCE SHELF

Vol. 30   No. 3

THE AMERICAN LABOR MOVEMENT

Edited by
WALTER M. DANIELS

THE H. W. WILSON COMPANY
NEW YORK   1958

19205

PREFACE

This volume discusses the American labor movement, with special emphasis on recent trends. It opens with a section on the 170-odd-year history of American labor's organizing efforts and struggle for recognition. The second section depicts labor's position today, after the merging of the American Federation of Labor and the Congress of Industrial Organizations into the first unified group ever to speak unchallenged for the vast majority of the nation's 18 million organized workers.

In the third section are discussed the problems posed by labor's activities and objectives in our economic and political society. Next the provisions of the National Labor Relations Act of 1947 (Taft-Hartley) and its application are discussed by labor, management, and government spokesmen.

The section on "right-to-work" laws, as they are called by their sponsors, offers a variety of opinions on this key controversy. The topic is discussed on one side as "compulsory unionism" and on the other side as "union security," or as "right-to-work" and "right-to-wreck" laws.

The book concludes with a section on violence and corruption in unions and on their internal democracy, what is being done about these problems, and what it is suggested may or should be done.

The compiler expresses appreciation to the writers and speakers who have consented to be quoted and to the publications in which these materials were originally published for permission to reprint them.

WALTER M. DANIELS

March 1958

A NOTE TO THE READER

For an earlier account of the labor movement with much useful information on the internal organization of labor unions, the reader is referred to *American Labor Unions: Organization, Aims, Power,* by Herbert L. Marx, Jr. (Volume 21, Number 5 of The Reference Shelf).

Further details on the issue of the Guaranteed Annual Wage, briefly discussed in Section III of this volume, are to be found in Section III of *Social Welfare in the United States,* by Poyntz Tyler (Volume 27, Number 2 of The Reference Shelf).

CONTENTS

III. Some Basic Problems

IV. The Taft-Hartley Act

V. "Right to Work" Laws

I. HISTORY OF UNIONS IN THE UNITED STATES

EDITOR'S INTRODUCTION

In the first article of this section, a long-time student and friend of labor describes the early struggles of workers to organize and to obtain recognition for their groups. He describes how labor has faced its responsibilities as a powerful factor in the American industrial and political society. Next, a survey by the United States Department of Labor shows the present strength of unions.

A group of three articles focuses the spotlight on the men now directing the policies of aggregations of 18 million organized workers. George Meany, president of the merged AFL-CIO is depicted by a newspaper labor reporter as a "crusader for clean unionism." A news magazine contributes a picture of Walter Reuther as a new type of leader whose ambition and far-reaching vision challenge the supremacy of the old-time leaders who have guided the American Federation of Labor since its founding. A national business magazine gives a revealing glimpse of the second-echelon "specialists" who blueprint labor's course and direct execution of its programs.

The functions of the Department of Labor and the Federal Mediation and Conciliation Service are described in releases from those agencies. Finally, a business magazine calls attention to the increasing role of arbitration in industrial disputes.

HISTORY OF UNIONISM IN THE UNITED STATES [1]

The trade union movement in the United States is today an accepted and permanent part of the American social scene. After decades of intense struggle, organized labor is now ad-

[1] From "A Brief Labor History," by Harry W. Laidler, executive director, League for Industrial Democracy. *Current History*. 27:1-6. July 1954. Reprinted by permission.

mitted, by friend and foe alike, to be a powerful factor in all phases of our economic, political and social life. . . .

In the early days of our country, there were few labor unions. . . . Few workers developed a feeling of class consciousness; few thought of trade union organization.

If a worker attempted to gain higher wages or otherwise to improve his position by organizing with his fellows, he frequently found himself opposed by the power of the law. For American jurisprudence had taken over bodily the English common law doctrine of conspiracy developed in the Middle Ages.

This doctrine of conspiracy involved two concepts. The first was that a maximum wage could be fixed by law. . . . The second was that workers could be compelled against their will to work. . . .

The combination of these two ancient ideas produced the rule that a workingman could be forced to work and at a prescribed wage—the average or standard rate in his particular occupation. Therefore, when workers struck in an effort to force a raise in wages, they were guilty of a "criminal conspiracy" at common law.

These concepts were applied to efforts of workers to organize in the United States on many occasions in the early nineteenth century. . . .

With the growth of industry and the factory system, workers found it increasingly necessary to organize (as a means of preventing ruthless exploitation) despite the opposition of the law. They found that there was no equality in bargaining power between an individual worker and a factory owner or corporation backed by large financial resources. Only through collective action could they bargain on anything like equal terms. They began to organize. History records a strike by Philadelphia printers as far back as 1786 for a minimum wage of $6 a week, and six years later, the formation among shoemakers of this Quaker City of the country's first permanent labor union.

Scattered unions were formed in the first two decades of the nineteenth century, but not until 1827 can we say that a labor *movement* appeared in this country. In that year for the first time workers in different trades united to form one central labor organization—the Mechanics Union of Trade Associations of Philadelphia—a body consisting of local unions of carpenters, bricklayers, printers, glaziers and others. After this, other central bodies sprang up in New York, Boston and other cities, and the 1830's even witnessed the beginnings of national unions.

The unions of those days fought on their economic and political fronts not only for better wages and hours, but for the extension of the suffrage, free education for workers' children, the ten-hour day, and the abolition of child labor and sweatshop conditions. As a means to this end, they organized a number of local labor parties. Some notable victories were won by labor during the 1820's and 1830's, but, in 1837, a severe economic depression gripped the country. Factories closed down. Workers were thrown out of work, union treasuries were wiped out, and locals, city-wide organizations and national unions went out of existence.

Many union members during the next decade or so looked to utopian experiments of the day for their economic salvation and became supporters and members of cooperative colonies established by the followers of the British industrialist and dreamer, Robert Owen, the French Utopian Socialists, etc.

Few of these colonies, however, survived; other economic schemes for improving labor's lot failed, and, in the 1850's, many workers turned again to the trade union movement. The increase in employment due to the building of the railroads, the discovery of gold in California, and the general growth of industry strengthened this trade union trend, and organized labor continued to advance steadily until the pre-Civil War depression of 1857.

Then came the Civil War and with it the establishment of new factories to supply the armies, the growth of transportation, the expansion of markets from one locality to the nation as a whole, and the growth of large corporate units.

The development of national markets compelled labor to organize increasingly on a national as well as local scale. In 1866 . . . the National Labor Union was formed, a loose federation of labor unions and of a variety of reform organizations. This organization, however, failed to develop a trade union program as we know it today. . . .

In 1869, another national labor organization was formed— the Knights of Labor. When a group of Philadelphia tailors organized this new body, many workers were fearful that discovery of their union activity would mean instant discharge and blacklist. The Knights therefore decided to meet in secret sessions in club rooms and at the homes of their members. To increase their strength in the community, they included in their locals or assemblies farmers, shopkeepers, members of professions and others, besides workers in a variety of trades. . . .

In the late 1870's, the K of L gave up its secrecy, and, during the 1880's—a period of marked industrial expansion— participated in some of the greatest industrial strikes the country had seen, including those against the giant Union Pacific and the Gould railroad systems. Among the union's greatest contributions was its emphasis on the dignity of labor and the need for working class solidarity. . . .

The K of L reached its zenith in 1886, with a membership of 700,000, but from that year on it rapidly declined in strength. In 1893, its membership had decreased to 70,000 as a result of several factors, . . . perhaps most important of all, the rise of a rival organization, the American Federation of Labor. . . .

The AFL was organized in 1881 and reorganized . . . in 1886. Samuel Gompers was its president from its inception until his death in 1924, with the exception of one year. . . . He concentrated largely in the beginning years on the organization of skilled workers into national unions, and in securing better labor conditions for these workers through collective bargaining and strikes. . . . He insisted on the need of strong trade union treasuries to be used in organization work, in servicing the union members and in strikes. At the same time, he discouraged the organization by trade unions of political parties, urged labor "to reward its friends" (primarily in the major parties) and "to punish its enemies," and sent labor representatives to Washington and the state capitals to oppose antilabor legislation.

The Federation started with a membership in 1886 of 138,000. In the next decade, it had an uphill fight for survival.

It suffered defeat in two steel strikes in which the strikers were
fought by every weapon at the steel companies' command. It
was weakened by the depression of 1893, and by many internal
fights within the labor and radical movement. By 1894, the
AFL membership had only grown to about 275,000.

During the 1890's labor was organized likewise in the railroad brotherhoods and in other organizations not affiliated with
the AFL. One of the most spectacular labor battles in the
railroad field during these days was the strike against the Pullman
Company led by the American Railway Union, of which Eugene
V. Debs was the moving spirit. When the strike was called, the
Federal Government ordered out troops to protect the property
of the Pullman Company. The presence of these troops, the
issuance of sweeping injunctions, and the arrest of Debs for
alleged contempt of court, among other things, resulted in the
breaking of the strike and in the death soon after of the ARU.

With the return of prosperity in the late 1890's, the labor
movement began steadily to advance. From a membership of less
than a half million, within and without the AFL, it grew by 1904
to a membership of over 2 million. One of the most important
labor events during this period was the five-and-a-half-month
strike of the miners in 1902 for union recognition, the nine-hour
day and other improvements. This strike evoked the intervention
of President Theodore Roosevelt, and ended in a union contract
with the entire anthracite coal industry.

The period from 1904 to 1917, when America entered the
First World War, witnessed a further growth of organized labor
from 2 to 3 million members; the strengthening of the building
trades, and the development of strong unions in the men's and
women's clothing industry following the dramatic strikes of
1909 and 1910 against tragic sweatshop conditions.

It was during this period (1905) that the Industrial Workers
of the World (the Wobblies) was founded, to organize the
unskilled and semiskilled workers into industrial unions. The
IWW during the next few years conducted a vigorous organization campaign among the lumbermen of the Pacific Coast, the
textile workers of the East, the Western miners, and migratory
agricultural workers, among others. It was involved before and

during the war in many free speech fights. William D. Haywood and other leaders of the IWW espoused the principles of French syndicalism, and, after the outbreak of the war, many IWW leaders were arrested, charged with "criminal syndicalism."

Due to government prosecution, to unsound administrative policies and the poverty of most of the union's membership, the IWW found it impossible to place the organization on a permanent basis, ceased its organization campaigns and, after a few years, went out of existence.

Since 1917, the history of labor in America may be divided into a number of stages:

1. 1917-1920—The Period of the First World War. In this period, employment was high, the cooperation of the AFL and the railroad brotherhoods in the war effort was strenuously sought by employers and all branches of government, and labor organizations flourished in 1920, reaching a peak of over 5 million members. During this period, hundreds of labor-management committees were organized to increase labor productivity and many proclaimed that the day of industrial democracy was at hand.

1920-1932—The Period of the New Capitalism and the Early Days of the Depression. Immediately after the war, many American employers took advantage of the slump in industry to start an all-out fight, under the guise of the American plan, against trade unionism. Though strong trade unions survived, many newer unions were wiped out following the loss of strikes called in a desperate effort to hold their war gains.

The temporary period of hard times and the employer attacks on labor turned the attention of many unions to more militant political action. The railroad unions and other labor and progressive groups formed the League for Progressive Political Action; the Executive Council of the AFL endorsed Robert La Follette, candidate of the Progressive party, as the Federation's presidential candidate in the 1924 elections. A number of labor unions during this period started labor banks, organized cooperatives, and gave increasing attention to educational and research activities. Several railroad brotherhoods agitated for railroad nationalization.

When employment increased in the late 1920's, many workers accepted the prevailing view among businessmen that the new capitalism had solved the problem of depression, and that the company-controlled unions and the increasing welfare services provided by employers provided sufficient protection for them. Many still remembered the coercive measures used by big business a few years earlier against members of unions. As a result, trade union organizers found much difficulty in bringing in new trade union recruits, and membership steadily declined.

On the credit side, however, labor in the railroad industry registered a distinct gain in the passage of the Railway Act of 1926, which, for the first time, affirmatively established by statute the rights of labor in that industry. This was followed six years later by the passage of the Norris-LaGuardia Act, which severely restricted the issuance of injunctions during labor disputes.

2. Labor Under the New Deal. With the defeat of President Hoover and the election of Franklin D. Roosevelt in 1932, labor entered a new era of cordial relations with the Federal Government. Despite the extreme difficulty of organizing workers during a great national depression, labor took advantage of Section 7A in the National Industrial Recovery Act of 1934, and used this as an important instrument in labor organization.

Armed with this legal weapon, and, a year later, with the legal protection given them by the National Labor Relations Act of 1935 [the Wagner Act] (which outlawed discriminatory practices against union members and interference with labor organization), they began a frontal organizational assault on the great corporations in the giant steel, automobile and other industries.

Many trade unionists soon became convinced that these campaigns could not succeed if new members were divided into dozens of craft organizations and they urged organization by industries rather than by crafts. Leaders of the miners, clothing workers and several other unions formed in 1935 the Committee for Industrial Organization under the leadership of John L. Lewis to organize industrial unions *inside* the AFL. Bitter disputes among AFL leaders followed; the 1936 Convention of the AFL expelled the unions affiliated with the CIO, charging them with starting a rival labor organization—a charge they denied—and, shortly thereafter, the Committee changed its name to Congress of Industrial Organizations, and organized the CIO on a permanent basis.

Both AFL and CIO put on nationwide organization drives, and, by 1952, when the New Deal and Fair Deal administrations of President Roosevelt and President Truman had ended, organized labor found that its 3 million membership (1930) had multiplied five-fold to over 15 million and that great corporations which, for decades, had conducted merciless fights against trade union organization, had accepted the principle of collective bargaining as an integral part of their labor management relations.

On the other hand, employers had mobilized their forces against the National Labor Relations Act and, in 1947, when the Republicans were in control of both Houses of Congress, had supplanted the Wagner Act with the Taft-Hartley Act, the Labor-Management Relations Act of that year claiming that the Wagner Act had been unfair to the employer.

The late 1940's under President Truman found labor increasingly active in politics through the AFL's Labor's League for Political Action and the CIO's Political Action Committee; witnessed the purging of Communist-controlled unions from the CIO; and saw labor in the midst of many legislative battles for the strengthening of social insurance, minimum wage and other labor and social legislation. Many unions during these years greatly increased their union welfare services and their educational activities, and gave increasing attention to the international situation. . . . The AFL and CIO developed close cooperative relations . . . in the international field through their membership in the International Confederation of Free Trade Unions.

3. Labor in the Eisenhower Administration. Both the CIO and the AFL . . . endorsed the Democratic candidate for President, Adlai E. Stevenson, in 1952 . . . and spent much time and energy in his behalf during the campaign. Shortly before the new administration came into power, William Green, president of the AFL since 1924, and Philip Murray, president of the CIO since 1940, died, and two able and vigorous leaders, George

Meany and Walter P. Reuther, respectively, were elected as their successors.

Following their elections, no-raiding pacts between these two federations were voted by their conventions, and both presidents pledged their best efforts toward the unification of the labor movement [achieved in December 1955].

The 1955 AFL convention, under the chairmanship of George Meany, voted overwhelmingly for the expulsion of the International Longshoremen's Union on charges of corruption. Both AFL and CIO have taken an increasing part in local, state and national community activities.

UNION STRENGTH TODAY [2]

Membership of national and international unions with headquarters in the United States was approximately 18 million at the beginning of 1955. . . . Membership reported or estimated was: AFL, 10.9 million; CIO, 5.2 million; and unaffiliated, 1.8 million. The 18 million total represents an increase of at least 1 million over the . . . Bureau of Labor Statistics estimate of 16.5 to 17 million for 1951. However, membership in 1954 was virtually unchanged compared with 1953. . . .

Nearly 77,000 local unions were affiliated with international unions. More than half of these were affiliated with nineteen unions, each with 1,000 or more locals. Some small, highly centralized unions had no local affiliates. Both local and international unions, in varying degrees, shared the responsibility for the negotiation and administration of at least 125,000 collective bargaining contracts.

Full-time personnel were employed in research capacities by eighty-one unions, and in educational work by sixty-seven. In twenty-four of ninety-five AFL or CIO state and territorial organizations, staff was similarly engaged. Staff members assigned to a position related to collectively bargained health, insurance, and pension plans were reported by ninety-two international unions.

[2] From United States Department of Labor *Directory of National and International Labor Unions in the United States, 1955.* (Bulletin no 1185) Superintendent of Documents. Washington 25, D.C. 1955. p 1-11.

Publications were issued by 166 international unions, usually on a monthly basis. Forty-nine state bodies also issued publications. Conventions were held at intervals ranging from less than a year to five years by 180 of the 199 international unions. . . . One of every four unions maintained its headquarters in Washington, D.C.

The series of steps which set the stage for merger activities of the AFL and CIO overshadowed all other trade union developments since . . . 1954. . . .

Almost since the AFL-CIO split developed nearly two decades ago, efforts toward permanent reunion have been made. . . .

Early in 1953, unity committees . . . were reactivated to discuss merger problems. Representatives from both federations agreed that a major obstacle was "raiding"—the attempt by rival unions to organize or represent employees already covered by an established bargaining relationship. The relatively fruitless expenditure of effort involved in "raiding" contests was demonstrated . . . through analysis of National Labor Board records. This disclosed that "the net change [from "raids" during 1951-1952] involving 366,470 employees was 8,000 or only approximately 2 per cent of the total number of employees involved." Subsequently, on June 17, 1953, a "no-raiding agreement" was drafted and on December 16, 1953, it was signed by officers of the AFL and CIO, after convention approval by both organizations. On June 9, 1954, the agreement was made effective for 65 AFL and 29 CIO affiliates whose representatives had signed the agreement. At the beginning of 1955, a total of 77 AFL unions and 30 CIO were signatory. The pact, due to expire December 31, 1955, was renewed for a two-year period at a joint AFL-CIO unity meeting in July . . . [1955].

The "no-raid" agreement embodied the following principle: "No union affiliated with either federation shall attempt to organize or to represent employees as to whom an established bargaining relationship exists between their employer and a union in the other federation." Dispute settlement procedures incorporated in the agreement provide for a final and binding decision by an impartial arbitrator, if other specified machinery leaves disputes unsettled.

Contributing to a harmonious atmosphere for further action were separate agreements formulated within the CIO and AFL to settle disputes concerning jurisdiction and representation rights involving their own affiliates. The CIO Organizational Disputes Agreement was adopted in 1951; the AFL Internal Disputes Plan was approved by convention action in 1954.

An "Agreement for the Merger of the American Federation of Labor and the Congress of Industrial Organizations" was reached on February 9, 1955. It opens with a declaration of intent by the AFL and CIO "to create a single trade union center in America, through the process of merger which will preserve the integrity of each affiliated national and international union." Unanimous agreement on this principle was enunciated earlier by the joint AFL-CIO Unity Committee meeting on October 15, 1954.

The AFL Executive Council and CIO Executive Board, at separate sessions held during February 1955, approved the merger agreement. In May a proposed constitution for the merged labor federation was approved by the executive bodies of the two federations. Final approval of this document was vested in the federation conventions.

Summarizing the constitution, the AFL and CIO presidents said:

It recognizes the equal status of craft and industrial unions.

It offers a closed-door policy to unions controlled or directed by Communists or other totalitarians.

It promotes democratic unionism. It recognizes that all workers, whatever their race, color, creed, or national origin, are entitled to share fully in the benefits of trade unionism.

It provides effective remedies for keeping the new organization free of both corruption and totalitarianism, and for quick and effective penalties against unions which fail to measure up to the high ethical and moral standards which the public has a right to expect of our affiliated organizations.

It is our belief that this constitution, an amalgam of the best of the CIO and AFL constitutions, is without peer as a fundamental charter for a democratically dedicated labor federation. . . .

[Merger was effected in December 1955.—Ed.]

Of the eleven unions expelled from the CIO during 1949-1950 on charges of Communist domination, only four remain as unions in 1955. Their combined membership is approximately a third of the 850,000 to 900,000 estimated for the eleven unions when the expulsions occurred. The membership decline for the group is traceable to several factors, including: (1) inroads by rival affiliated unions such as the CIO Electrical Workers and the CIO Auto Workers; (2) the collapse of some left-wing unions and absorption of their membership by affiliated unions; (3) the entrance of some into affiliated ranks through merger action; and (4) opposition to Communist-dominated organizations both by labor leaders and American workers. . . . [The four unions are still in existence with a combined membership of 277,500 as of November 1957.—Ed.]

There are three organizations which function as federations or have some of the characteristics of a federation such as the issuance of charters to, or the maintenance of a formal affiliation among, autonomous labor organizations in more than one industry—The Confederated Unions of America, the Engineers and Scientists of America, and the National Independent Union Council. Unions affiliated with these organizations which had negotiated agreements covering different employers in more than one state are included among the unaffiliated or independent unions discussed below.

A total of fifty-seven national or international unions not affiliated with the AFL or CIO were known to the Bureau in 1955. Their combined membership for 1954 was estimated at 1.8 million. This group includes such long-established and well-known organizations as the four "operating" railroad brotherhoods and the United Mine Workers of America. . . .

From 1930 to 1945, union membership as a percentage of the labor force grew from 7 per cent to 22 per cent. By 1954, it had increased further to about 25 per cent of the total labor force. In terms of total nonagricultural employment—where most union members are found—these ratios were somewhat higher, moving from 12 per cent in 1930 to almost 36 per cent in 1945 at the close of World War II. Since that time, the growth of union organization, in terms of membership, has matched but not exceeded the employment expansion in nonagricultural industries. Thus a ratio of about one union member to every three non-agricultural workers has typically prevailed during the past decade. . . .

The heavy concentration of membership in a few unions remains a characteristic of the labor movement. Thirteen of the 199 unions had nearly half of the total membership. Sheer size, however, is not necessarily the key index to union strength that it appears to be. The larger international unions can, of course, muster greater support, financial and otherwise, to help their affiliated locals. However, smaller unions organizing in industries with a small labor force, or those strategically situated because of the nature of the work done by members, have an inherent strength not readily apparent from membership figures.

BIOGRAPHY OF LABOR'S TOP MAN [3]

Two hundred and thirty pounds of Bronx granite, [George] Meany [AFL-CIO president] stands against the tides of expediency that so often in the past have washed away the virtuous resolves of labor's top echelon. He knows that James R. Hoffa, the teamsters' brassy president-elect, is prepared to offer substantial concessions to stay in the federation. He knows, too, that a majority of his own executive council would welcome almost any face-saving formula as a means of avoiding war to the death with the teamsters, a union that wields make-or-break power in strikes and organizing campaigns. . . .

It is a measure of Meany's dedication to the cause of clean unionism that he would stand against these considerations, even if he felt the only vote for what he thought was right would be his own. It is a measure of his status as a leader that he will not have to stand alone. . . .

Before he took hold in 1952, the teamsters bossed the executive council with shameless arrogance. Daniel J. Tobin, then head of the truck union, bragged of controlling six of the thirteen votes on the old council. . . . Meany did not even wait

[3] From "Crusader for Clean Unionism," article by A. H. Raskin, New York *Times* labor reporter. New York *Times Magazine.* p 19+. October 20, 1957. Reprinted by permission.

to get his feet under the desk before letting Tobin know things would be different in his regime.

The first test of strength came at the very meeting at which Meany was elected president. The teamster chief, who had backed Meany for the top job, decided he would dictate the choice of a man for the No. 2 spot as secretary-treasurer. That did not fit in with Meany's ideas of being boss in his headquarters. He insisted on the election of his own choice, William F. Schnitzler. He won, 7 to 6.

When [teamster president] Dave Beck came on to the council four years ago, Meany quickly wrote him off as a loud-mouth, more interested in money than in the welfare of his members. . . .

When Beck and Hoffa began flirting with the old International Longshoremen's Association, it was Meany who blew the whistle. He made the teamsters tear up their mutual assistance pact with the pier union and cancel a $400,000 loan after the checks had been drawn on the international treasury. [The AFL expelled the ILA. See the first article in this section.—Ed.] And it was Meany who initiated the present charges that the truck union is dominated by corrupt influences and who forced out Beck as a federation vice president.

The advent of the suspension test has caused the teamsters to start a grassroots pressure campaign based on threats to cut the economic lifeline of unions whose presidents fail to support them in the executive council. Meany is so disdainful of this kind of blackmail that he is not even in his Washington office to counteract it.

Instead he is functioning as a global statesman in the United Nations headquarters in New York. President Eisenhower appointed him as a member of the United States delegation to the General Assembly and he began serving on a full-time basis [in September 1957].

He passed up the UN salary of $22,500 a year and he insisted that the AFL-CIO, rather than the Government, foot the bill for his hotel suite here and the taxis he uses in connection with his UN duties. For a man as blunt as Meany, being an official diplomatic spokesman is tough enough without the ties of financial obligation.

Thus far Meany, the former plumber's helper from the Bronx, and the protocol-conscious representatives of the State Department have been getting along quite amicably, despite the gloomy expectation of some of Meany's union associates that he would eventually find his diplomatic striped pants too tight.

His understanding with Secretary of State Dulles and UN Ambassador Henry Cabot Lodge is that he will take the floor only on issues on which his views and those of the Government run parallel. . . .

He made an impressive debut with a speech on the explosive issue of race relations. As the head of the biggest labor organization in the free world, he did much to offset the damage done in the minds of Asian and African delegates by the school disorders in Little Rock. . . .

In appearance he is a cross between bull and bulldog, with resolute head set on short, massive neck, powerful hands and a bulk that bespeaks solidity rather than flabbiness. Custom-made suits and shirts have done little to give him elegance. High black shoes (a concession to a high school football injury), dollar ties and an omnipresent cigar of the three-for-a-half-dollar variety would make him look more at home behind his old desk as a plumbers' business agent than in the glass and marble corridors of the UN.

His wanderings about the world have made him a connoisseur of fine food and wine, but his preference still runs to steak and beer or a thick delicatessen sandwich on rye bread. He is a better-than-average golfer, a surprisingly agile dancer and the possessor of a fine baritone voice. He has developed a Churchillian fondness for oil painting, a pursuit that is displacing duck-shooting in his list of pastimes.

In personal demeanor he is probably the gruffest man ever to carry a diplomat's card. In the AFL-CIO he sets forth his views with such disregard of the sensibilities of those around him that almost every close associate has felt the itch to quit at one time or another. Only the strong urging of friends prevented Walter P. Reuther from delivering his resignation as a federation vice president last summer. The list could be extended to include at least a half dozen others.

He is not much on consulting his fellow leaders. Sometimes this lack of advance discussion prompts the executive council to charge off in a direction Meany does not want it to go. That happened . . . [in 1956] when he felt it would be a mistake for the federation to give its official support to any presidential candidate. By the time he made his own opinion known, so many council members had declared for Adlai E. Stevenson that it was impossible to block an endorsement. . . .

Meany's targets in the underworld fringe of labor charge that his zeal for purification stems from a desire to outdo the crusading vigor of Walter Reuther, James B. Carey and other militants of the old CIO. His adversaries recall that his own early rise to the presidency of the State Federation of Labor would have been impossible without the support of two notorious crooks, Joseph P. Ryan of the ILA and Joseph A. Fay of the Operating Engineers Union, then the dominant figures in New York labor. In short, the racket boys view him as a "traitor to his class' in much the same way that industrialists regarded Franklin D. Roosevelt, the squire of Hyde Park, for his attacks on "economic royalists." They predict that expulsions and secessions will eventually take so many of the old AFL unions out of the merged federation that Meany will wind up as president of the CIO.

This kind of baiting does not bother Meany at all, nor those who share his passion for cleaning up messy unions. Meany started his reform drive long before the merger two years ago. Even before he became president of the AFL, he teamed up with David Dubinsky to force revocation of Johnny Dio's first union charter. He led the fight to oust the ILA and he was as insistent as any CIO leader on the inclusion in the unity compact of workable sanctions against racket-controlled unions. Far from accepting the view that the federation will be destroyed if it throws out too many tainted unions, Meany is convinced it will be destroyed if it keeps them in. This may be an unbusinesslike attitude for a man nurtured in the traditions of business unionism, but Meany is one who believes a labor movement has no reason for being if it does not stand for more exacting standards of morality than prevail in the market place—regardless of what such morality may cost in dues revenue and economic strength.

Few of Meany's associates welcome his cooperation with the McClellan [Senate] committee in its inquiry into seamy union practices. They worry about the possibility that the senators will sponsor a national "right to work" law or other restrictive legislation. They worry, too, about who will be next on the committee's list, and whether unions involved legitimately in big strikes or bargaining drives may be attacked at critical moments.

Meany's view is that labor, with no subpoena power and no independent organization like the FBI, must rely on the fact-finding efforts of government investigators to expose union corruption. It is no secret to him that congressional committees are imperfect instruments, with great potentiality for harm as well as good. But he is convinced that labor will be better able to resist unfair assaults on its member unions and unjust attempts to clamp legislative handcuffs on all unions if it proceeds uncompromisingly in its own house-cleaning.

The feeling of some of his more timorous vice presidents that the teamsters are invincible wins no agreement from the sixty-three-year-old Meany. As he prepares for the test on which he has staked his career, he asks no favors, seeks no allies. When his twenty-eight colleagues gather around him in the opulent council room at AFL-CIO headquarters, he will tell them exactly what he thinks and why. Then it will be up to them. Powerful as the teamsters are, it is doubtful they can beat this president in a roomful of presidents. More than any other man, he unified the labor movement. Now he expects he will keep it united in a crusade for decency. [The Teamsters were ousted from the AFL-CIO in December 1957.—Ed.]

THE CHALLENGE OF REUTHER [4]

When Walter Reuther first went to Detroit, he was nineteen years old and not quite sure of himself—a youthful weakness

[4] From "The G. A. W. Man." *Time.* 65:20-2. June 20, 1955. Courtesy *Time;* copyright Time Inc. 1955.

that he has long since corrected. According to a Detroit YMCA questionnaire which he filled out in 1927, he wanted to be either (1) a chicken farmer or (2) a labor leader. Within a decade, he was leading thousands of men in the great sitdown strikes of Depression-era Detroit. By now, restless, redheaded, hard-driving Walter Reuther, who could never have confined himself long to a hen house, has reached the top of the heap in the alternate career: he has more personal power—although not more popularity—than any other leader of United States labor.

Reuther runs—with managerial efficiency—the largest United States labor union: the 1.5 million-man CIO United Automobile Workers (UAW); he has signed up 250,000 new workers in the last four years. . . . [In the summer of 1955] he achieved a triumph and a great victory for labor, winning . . . a form of guaranteed semiannual wage for laid-off workers. [See "Guaranteed Annual Wage—Threat or Promise?" in Section III, below.—Ed.]

A third-generation Socialist born in Wheeling, West Virginia, Walter Philip Reuther was bred to worship God and to translate brotherhood into Socialist terms. His grandfather Jacob was a German Social Democrat who emigrated to the United States in 1892 to save his sons from military service. . . .

Walter Reuther's pattern of life was molded by his father, Jacob's son Valentine, a union organizer and an ardent Socialist. Walter retains a vivid boyhood memory of going to Moundsville Penitentiary with his father to visit Socialist Eugene Debs, sentenced to ten years under the Espionage Act.

On Sundays at home, Valentine Reuther conducted debates on issues like capital punishment and the right to strike. "It was no accident," says Valentine Reuther, that three of his four sons became labor officials, all in the CIO. It is also no accident that Walter Reuther can debate Detroit's most fluent corporate talent to a standstill.

Of the brothers, Walter was the smallest (now 5 feet 8½ inches) and the least brilliant in school. He flunked English and algebra. At sixteen, he quit to become an apprentice

machinist at Wheeling Steel (11 cents an hour). In 1927 he
went to Detroit to make big money. . . .

Working nights, he went to high school and then to Wayne
University, came out of classes frothing ideals. When the depression (of the early thirties) hit Detroit . . . , he joined picket
lines and soapboxed at breadlines, organized soup kitchens and
leftist students clubs. . . .

Breaking company commandments, he tried to organize Ford
workers. . . . In 1932 Walter Reuther was fired by Ford. He
and his brother Victor withdrew their savings (some $900) just
before the 1933 bank closing and sailed on a world "tour of
social engineering." . . .

They got visas to Soviet Russia and worked for sixteen
months with other Americans and foreigners at the American-
built automobile plant at Gorky. . . .

On leaving Gorky, the brothers traveled 18,000 miles across
the U.S.S.R., came home via Japan. At twenty-eight, Walter
Reuther had completed his education and was ready to get to
work in an auspicious environment, depression-haunted Detroit. . . . Reuther set out in 1936 to organize West Side
Detroit for the struggling automobile workers union. . . .

Reuther has displayed the winner-take-all talents of a Com-
mando leader in his strike strategy. In 1939, to save strike funds,
he pulled out General Motors tool-and-die men at exactly the
right moment to stop all production; the other workers, technically non-strikers, collected state unemployment compensation.
In 1937, during the bitter GM sitdown at Flint, Michigan, he
helped to organize the seizure of a key building and stop
production. . . .

After forty-four days, the UAW won the strike, organized
General Motors and within a year had four hundred contracts
covering most carmakers, except, notably, Ford (where company
police beat up Reuther and his associates during 1937's "Battle
of the Overpass"). In 1941, with war production booming,
Ford capitulated after a ten-day strike. Even since then the UAW
has been virtually unchallenged in its control of automobile
labor. In postwar strikes, the automakers never even tried to
keep open.

Despite—or because of—his trip to Russia, Reuther has a good anti-Red record. . . . He pushed an anti-Communist resolution through the 1941 UAW convention. Thereafter, as a rambunctious union vice president, he fought the Communists relentlessly and effectively.

When the 1946 union convention at Atlantic City came around, Reuther was ready to take on the Communist-line clique that controlled the UAW's president, R. J. Thomas. . . . When the vote came, the Communists and their followers lost; by the narrowest of margins, Walter Reuther beat R. J. Thomas for president of the UAW. . . .

On Friday, March 13, 1936, Reuther married pretty, auburn-haired Mae Wolf, a physical-education instructor whom he met before his European trip. He never wrote to her, but began courting on his return. "On our wedding night," Mrs. Reuther recalls, "we took a drive out of town somewhere. Walter had to make a speech."

At first, during the early, hectic organizing drives, they lived in Detroit's Knickerbocker Apartments, a nest of friendly, frenzied CIO officials. "We hardly ever slept at all," Reuther remembers. Thugs once beat him up in his own apartment. Later he moved to the north side, where a gun blast fired by a would-be assassin ripped into his right arm. Reuther lost blood copiously but never lost consciousness. "I decided," he said later, "to fight harder than ever."

A bodyguard follows him everywhere, and Detroit newspapers never mention his present address. . . .

Outside his family, Reuther has no intimates and few friends. Glowering John L. Lewis, the founder of the CIO, is one of the few labor leaders who have publicly expressed themselves on the subject of Walter Reuther. He referred to him as a "pseudo-intellectual nitwit." Labor leaders generally dislike his metallic personal qualities—the iron will, the tinny personality, the brass nerve. They distrust his power and his policies.

"His early training sharpened him," said one top labor leader, "but it also put him on the wrong track so far as trade-union philosophy in the United States is concerned. He started out trained in Marxist concepts, and he believed in the elimination of private ownership. He was one of those youngsters we used to call a 'Yipsol' [from Young People's Socialist League]. They could talk like hell, but they could not produce anything."

But the same critical labor leader admits that Reuther is changing; he is becoming more a "bread-and-butter unionist" and less a social engineer out to "remake the world." Not that he has dropped his habit of making grandiose plans. He prepared a wartime plan to raise the sunken liner *Normandie;* later he blueprinted a "hundred-year plan" under which the United States would give the rest of the world $1,300 billion for peace. . . .

Time and success have mellowed both Reuther and the mass movement that swept up the distressed workers of Detroit two decades ago. . . .

Reuther still uses some of the old mechanical clichés of class-struggle philosophy. But he is too alert a man not to realize how much he has won for his followers within the framework of capitalism—and how much the picture holds within that same framework. In a recent speech Reuther said: "Movements release tremendous emotional forces, and they get into motion great dynamic qualities; then they tend to dissipate themselves. They sort of spend themselves. You always need to find a way to re-create enthusiasm and spiritual power."

LABOR'S ADVISORY ECHELON [5]

Key men inside AFL-CIO whose influence and work will have the most impact include:

John W. Livingston, who is directing big labor's drive for 26 million more members and is giving most immediate attention to unorganized workers in chemical, oil, textile, paper, wood, furniture, shoe and leather industries and to white-collar workers in all industries.

James L. McDevitt, director of the AFL-CIO political machine that sought to help elect Adlai Stevenson, and more friends to Congress.

[5] From "Experts Who Guide Labor's Leaders." *Nation's Business.* 45:36-7+. February 1957. Reprinted by permission.

Stanley H. Ruttenberg, whose economic views and research guide AFL-CIO economic policies and influence union bargaining demands.

Andrew J. Biemiller, former Wisconsin congressman, who is the new director of AFL-CIO lobbying activities on Capitol Hill.

J. Albert Woll, who is retained as outside counsel to fight AFL-CIO's legal battles with the Taft-Hartley, Hobbs Anti-Racketeering, Walsh-Healey Public Contracts, minimum wage and other Federal laws.

These five are by no means all of the top staff people, but they are the experts whose work is most likely to be felt by business groups. . . .

Jack Livingston, AFL-CIO's director of organization, is a product of General Motors' Fisher Body plant in St. Louis who fought his way up in the United Automobile Workers alongside [Walter] Reuther. He was a UAW vice president and director of the union's General Motors and aircraft departments when he assumed his duties after the merger.

Mr. Livingston, not yet fifty, has had notable success as an organizer, although he is better known as a negotiator. In eighteen months as director of a UAW region he increased the size of his jurisdiction's membership thirteen times; General Motors became almost 100 per cent unionized under his leadership, and he scored heavy gains in aircraft.

Big organizing gains are the first objective of AFL-CIO. Mr. Livingston believes that the success of the AFL-CIO merger will be measured by its progress in organizing employees and, conversely, that the AFL-CIO will progress toward its over-all objectives only as long as its organizing is successful. . . .

AFL-CIO organizing targets can be anticipated from a survey by Mr. Livingston and his staff of three hundred organizers in twenty-two regions. Confined to AFL-CIO organizations, it shows:

Thirteen states with less than 20 per cent of employees organized are mostly in the South; only seven states are more than 40 per cent organized, and only one (Washington) is more than 50 per cent organized. Washington, which was Teamster Boss Dave Beck's base for years, is 59 per cent organized.

Least organized groups are employed in wholesale and retail trade; banking, insurance and real estate, only 5 per cent unionized. Others are: government, 7 per cent; service industries, 10 per cent; crude oil and natural gas production, 30 per cent; public utilities and communication, 45 per cent; manufacturing, 55 per cent; coal and metal mining, 75 per cent, and construction and transportation, 80 per cent.

Total organizable among 41 million employees considered eligible for union membership: 26 million.

Jim McDevitt, director of the Committee on Political Education, hopes to increase labor's political activity and make it more effective as AFL and CIO mergers are completed in the states this year. Thus far merger of state labor organizations has occurred in only nineteen states, and it is in those states that COPE claims to have made its best showing last fall.

COPE feels it must get even more active politically, on a year-round basis, to offset the apparent collapse of once powerful Democratic political organizations in major cities, such as Jersey City, Memphis, Chicago and New York.

In . . . [the 85th] Congress, labor claims about 190 friends in the House and 41 in the Senate, about the same as in the last Congress. But it looks for some members who were previously cool to labor's views, to warm up because of labor's increasing political effectiveness.

McDevitt expects labor to make some gains in the next election and to support a presidential candidate again in 1960, despite Eisenhower's tremendous victory last fall over COPE opposition.

Mr. McDevitt is a product of Pennsylvania's school of practical politics. While president of the AFL organization in the state for thirteen years, he spent much of his time in legislative work, or lobbying, and participating in Democratic political campaigns. He's a Democrat.

In 1954 he took leave from directing the AFL League for Political Education to help Pennsylvania elect its first Democratic governor in twenty years, Governor George M. Leader. . . .

A spry fifty-eight, Mr. McDevitt believes there is no substitute for hard work in politics and legislative activity. He also believes that labor can be more effective politically by working quietly, letting the politicians know where it stands, educating the public and getting voters to the polls. He's no drum-beater.

COPE's political machinery is organized down to the state, county and precinct level and inside the individual unions. Union funds are being used for political education and, to get around the Federal ban on union political spending, about $2 million was solicited in voluntary $1 contributions from union members for direct contributions to candidates for Federal office.

Part of the educational phase was the mailing of the voting records of members of Congress to the homes of all 15 million AFL-CIO members.

Mr. McDevitt, a plasterer by trade, is an executive-type union leader and a clean-desk man. He has served in union and many government advisory posts for more than twenty years. . . .

Stanley Ruttenberg, director of the Department of Research, considers himself a practical economist close to the philosophy of the late Philip Murray, who brought him into the CIO as a young graduate of the University of Pittsburgh.

I try to take a practical, rather than theoretical or academic approach to problems [the thirty-nine-year-old Ruttenberg said in an interview with *Nation's Business*]. I don't discuss economic issues except in the framework of political realities—whether the political realities be of government or the trade union movement.

I try to adapt sound and basic economic principles to the realities of everyday life. Because I believe in the objectives of the trade union movement, I have no difficulty in feeling perfectly at home with its basic economic philosophy.

Mr. Ruttenberg likens himself to economists in other organizations. He says he weighs the pros and cons of a problem against the objectives of the labor movement, and then hits as hard as he can those which support the labor view.

He believes strongly—"I will preach it from the housetops" —that wage increases can take place without price increases and their cost borne through higher productivity and reduced profit margins.

From 1951 until recently, Mr. Ruttenberg says, we have had relative wage stability while prices and productivity have gone up. He sees trouble if workers' wages do not keep up with the rise in productivity. . . .

Like other staff departments, Mr. Ruttenberg and his staff work under AFL-CIO President George Meany and service AFL-CIO committees which make recommendations to the twenty-nine-man Executive Council, the policy-making body.

Mr. Ruttenberg is also staff director for the Economic Policy Committee and regularly prepares a detailed report for the committee on the economic trends as they are developing. A report last spring, approved by the committee and adopted by the Executive Council, saw a mild decline in business activity during the summer and fall and recommended a $3 billion tax cut immediately to bolster consumer income and spending to prevent a serious decline. . . .

As for automation, Mr. Ruttenberg believes it can, and will, bring a tremendous increase in the standard of living—"but we can't take this for granted."

In other words, labor must see to it that workers share in its benefits, just as they now share in the benefits of rising productivity. Automation views are contained in an AFL-CIO pamphlet, *Labor Looks at Automation.* . . .

The Department of Legislation, the AFL-CIO's lobbying arm, was run by the veteran Bill Hushing, and Robert Oliver, former director of the CIO legislative staff, as codirectors, until Mr. Hushing retired and Mr. Oliver resigned. . . . Andy Biemiller was promoted from the staff to take their place.

Mr. Biemiller is in basic agreement with [George] Meany that it is up to the union leadership to convince members of Congress that the AFL-CIO's position is the right one, rather than trying to pressure a legislator by a mass lobby from back home. . . .

Mr. Biemiller, who is fifty, got his labor training in Wisconsin, although he is a native of Sandusky, Ohio. He has had extensive labor and legislative experience.

As a New Deal Democrat, he was elected to the House of Representatives from Milwaukee in 1944 and 1948. He has remained in Washington in various union capacities and as a labor consultant to government agencies.

Before entering Congress, Mr. Biemiller was graduated from Cornell University, taught at the University of Syracuse and University of Pennsylvania, engaged in newspaper and labor education activities, served in the Wisconsin Legislature as party floor leader while an organizer for the Wisconsin AFL and during World War II was on the War Production Board staff.

As one of four AFL-CIO legislative staff members . . . on Capitol Hill, Mr. Biemiller worked mainly on social security, foreign aid, schools, education and atomic energy legislation. He doesn't feel his background as a New Deal member of Congress is a handicap in trying to influence Republicans or conservatives of either party. . . .

Al Woll, the AFL-CIO's lawyer, has his own firm for general legal practice in Washington, but it happens that all of the practice involves unions because, he says, when you do work for unions you don't get anything else.

He is general counsel for the AFL-CIO and the Teamsters' Union and gets some work from other unions. There are five attorneys in the office. One is William S. Tyson, former solicitor in the Department of Labor.

Mr. Woll, son of the recently deceased Matthew Woll, AFL-CIO vice president, represented the AFL from 1947 until the merger.

Mr. Woll's legal experience after his graduation from the University of Illinois Law School in 1927 was in government activity not related to labor relations matters. He had been United States District Attorney in Chicago for seven years, under a Roosevelt appointment, when he went to Washington as AFL counsel. Highlight of that service was prosecution of German saboteurs in 1942. Previously he had done appellate work in the state's attorney's office in Chicago and, as special assistant to the attorney general in Washington, he handled matters involving mail fraud, the Securities Act and the Public Utility Holding Act.

Mr. Woll does not try to influence AFL-CIO policies, but does try to help make them effective. On legislative matters, he analyzes the effect of pending bills and legislation already passed from the viewpoint of labor's interests. He seldom is seen in the Capitol.

The Taft-Hartley law was passed just before Mr. Woll left Chicago so he was not involved in the fight over that legislation. But he has followed closely the application of Taft-Hartley, the Hobbs Anti-Racketeering Act and other labor laws by government agencies and their interpretation by the courts, and sometimes he has initiated test cases.

For example, if he thinks an agency or court decision will have an adverse effect from the AFL-CIO's standpoint, he calls it to Mr. Meany's attention. Mr. Meany may authorize an appeal or take the question up with the Executive Council. Often the AFL-CIO itself is not involved in the situation directly and intervenes as a "friend of the court."

THE DEPARTMENT OF LABOR [6]

The Department of Labor was established by Congress to promote and develop the welfare of wage earners. The Department's organic act instructed the Secretary to improve our people's working conditions and advance their opportunities for profitable employment. In carrying out this directive, and many later and more specific provisions of law, the Department is dedicated to the improvement of the economy and raising America's standard of living.

While each bureau in the Department collects and releases data gathered for its own specific program purposes, the job of collecting information on matters of over-all economic significance is concentrated in a bureau (Bureau of Labor Statistics) specializing in labor statistics.

Many of the data collected by this bureau are obtained from employer records, either by mail or through plant visits. . . .

Over-all factual and statistical studies are published by the Department in the *Monthly Labor Review*. Specialized studies are also published.

[6] From "The United States Department of Labor . . . and What It Does," pamphlet prepared by the Department of Labor. Superintendent of Documents. Washington 25, D.C. 1956. p 1-20.

The Department publishes studies and reports on the prices of foods, goods, services, and rents. It also maintains the Consumer Price Index and publishes monthly, weekly, and daily indexes of prices at primary markets.

It collects data on nonagricultural employment, payrolls, hours of work, labor turnover, and earnings, publishing detailed information for manufacturing industries, and state breakdowns and data by industry for major industrial cities. It also makes studies of employment opportunities in a wide variety of occupations, and provides estimates of manpower resources and demands. . . .

Two important functions of the Department of Labor are: promoting and helping to maintain a Federal-state system of public employment offices to assist workers seeking employment and employers seeking workers; and promoting a Federal-state program of unemployment insurance for workers unemployed due to lack of work. . . .

Technical help is given to employers in solving their manpower problems, especially as regards the selection, assignment, and retention of workers. Technical help is also given in selecting communities where needed workers are available for locating new plant sites. These services help to reduce labor turnover and to improve the mobility of labor. Through a nation-wide job-clearance service, workers and employers are brought together, even when in different communities or states.

Where communities have serious unemployment problems, technical help is given in improving job opportunities and employment conditions.

At the local, state, and national levels, the Department of Labor and its affiliated state employment security agencies provide continuous labor market information for employers, workers, and others. . . .

The Department of Labor is the Federal partner in the Federal-state unemployment insurance program under the Social Security Act, the Federal Unemployment Tax Act, and the state employment security laws. It continuously provides assistance to state agencies in legislative, interpretative, administrative, and financing aspects of the state programs. . . .

The Department of Labor, as the civilian manpower agency, plays a significant part in determining manpower policies. . . .

It is particularly concerned with the training and utilization of the labor force and the deferment of workers in occupations of critical importance to the production needs of the nation. . . .

The Department also encourages employers and labor to develop training programs to improve the skills and knowledge of the entire work force.

Technical service based on analysis of need is provided to industry upon request. The objective is to fit the training to the need of the establishment, and to broaden the opportunities of the worker to advance to better paying or more satisfying jobs.

The Department does not provide instruction. It encourages management and labor to make use of the services of the local vocational schools for subjects requiring classroom instruction. . . .

A major function is to administer and enforce the minimum wage, overtime pay, and child-labor provisions of the Fair Labor Standards Act. . . .

Upon request, the Secretary of Labor may bring actions in behalf of workers for unpaid minimum wages or unpaid overtime compensation owed them under the Fair Labor Standards Act. The Department also supervises the payment of back wages found due under the law.

The Secretary of Labor also initiates appropriate civil and criminal actions to protect the public interest against violations of the Fair Labor Standards Act.

The Department also administers the Walsh-Healey Act relating to public contracts in excess of $10,000 for supplies for government use. This act provides for the payment of time and a half for work in excess of eight hours a day or forty hours a week. It prohibits home work, convict labor, and child labor on the contracts. It authorizes the determination of prevailing minimum wages for the government work, and requires government suppliers to maintain safe and healthful working conditions. . . .

The law which prohibits employers from forcing employees on Federal and federally financed or assisted contracts to kick back any part of their wages is administered by the Department of Labor.

In general the Department of Labor is authorized to coordinate the administration and enforcement of labor standards which the law makes applicable to contracts covering federally financed and federally assisted construction. . . .

The administration of these laws involves consideration of all claims made by employees or other persons covered by such laws for workmen's injury compensation and other related benefits. . . .

The Department analyzes proposed and existing state and Federal labor legislation, and prepares information about it for the use of state labor departments, legislative commissions, civic groups, unions, management or the general public. It serves as a national repository for technical information on all aspects of labor law and administration. . . .

The promotion of industrial safety is one of the Department's chief interests. It helps state labor officials to strengthen their accident-prevention programs, and offers training courses to their safety inspectors. It develops with the state authorities various industry-wide programs to reduce work injuries. It also provides the staffing for the President's Conference on Occupational Safety, which brings to bear on the nation's industrial safety problems the best knowledge and methods available for the reduction of work accidents. . . .

The Department is also one of four Federal agencies which by law are represented on the Board of the Foreign Service, with responsibility for advising the Secretary of State on the over-all administration of the Foreign Service. In this connection the Department is chiefly concerned with development of the labor attaché program in our missions abroad.

The Department takes part in discussions within the United States Government, and in the United Nations and its specialized agencies, and particularly in the International Labor Organization, on matters relating to international labor problems.

Under the Department's international labor affairs program, the various bureaus in the Department cooperate to give training in labor matters to foreign trade union leaders, government officials, technicians, and women leaders who visit the United States under official programs. The Department also cooperates with the Department of State and the International Cooperation Administration in arranging for the loan of United States experts in economic and labor problems of various kinds to other countries, and provides those countries with technical materials and information relating to labor matters. . . .

The Library of the Department of Labor maintains a research collection of approximately 345,000 items. . . . It is open to the public and lends materials to other libraries for research purposes.

FEDERAL MEDIATION SERVICE [7]

The Federal Mediation and Conciliation Service is an independent government agency. Its mediators assist labor and management, in industries affecting interstate commerce, to resolve issues and settle differences affecting their working relationship through collective bargaining. . . .

Throughout the free world, the mediation of labor-management controversies has generally developed as an important and continuing governmental function. In the United States, where our basic principles of free collective bargaining decry government control or dictation, mediation plays a most vital role, the alternative to some element of governmental control.

The mediator's job is not to decide issues but to help the parties reconcile any differences which may exist between them. More effective use of mediation can be achieved if the parties are frank with the mediator, and are willing to discuss candidly with him the limits of their respective positions. The mediator has a statutory duty to explore fully all possible solutions and alternatives.

The mediator always steps into a case, no matter how difficult it may be, with the idea that a settlement is possible. He is not a magician nor a soothsayer and he can be effective only to the extent the parties are receptive to reaching agreement and want to seek a way out of their deadlock.

[7] From "Facts Behind the Headlines in Labor-Management Disputes," pamphlet prepared by the Federal Mediation and Conciliation Service. Superintendent of Documents. Washington 25, D.C. 1957. p 1-7.

Primary responsibility for reaching and maintaining agreements always rests with the parties. The efforts and desires of labor and management—not the government—determine whether industrial peace or work stoppages exist. The sole duty of the Mediation Service is to help parties reach their own agreements. It does not decide the outcome. . . .

Mediation is completely noncompulsory, and without cost to the parties.

Effective use of it is an important factor in making free collective bargaining a continuing, dynamic process.

At times when no contract dispute exists, parties often request a mediator to assist them in improving their relationships. Mediators are available at any time when their services may assist in preventing or minimizing labor-management disputes in industries substantially affecting interstate commerce. . . .

The Labor-Management Relations Act of 1947 . . . requires that if either a company or a union wants to change, modify or terminate a contract it must give the other party sixty days' advance notice. If within thirty days thereafter, agreement has not been reached, the party that made the initial request must notify the Federal Mediation and Conciliation Service and the appropriate state or territorial mediation agency that a dispute exists. . . .

The assignment of a mediator to a dispute situation is a free offer of assistance. No formal processes are involved, and mediation can be terminated as informally as it originates. . . .

Disclosures to the mediator, as well as any facts he learns during mediation, are held in strictest confidence. The procedures of the Service provide that a mediator cannot testify concerning such information in court, before boards or commissions or in arbitration. . . .

Mediators of the Service do not arbitrate disputes, nor does the Service employ arbitrators. The Service does, however, maintain a nation-wide roster of available private arbitrators and, upon joint request of labor and management, assists in the selection of arbitrators by the parties.

ARBITRATION'S EXPANDING ROLE [8]

Arbitration has expanded steadily with the spread of collective bargaining—90 to 95 per cent of an estimated 125,000 collective bargaining contracts contain arbitration clauses. The growing practice of signing contracts running as long as three to five years makes the role of the "third man" crucial.

[Under an arbitration clause, issues on which labor and management are unable to reach agreement are referred to an impartial umpire, whose decision both parties usually agree in advance to accept. The United States Supreme Court ruled in June 1957 that District Courts might require employers or unions to carry out the provisions of arbitration clauses.—Ed.]

The American Arbitration Association reports that its case load reached a new high of 2,175 cases in 1956, a 7.4 per cent gain over the previous year. This year's case load runs 14 per cent ahead of last year.

The Federal Mediation and Conciliation Service also reports a "wider acceptance of arbitration." Its arbitration case load in 1956 topped the previous year by 21 per cent. So far this year, the service is handling 11 per cent more cases than last year. . . .

The American Arbitration Association recently . . . found:

Most cases (81.6 per cent) were handled by a single arbitrator.

Where three-man boards were used, only a few decisions (15.5 per cent) were unanimous.

Most arbitrators are educators (41.8 per cent); about half of these teach in law schools. Practicing attorneys account for another 34.2 per cent of the arbitrators. Professional arbitrators make up about 14.4 per cent of the total group.

The average case took two to three months from the time it was submitted for arbitration to a decision. . . .

Dr. George W. Taylor, professor of industry at the University of Pennsylvania's Wharton School, consultant to both industries and unions, . . . [believes] it is important . . . to develop a

[8] From "Third Man Grows in Importance." *Business Week.* p 174. September 7, 1957. Reprinted by permission.

body of precedent in arbitration so that you do not have "ad hoc" arbitrators ruling one way in one case, a different way in the next.

The veteran arbitrator feels that the permanent umpire is of particular benefit in handling the big, complicated cases. For one thing, his knowledge of industry conditions increases his understanding of the problems brought to him and can speed his work in settling disputes.

The parties to a dispute can call on him, discuss a case, and perhaps settle it without resorting to formal proceedings. In effect, the permanent umpire can practice a "preventative arbitration."

The two largest companies in the two largest industries in the United States . . . , General Motors and United States Steel, pioneered with their respective unions in devising methods for handling disputes arising under their contracts. . . .

The General Motors-United Auto Workers system is an "umpire system in the strictest sense," according to a GM spokesman. No latitude is allowed for making rules that are not in the contract. The arbitrator is Nathan Feisinger.

Actually, Feisinger handles only a small percentage—3 per cent—of all grievances that arise over the interpretation of the contract. The bulk of disputes are handled directly by the union and management at various levels. Only the thorniest of them pass to the top. Feisinger gets an annual fee of around $35,000 —payment of which is split between UAW and GM. He has a yearly contract, which each party need not renew.

US Steel and United Steelworkers arbitration system is a good example of one in which a three-man board evolved into a single, permanent arbitrator. At the end of World War II, the steel arbitration board was a three-man affair, with one representative from USW, one from US Steel, plus an independent. This system was discarded a few years later—the labor and management representatives invariably were at odds with one another, and the independent arbitrator was making most of the decisions anyway.

In steel, both sides may use written and oral arguments, briefs and witnesses. It's estimated that witnesses appear at the hearings in as many as 90 per cent of the cases.

The US Steel-USW arbitrator, Sylvester Garrett, . . . technically heads a board of arbitration: as chairman, he can call up the two other men (specified in the contract) for consultation, one appointed by the union, the other by management. In addition, Garrett on occasion retains someone to hear individual cases and to recommend a solution to him. However, Garrett makes the final decisions in all cases.

Garrett's term of office is indefinite as long as he meets "conditions mutually agreed upon." Arbitration expenses, shared equally by the company and the union, come to approximately $100,000 a year for the whole package.

Both US Steel and USW consider arbitration an integral part of modern large-scale industrial relations. But, as in the case of General Motors and the UAW, other procedures are used first in an attempt to settle disputes. Arbitration is mandatory, however, if an issue can't otherwise be settled. And the findings of the arbitrator are binding.

Disciplinary layoff and discharge cases are the most frequent among those to reach arbitration, according to arbitration agencies. Cases involving job evaluation, work load and assignments, individual wage scales place second on the arbitration docket. Seniority cases, formerly in second place, have slipped into third, say the agencies. . . .

Arbitrators seemingly are becoming more firm in upholding management in discipline cases. Unions are not winning as many cases as they used to, says one arbitrator. Management has learned how to settle "bad" cases before they reach the arbitration stage, and is making better presentations of cases being arbitrated. Management also is less bothered than unions by considerations of what its followers will think. Unions, the arbitrator feels, take many cases to arbitration they know they can't win.

Arbitration became solidly established as the unions became more sure of themselves in dealing with management. The long-term contract was a further impetus. While the really big issues between labor and management may be postponed until new contract negotiations are scheduled, most disputes can't wait and go directly into the grievance hopper. The actual number of disputes coming before the arbitrator may be small. But the precedents he has established in the past and the fact that he is available if other efforts fail serve as pressures on both parties to settle the grievances on the lower levels. The impact of arbitration, therefore, is greater than the number of cases reaching arbitration procedure.

As for the future, arbitrators themselves point to these trends:

Arbitration of wage questions under reopener clauses in long-term agreements probably will increase. Arbitration, however, will not substitute for collective bargaining when contracts terminate. Neither unions nor management wish to turn basic decisions over to a third party.

Arbitration case loads may grow as contracts grow longer. Already in some industries where one umpire formerly sufficed, two or three associates now are the rule. General Motors' experience indicates, though, that this may be a temporary condition. From 1950 to 1956, the number of grievances filed by the company and union increased from 44,000 a year to 114,500; at the same time, arbitration decisions dropped from 85 a year to 47. As a backlog of precedent builds up, it may cut deeply into the number of cases reaching the arbitration stage.

Mediation probably will increase as a method of settling grievances headed for arbitration. Some arbitrators report success in using a mediation "half-step" between the top grievance level and final arbitration. It eases their case load.

II. LABOR UNITED

EDITOR'S INTRODUCTION

This section is concerned primarily with the significance of the merger of the American Federation of Labor and the Congress of Industrial Organizations. It opens with an analysis, by a university discussion bureau, of the basic rights of workers in an industrial society, followed by excerpts from the AFL-CIO Constitution, setting forth the philosophy and principles of the merged groups.

Next, two articles describe "the new look" in labor and management. In the first of these, a union educational director tells of labor's changing approach to management. In the other, two university faculty members analyze changes in management's attitude toward labor.

A newspaper columnist draws attention to the great concentration of power in a single great labor organization and inquires into the implication of such power. In two final articles, leading representatives of organized labor and management tell what their groups expect of each other.

THE WORKER IN THE INDUSTRIAL ECONOMY [1]

When great machines were built that changed the whole pattern of our living and working, making each worker a specialist who works outside his home to produce some one thing or service that has value for him only as he can exchange it for other things he wants, then the question of who should own and control the use of property took on a bewildering new importance. . . .

The question of the need for special controls over the ownership of property in an industrial society was raised when the

[1] From "How Free Should the Individual Be to Earn and to Own?" (Package Library Briefs. v 13, no3) Mimeographed. Indiana University. Bureau of Public Discussion. Bloomington. November 1956. p4-6, 16, 20, 26-7. Reprinted by permission.

workers found that those who owned the means of production could not assure them even so much security or comfort or joy in working as they had known before the days of factories. As poverty and despair came to be a distinguishing mark of life among factory workers, it was recognized that the men who owned the only means by which these people could provide for their needs had a dangerous amount of power over too many lives. The first effective limit on this power to own and to use machines and factories came about when workers organized into groups that could refuse to work unless the factory owner met certain of their demands. . . . This organization of labor that gave working people a defense against the power of ownership of the means of production established limits to earn and to own that led to great changes in the lives of both factory owners and workers. In some countries labor organization and other social controls have not accomplished the reforms that were needed and so the governments have taken over the ownership and control of the means of production; in these cases industry is owned and controlled by the state. A society that controls its means of production in this way is not capitalist; it is communist or socialist.

Another important question in industrialized societies is how much of the goods and services produced by the machines belongs to the owners of the machines and how much to the persons who operate them and do the other work involved in keeping the industries running. . . .

The question of what part of the benefits from the work belongs then to the man and what part to the tool is impossible to answer. The question had little importance so long as workers made or owned the tools by which they earned their living, but when they came to depend for their "means of production" on very costly tools provided by other people it became important to find some answer to the question, How much of the fruits of modern industry belongs to the man who operates the machines and how much to the man who provides them? . . .

The way industrial profits are divided between capital and labor—the machines and their operators—will determine whether individuals will voluntarily make the sacrifice of saving and risking their property in order to provide the means of production for the nation. Unless people feel there is likelihood of sufficient reward for their sacrifice and risk, they will tend to use their property on their own immediate enjoyment and so not accumulate property or risk it in industrial enterprise. When this happens, a nation that wishes to develop industries or other costly enterprises can accumulate the capital for them only through a government that takes property from the people and "saves" it until sufficient amounts are available for the needed developments. Where capital has been collected and expended in this way, freedom of enterprise has been supplanted by strict controls; "capitalism" has been supplanted by socialism or communism. . . .

By the 1840's and 1850's when factories began to become significant in the life of the nation, . . . the owners and managers of these new means of production generally reflected the attitudes of the western settlers that people should be left free to earn and to own as they pleased. They wanted freedom to develop industries in their own way and to use the profits as they pleased. And they were the people who largely influenced government policy. . . . The courts expressed the popular belief that the economic welfare of the nation would best be encouraged when everybody was free to earn and to own as he pleased. They also believed that the most important principle involved was that of basic freedom of the individual to develop his life and his activities according to his own inclinations and his own conscience in so far as possible.

As industry developed, more and more people left the farms and came to the cities to work in factories. . . . The farmer-turned-factory-worker sacrificed many freedoms—the freedom to plan his own schedule and to manage his own business, among many. He also lost much of his independence, for he no longer owned the tools he had to have or the land from which he could produce. He became dependent for his food and shelter and all that he needed for his daily living on the owners of the machines and the factories and the other businesses that paid his wages. . . .

It came to be realized by many people that one of the basic problems of democracy was to establish a system of laws under which there would be seeming contradictions: Wage earners must be protected against those who owned the means of production or against those circumstances in which there did not seem to be adequate goods for them, and people must be left free to develop their businesses as they wanted to develop them. The industrialist and the businessman . . . should have freedom to handle their own property as they saw fit. . . . A manufacturer should be free to pay whatever wages he felt that he could and wanted to, to hire and to fire workers and to provide working conditions without interference from anybody, to make whatever kinds of goods or provide whatever kinds of services he wanted to and to charge what he pleased for them. But in spite of the great power held by those who owned the means of production, changes began to appear; law increasingly limited the rights of the owners of means of production to earn and to own. . . .

Society finally agreed also that those who owned the means of production must be made to provide opportunity for wholesome living and the fullest possible development of workers and their children. Deplorable conditions in factories, mines, and city slums gradually called forth legislation designed to remedy the worst exploitation of workers. Acts were passed regulating length of working days, and standards of health and safety, and wage rates. All such laws were, of course, technically encroachments on the right of persons to earn, own, and handle their own property.

Freedom to carry on business according to the owner's wishes was further limited as unions became a significant part of the American economic scene. . . . Workers had learned that plant owners were dependent on them. Then when enough of them joined together they were able to develop the powerful weapon, the "strike," by which they could force their employers to give them much that they wanted. The government finally declared legal this labor "union" activity that limited employers' freedom to carry on their business as they wanted to.

In the 1920's many people felt that the United States had indeed found the secret of perpetual prosperity and a good many—particularly the successful people—believed that freedom to earn and to own was at the bottom of this success. But soon came a great collapse of our whole economy that showed that something was wrong with the system. The nation thought deeply then about the difficult problem that we set ourselves— to permit as great freedom as possible to everybody but at the same time to preserve the security and the prosperity of the nation and to reduce the destructive force of poverty as much as possible.

New limits were set on the freedom to earn and to own in an effort to increase the security and welfare of the nation. For a period of several years it seemed to many people that individual freedom was being sacrificed to a dangerous extent for national welfare. Among policies that were established in that period, though, are many that we have agreed should be retained as a part of our economic system.

Perhaps one of the most radical departures from the old freedoms was a system of compulsory insurance that required large numbers of workers to turn over to the government a part of every pay check to be kept for them as premiums on insurance policies that would be paid back in the form of regular income after the worker was too old to continue earning. This system imposed a strictly controlled limit on the right of even the poor worker to use his income as he wanted to, but it protected his chances of having some economic security in his old age.

Another system of insurance provided that workers who were forced out of employment should have some guaranteed income. Unemployment insurance put a tax on employers to meet part of the costs of this insurance; government funds covered the rest. Again welfare considerations won over the freedom of employers to spend their money as they pleased. . . .

In the economy of our nation today we find evidence that the pressures for freedom and the pressures for control have continually worked together in the shaping of a system that provides for a maximum of freedom combined with sufficient controls to protect the welfare of the nation and of those in-dividuals whose freedoms are lost unless society offers them some special protection.

In the United States today certain economic freedoms are assured everyone. Everyone in the United States is legally free to choose the kind of economic activity he will engage in—to earn his living in whatever way his talents and natural inclinations lead him to. This freedom is, however, limited by standards of proficiency that must be met in many occupations for which licensing requirements have been established. In the United States every individual is free to earn as much money as he can get, to bargain for higher wages, or to charge as high prices as people will willingly pay him. (This principle was departed from in the wartime emergency when certain limits, which have since been abandoned, were set to prices that could legally be charged.)

Against these guarantees of freedom must then be weighed those social controls that impose limitations on the freedoms of individuals. The most important of these can perhaps be summarized under the general headings of:

Taxes—especially the income and social security taxes

Prevention of monopoly

Legal controls over wages and working conditions

Labor union activity

Another development in our country that is viewed by many as a threat to individual freedom to earn and to own is the growing power of organized labor. Here a group that does not represent the government has organized into what in some instances amounts to a monopoly threat to employers and even to workers who prefer to remain outside these organizations. . . .

The freedom of owners and their chosen representatives to manage their businesses is seen by some to be threatened by the power of organized labor to dictate terms to management— terms of wages and hours of work, working conditions, pensions, and other benefits for workers. Natural forces, primarily the increasing sharing of viewpoints by labor and management, are seen to be relieving some of the conflict in this area, but many problems continually arise in the dealings between labor and management that demand a clear examination of the basic problem of freedom *versus* controls.

The freedom of the individual to earn as he pleases is also thought by some to be threatened by the growing power of organized labor. In some instances a person who chooses to accept a wage that is offered him, to work under conditions that exist, or to work longer hours than those his union permits feels that his individual freedom is being restricted by the very organization that is set up to protect his interests against those of the owners of the capital that employs him.

CONSTITUTION OF THE MERGED AFL-CIO [2]

Preamble. The establishment of this Federation through the merger of the American Federation of Labor and the Congress of Industrial Organizations is an expression of the hopes and aspirations of the working people of America.

We seek the fulfillment of these hopes and aspirations through democratic processes within the framework of our constitutional government and consistent with our institutions and traditions.

At the collective bargaining table, in the community, in the exercise of the rights and responsibilities of citizenship, we shall responsibly serve the interests of all the American people.

We pledge ourselves to the more effective organization of working men and women; to the securing to them of full recognition and enjoyment of the rights to which they are justly entitled; to the achievement of ever higher standards of living and working conditions; to the attainment of security for all the people; to the enjoyment of the leisure which their skills make possible; and to the strengthening and extension of our way of life and the fundamental freedoms which are the basis of our democratic society.

We shall combat resolutely the forces which seek to undermine the democratic institutions of our nation and to enslave the human soul. We shall strive always to win full respect for the dignity of the human individual whom our unions serve.

[2] From AFL-CIO Constitution. (Publication no 1) AFL-CIO. Division of Publications. 815 16th St. Washington 6, D.C. 1955. p 1-5, 22-6, 37-8. Reprinted by permission.

With divine guidance, grateful for the fine traditions of our past, confident of meeting the challenge of the future, we proclaim this constitution. . . .

Article II. Objects and Principles. The objects and principles of this Federation are:

1. To aid workers in securing improved wages, hours and working conditions with due regard for the autonomy, integrity and jurisdiction of affiliated unions.

2. To aid and assist affiliated unions in extending the benefits of mutual assistance and collective bargaining to workers and to promote the organization of the unorganized into unions of their own choosing for their mutual aid, protection and advancement, giving recognition to the principle that both craft and industrial unions are appropriate, equal and necessary as methods of union organization.

3. To affiliate national and international unions with this Federation and to establish such unions; to form organizing committees and directly affiliated local unions and to secure their affiliation to appropriate national and international unions affiliated with or chartered by the Federation; to establish, assist and promote state and local central bodies composed of local unions of all affiliated organizations and directly affiliated local unions; to establish and assist trade departments composed of affiliated national and international unions and organizing committees.

4. To encourage all workers without regard to race, creed, color, national origin or ancestry to share equally in the full benefits of union organization.

5. To secure legislation which will safeguard and promote the principle of free collective bargaining, the rights of workers, farmers and consumers, and the security and welfare of all the people and to oppose legislation inimical to these objectives.

6. To protect and strengthen our democratic institutions, to secure full recognition and enjoyment of the rights and liberties to which we are justly entitled, and to preserve and perpetuate the cherished traditions of our democracy.

7. To give constructive aid in promoting the cause of peace and freedom in the world and to aid, assist and cooperate with free and democratic labor movements throughout the world.

8. To preserve and maintain the integrity of each affiliated union in the organization to the end that each affiliate shall respect the established bargaining relationships of every other affiliate and that each affiliate shall refrain from raiding the established bargaining relationship of any other affiliate and, at the same time, to encourage the elimination of conflicting and duplicating organizations and jurisdictions through the process of voluntary agreement or voluntary merger in consultation with the appropriate officials of the Federation, to preserve, subject to the foregoing, the organizing jurisdiction of each affiliate.

9. To aid and encourage the sale and use of union made goods and union services through the use of the union label and other symbols; to promote the labor press and other means of furthering the education of the labor movement.

10. To protect the labor movement from any and all corrupt influences and from the undermining efforts of Communist agencies and all others who are opposed to the basic principles of our democracy and free and democratic unionism.

11. To safeguard the democratic character of the labor movement and to protect the autonomy of each affiliated national and international union.

12. While preserving the independence of the labor movement from political control, to encourage workers to register and vote, to exercise their full rights and responsibilities of citizenship, and to perform their rightful part in the political life of the local state and national communities. . . .

Article III. Executive Council. Section 1. The Executive Council shall consist of the president, the vice presidents and the secretary-treasurer.

Sec. 2. The Executive Council shall be the governing body of this Federation between conventions. It is authorized and empowered to take such action and render such decisions as may be necessary to carry out fully and adequately the decisions and instructions of the conventions and to enforce the provisions contained in this constitution. Between conventions it shall have the power to direct the affairs of the Federation and to take such actions and render such decisions as are necessary and appropriate to safeguard and promote the best interests of the Federation and its affiliated unions, including the organization of unorganized industries by means most appropriate for that purpose. . . .

Sec. 7. It is a basic principle of this Federation that it must be and remain free from any and all corrupt influences and from the undermining efforts of Communist, Fascist or other totalitarian agencies who are opposed to the basic principles of our democracy and of free and democratic trade unionism. The Executive Council, when requested to do so by the president or by any other member of the Executive Council, shall have the power to conduct an investigation, directly or through an appropriate standing or special committee appointed by the president, of any situation in which there is reason to believe that any affiliate is dominated, controlled or substantially influenced in the conduct of its affairs by such corrupt influence, or that the policies or activities of any affiliate are consistently directed toward the advocacy, support, advancement or achievement of the program or of the purposes of the Communist party, any Fascist organization or other totalitarian movement. Upon the completion of such an investigation, including a hearing if requested, the Executive Council shall have the authority to make recommendations or to give directions to the affiliate involved and shall have the further authority, upon a two-thirds vote, to suspend any affiliate found guilty of a violation of this section. Any action of the Executive Council under this section may be appealed to the convention, provided, however, that such action shall remain in full force and effect pending any appeal. . . .

Sec. 11. The Executive Council shall have the power to file charges and conduct hearings on such charges against any executive officer of the Federation or other member of the Executive Council on the ground that such person is guilty of malfeasance or maladministration, and to make a report to the convention recommending appropriate action. The Executive

Council must serve such officer with a copy of the written charges a reasonable time before the hearing.

Sec. 12. The Executive Council shall have the further power to refuse to seat or to remove from office any member of the Executive Council, or to remove from office any officer, who is found by the Council, by a two-thirds vote after notice and hearing, to be ineligible to serve. . . . Any action of the Executive Council under this section may be appealed to the convention, provided, however, that such action shall be effective when taken and shall remain in full force and effect pending any appeal.

Sec. 13. In any case in which an affiliate has been suspended from membership in the Federation by the convention, or by a two-thirds vote of the Executive Council in the cases set forth in Section 7 of this Article, and in which it is shown that the cause for such suspension no longer exists, the Executive Council shall have the power, upon a two-thirds vote, to terminate such suspension.

Article XV. Local Unions Directly Affiliated to the Federation, Organizing Committees, and National Councils. . . . Sec. 2. The Executive Council of the Federation shall issue rules governing the conduct, activities, affairs, finances and property of organizing committees, national councils, and directly affiliated local unions, and governing the suspension, expulsion and termination of such organizations. Such rules shall define the powers of the president, or his designee, with respect to disciplinary action against such organizations, or their officers. They shall provide for notice and hearing in all cases in which such action is taken with respect to directly affiliated local unions, but shall permit emergency action (including the authority to suspend officers and establish a trusteeship over such local unions and their property) prior to hearing where in the opinion of the president the interests of the Federation so require. The rules shall further provide for appeals to the Executive Council and to the convention, but shall provide that decisions appealed from shall remain in full force and effect pending any appeal.

Upon the dissolution, suspension or revocation of the charter of any such organizations, all funds and property of any character

shall revert to the Federation, which shall to the extent appropriate hold such funds and property in trust until such time
that the suspended or defunct organization may be reorganized
and be able to confine its activities and actions to conform with
the constitution and laws of this Federation. It shall be the
duty of the officers of any such organization which has been
dissolved or whose charter has been suspended or revoked to
deliver all funds and property to the president of the Federation or his designated representative. In the event of a failure
or refusal to so deliver such funds and property, all expenses
incurred by the Federation in recovering such funds and property
shall be a lawful charge upon the funds and property involved
and, on recovery thereof, the Federation shall reimburse itself
from the funds and property recovered.

THE NEW LOOK IN UNIONS [3]

The most important single factor affecting labor unions is
the attitude of the employer. This is particularly true in the
United States, where workingmen depend exclusively upon the
union (among forms of labor organization) for the articulation
and achievement of their aspirations. Here, to a far greater
degree than elsewhere, the employer is the source of all good
things. This sound working rule has acquired during the past
twenty years a firm ideological base, a virtually complete acceptance of that set of beliefs which may be roughly described
as "capitalism." This ideological structure is buttressed by a
specific faith in the capacities of American management, shared
alike by trade union members and trade union leaders. . . .

From the union's point of view, the significance of the new
attitude is that the employer's door is really open to the representatives of the union, especially the representative of the
national union. Nowadays, employers are far more likely to say
that local people are "difficult and unreasonable," while national
union representatives "understand the employer's problems."

[3] From "Observations on the Changing Nature of American Unions," by
George W. Brooks, research and educational director, International Brotherhood of
Pulp, Sulphite and Paper Mill Workers. Monthly Labor Review. 80:151-5.
February 1957. (From a paper read at the annual meeting of the Industrial
Relations Research Association, Cleveland, Ohio, December 28-29, 1956) Re-
printed by permission.

Some observers have professed inability to understand why, in the light of the attitudes of unions a quarter of a century ago, the union representative was so ready to walk through the open door. The question reflects a misunderstanding of what was happening a quarter of a century ago, and not of what is happening now. Before the passage of the Wagner Act, unions were traditionally antiemployer. But the earlier ideologies were not theirs by choice. They were forced upon the unions by systematic employer antiunionism. . . .

When antiunionism was abandoned in the forties and fifties by significant segments of American industry, a new world was created for the unions. For it now turned out that the imperative requirements of the union—the regular flow of new members and dues—could be underwritten by the employer with considerable more reliability than was possible under earlier arrangements. . . .

The outstanding change for the union, in its own mind, is its success. This colors every action and attitude of leadership. Labor leaders see their achievements mirrored in the new attitudes of management. They have every reason to belive that the trends of the last twenty years are all to the good, and that their systematic encouragement will lead to more good. . . .

The great change in American labor unions during the past twenty years has been a general shift in power and control from the members to the leaders. The change was far reaching; it appears to be permanent. The change had taken place almost wholly without constitutional reform. . . .

Before the forties, any strong central tendencies were offset, and frequently more than offset, by two omnipresent, disagreeable facts: widespread employer antiunionism and rival unionism, the latter often with a left-wing spice. . . .

Faced with an arrogant official attitude, a fundamental mistake in judgment, or a failure to respond to local wishes, a local union could leave the national union. If it simply wished to withdraw, the employer was always ready to be helpful. Or, if the local members were persuaded of the value of unionism, but not of this union, there was always a rival ready to welcome them with open arms.

Both of these routes are now closed, in the "protected" sections of industry. The employer typically does not now welcome withdrawal from the international union. . . . The local dissenters thus find themselves confronted today by a solid front of opposition which includes both the national union and the company. Within the past two years, the alternate route has been closed by the no-raid agreements and the AFL-CIO merger. Except in unorganized plants, therefore, the local people have a very restricted freedom of choice. These changes, whether good or bad, have completely altered the old balance between local and national unions. . . .

Union people, by and large, believe nowadays that a union should be big to be effective. It is not surprising that union leaders favor large unions, but the membership generally share this view, in the apparent belief that a large union is necessarily more competent and more powerful. Management contributes to this belief by "viewing with alarm" the growth of large unions. . . .

The emphasis on big national unions has been accomplished by a de-emphasis on the importance of local unions and local union activity. This has happened in two ways. First, the pursuit of bigness has made members willing to give up a good deal of local autonomy. Secondly, and more important, the very fact of bigness, especially when accompanied by large-scale multi-plant bargaining, has inevitably resulted in a diminution of local activity and a transfer of functions from local unions to national unions. . . .

As the [collective bargaining] process is removed further from local plants and local unions, the bargaining takes on a less personal character and tends to become more of a pageant or drama. There is much less of the "give and take"of negotiators who are familiar with local details and, therefore, willing to agree to variety and deviations. The role of the union negotiator himself has undergone subtle but fundamental changes. He enjoys the confidence of management, more often than not. He finds that management has been surprisingly willing . . . to grant significant concessions on wages, hours, and working conditions. He tends to believe that this state of affairs is permanent and reliable. His primary responsibility is to get a settlement. In his efforts to bring about an agreement, he frequently finds that it is the local union and not the company which is the stumbling block. His role changes, therefore; he becomes more and more a mediator. Collective bargaining itself becomes a kind of sociodrama enacted to convince the membership that the results were "fair" or at least "all that could be gotten.". . .

Union leaders whose experience goes back more than twenty years are now a tiny minority of the total number of persons employed by unions on a full-time basis. Their influence is still very great, but it is diminishing. And their like will never be employed again, if one may assume a continuation of the trends . . . for the past fifteen years. The change of attitude as to what type of men are to be employed by unions is largely due to these very leaders. Naturally, the first requirement is that they be able to "get along with management." It is not nearly so necessary that they be able to capture and retain the "loyalty" of workers. These changes of attitude are significant in their effect upon local unions, because they affect the type of man who will rise to leadership in local unions. . . .

The recent growth in the use of "experts" [on union staffs] . . . has been largely a matter of turning over to the experts significant aspects of collective bargaining or internal union processes. In its worst form, the officer or representative of the union abandons his role as spokesman for the union and contents himself with vouching for the qualifications of the expert, who then performs, independently of the machinery of the union, the decision-making function.

The process of blind reliance on experts has been accelerated by the growth of what is known as technical bargaining on pensions, insurance plans, and so on, where the union permits or even encourages the actuaries to make decisions of policy under the guise of performing purely technical functions. The union may even accept the statements made by the company's actuary, in the belief that his conclusions are dictated by facts and are untouched by considerations related to the interests of the company.

Regrettably, the arbitration process may have the same effect. Very few unions today would sign a no-strike clause without an arbitration provision, but few of them could have contemplated the extent to which the arbitration process would be elaborated. Arbitration is a necessary safeguard, but to be used, like the strike, sparingly. . . .

There has no doubt been a significant increase in union "responsibility" and "statesmanship" as a concomitant of these changes. I think a more important advantage is the nearly universal consent which the unions in manufacturing industries now give to technological change. . . . Local union members are always uneasy about, and usually opposed to, technological change. The national union, on the other hand is likely to take the statesmanlike view. A shift in power to the national union therefore strengthens the hand of management in making technological change.

It is argued on the other side that these advantages are far less than the disadvantages of the decline of local and membership participation in the internal processes of the union and in the processes of collective bargaining. The overt evidences of the problem press themselves upon [the union president] insistently. The unavailability of competent men, the drift of both local and national leaders into management, and the growth of the "professional delegate" are all phenomena which cause him acute pain.

But these phemomena are merely the surface manifestations of the problem. Those who most regret the current developments argue that the real loss is in local participation in the processes for which the union was created. Among the less cynical, there is a conviction that the union performs its historic function only when, and to the extent to which, there is direct and understanding participation by members and local officers in the union and in the bargaining.

THE NEW LOOK IN MANAGEMENT [4]

Three strands stand out . . . in the prevailing [management] philosophies of the 1920's and early 1930's: (1) The concept that the authority of the employer was supreme; (2) certain aspects of Taylorism [the principles developed by Frederick W. Taylor], particularly the importance of fitting the man to the job and the job to the man; (3) the welfare concept.

These strands had a number of points in common. First, the employee was viewed as a malleable factor in production. It was the employer who gave the orders, did the thinking. Second, incentive was conceived of in financial terms. . . . Third, unions and union members had no place in the scheme of things. Fourth, the term "management prerogatives" was a redundancy, not a discussable issue. Fifth, the concept of identity of interests prevailed. The identity was defined and implemented by management. . . .

Management still insists on the "right to direct the working force." It is recognized, however, that this right is subject to many limitations. Some of these restrictions are formally incorporated in union agreements. But whether or not they are thus embodied, the concept of limited sovereignty is now grounded in the philosophy and mores of management to a degree that contrasts strikingly with the situation earlier.

Increasingly the idea has gained ground that employees may have something to contribute to the productive process, over and above the performance of their specifically assigned tasks. This belief is part of the basis for the current emphasis on "two-way communication." It is intimately bound up with the increasing discussion of "participation.". . .

However grudging, there has been an increased willingness on the part of management to admit that the interests of management and employees are not in all instances identical. Correspondingly, there seems to have been a diminution in the conviction that management is the best judge of the interests of

[4] From "Management's Attitudes Toward Employes and Unions," by Douglass V. Brown and Charles A. Myers, of the faculty of the Massachusetts Institute of Technology. *Monthly Labor Review*. 80:157-60. February 1957. (From a paper read at the annual meeting of the Industrial Relations Research Association, Cleveland, Ohio. December 28-29, 1956) Reprinted by permission.

its employees. Two notes of caution, however, should be injected here. In the first place, we should not exaggerate either the magnitude of the changes in philosophy or the certainty of their performance. Second, while management may not be held to be the best judge of employees' interests, it may regard itself as a better judge than, say, the union. . . .

The most obvious fact is that managements have recognized unions and are dealing with them to an extent undreamed of twenty-five years ago. To this extent, at least, it can be said that management has accepted unions, both in its philosophy and in its practice. . . .

Management philosophy toward unions is reflected not only in the degree of its acceptance of unions as coexisting institutions, but also in the conduct of bargaining and the substance of the bargains made with unions. One focal area in this latter connection is that which centers around the concept of management prerogatives. Here again, it seems to us that there have been marked changes in management philosophy. Put briefly, the changes reflect a shift from the concept that management's decisions are unchallengeable simply because they are management's decisions. [The shift] permits discussion of matters which had to be at least discussable if the institutional needs of the unions were to be met.

There is, we feel, an increased awareness by management of the kind of organization a union is, of the compulsions that occur within and around it, and of the problems facing the leadership of a democratic union. There is a readier acceptance of the necessity for acting in ways that are in conflict with the traditions of sound business methods (or, as the unions might say, in conflict with management's stereotypes of itself). . . .

In the last few years, there seems to us to have been a trend in the direction of a stiffer attitude toward unions on the part of management. More significant, in our judgment, are those instances in which the stiffening has taken the form, not of opposition to unionism as such, but of more vigorous efforts to contain the union on substantive matters or to control the avenues along which the substantive matters would come to rest.

In the area of management's philosophies and attitudes toward employees as union members, the important issues may perhaps be phrased in terms of questions involving loyalties. Where employees are unionized, must there always be conflicts between loyalty to the union and loyalty to management? Does an increase in loyalty to one necessarily mean a decrease in loyalty to the other? Is it possible to have divided loyalties, with the relative pull varying with circumstances and issues? What approaches should management adopt, and by what philosophies should it be guided in this whole area of loyalties? . . .

We would . . . call attention to the obvious expansion of the role of staff services in personnel administration and labor relations. Efforts and expenditures of current magnitudes could not have been justified under the framework of philosophies of earlier eras.

Second, the role of supervision, and particularly firstline supervision, in the personnel area has come in for increasing attention. Here we need only refer to the prevalence of the belief that "technical competence in a foreman is not enough" and to the multitude of foreman training courses, with their emphasis on human relations, that have sprung up in every corner of the country.

Thirdly, even a cursory examination of the literature will attest to the widespread acceptance of the necessity for top management support in an effective program of personnel and labor relations.

Fourth, reference should be made to the growth of multi-employer bargaining. Typically, the idea of association with other employers in bargaining seems to have been repugnant to most American managements. The gradual weakening of their resistance we view as evidence, first, of the greater acceptance of unionism as a continuing phenomenon and, second, of the belief that association strengthens management's hands. . . .

Fifth, . . . there is evidence that, in recent years, there has been an increasing tendency on the part of management to take the initiative in collective bargaining negotiations.

Sixth, certainly one of the most striking contrasts between today and twenty-five years ago is to be found in the current prevalence and scope of grievance procedures, culminating usually in private voluntary arbitration.

Seventh, there have been adventures into joint administration of matters which would earlier have been the unquestioned province of management.

Eighth, the vastly different modes of behavior during work stoppages. Where there are still instances of bloodshed and violence, the general picture contrasts sharply with earlier days.

These changes . . . did not come about primarily because of internal changes in management organization and outlook. The main pressures . . . were external, forcing many managements to reevaluate their existing organization and policies and to adopt new ones to fit new conditions. Among these pressures were:

1. Growing labor shortages, starting with the end of immigration but really beginning to pinch with the onset of World War II.

2. Increasing governmental intervention in labor-management relations beginning with the New Deal period. . . .

3. The increased strength of unions. This clearly put pressure on management to change the earlier methods of dealing with workers.

4. Increasing size of business enterprises. Larger firms require more staff personnel. Industrial relations has become a specialized branch of management.

5. Separation of ownership and management, and the growth of a professional managerial group. This separation has led to the development of a professional, rather than family-oriented management, with fewer emotional reactions to the challenge of managerial prerogatives.

IMPLICATIONS OF AFL-CIO MERGER [5]

Big unionism has found no allure in a third party but it has become a lusty third force in American politics. . . .

[5] From "Labor a Lusty Force in Politics," by Charles Lucey, Scripps-Howard staff writer. New York *World Telegram & Sun.* p 1. October 11, 1957. (Article 4 in a series of eight articles titled "Big Labor—A Giant on a Tightrope," published October 8-16, 1957, in the New York *World Telegram & Sun* and other Scripps-Howard newspapers) Reprinted by permission.

Labor's political leverage is substantially responsible for the fact that, despite an Eisenhower, Democrats are today in control of Congress.

The unions have helped elect and defeat state governors, mayors, city councilmen, state legislators. Union leaders serve on scores of boards and commissions. They are skilled at lobbying in Washington and in state capitals; it is almost an axiom that getting the right law passed is an easier way of achieving an end than hitting the picket line in a strike.

Tick off Senate seats the Democrats won just a year ago— Pennsylvania, Oregon, Washington, Colorado, Idaho—and find labor playing an important role in all, a controlling role in some. Without those victories Democrats would not be running the United States Senate.

Just two months ago labor politicians were a vitally effective part of the force which made a dead pigeon of Walter Kohler in Wisconsin and elected William Proximire to the Senate.

So with the House—labor's political captains mount determined offensives in fifty or sixty industrial areas. They have no veneration for political folklore, have developed new campaigning skills of their own and improved on old ones.

When AFL-CIO merger became fact in 1955 many feared this held ominous political portent for the United States. They visualized a great monolith, a bulldozer capable of pushing to the polls each election day 15 million union members, plus families, to vote as union bosses decide.

It hasn't happened that way. There are no present signs it will. Union members are individuals first. Most will vote by conviction. Unions can influence but not control members in forming those convictions. There are many instances of members' failure to follow union leaders' guidance—the manner in which the late Senator Robert A. Taft clobbered them in Ohio in 1950 is cited often, and failure to elect a trade unionist mayor of Detroit.

Union politicians sometimes have paid dearly for overplaying their hand—for talking too big, for putting labor's stamp too prominently on a candidate or a campaign. They've learned to curb these earlier mistakes.

Labor's political techniques are improving. It shows up sometimes in little things—like finding that political campaign comic books, such as those which derided Mr. Taft in that Ohio campaign, actually lose votes by seeming to insult people's intelligence. Labor shies away now from campaigns of pure bitterness and hatred because most people have a basic sense of fair play. . . .

It's still a new thing for the trade unions to seek to channel their membership into a political force. Samuel Gompers and William Green weren't the Make-America-Over type and were chary of trying to swing labor's political weight. Usually they were for Democrats, though in 1924 the AFL executive council indorsed old Bob La Follette and Burton K. Wheeler on the Progressive ticket.

But from Franklin Roosevelt's time onward, the unions began, by formal political organization, to give aggressive attention to supporting their friends and opposing their enemies at the polls. John L. Lewis and Sidney Hillman set up Labor's Non-Partisan League in 1936, with branches in many states, but it was handicapped in succeeding years by the AFL-CIO split.

In 1943 the CIO established its new Political Action Committee. It performed almost spectacularly well in 1944 but in 1946, when the Republicans grabbed Congress, it lost some of its luster. In 1947 the AFL created its own political arm, called Labor's League for Political Education.

Now, a decade later and after labor unity, the political show has been rolled together in the Committee on Political Education —COPE—headed by James L. McDevitt.

"Organized labor," said the head of the National Association of Manufacturers in the 1956 campaign, "is boldly attempting to seize political control of the United States." The "outspokenness" of AFL-CIO political activity was compared to Hitler's *Mein Kampf* and Karl Marx' *Das Kapital*.

Now, there's a small Socialist fringe in labor, but no deep dedication—as in some European countries—to the idea of a purely labor government. Such statements would make more sense if labor's bosses could deliver anything like the 15 million labor votes, or if, say, 30 million of the 65-million work force were strapped into AFL-CIO. But John L. Lewis, who in 1940 at the height of his power tried futilely to swing labor's vote against Franklin Roosevelt, could give evidence on this point. And last year, despite the unions' pro-Adlai Stevenson bent, millions of card-carrying unionists voted for Mr. Eisenhower.

There's no question that, especially from the CIO side, the unions have helped the Democrats mightily. They did a tremendous job in getting people registered in big industrial centers in 1956. They distributed some 12 million printed voting records of senators and House members, with "right" and "wrong" scores shown on major issues in which labor had a stake. In many states they ran "boiler factories"—headquarters in which women manned batteries of phones to rouse out the vote for labor-favored candidates.

The Taft-Hartley law specified that regular union funds— union dues which come from members of diverse political belief —cannot be used for political activity. Yet court decisions since 1947 have opened a wide gap in this prohibition. In an early test, the Supreme Court said distribution of the CIO newspaper, plugging for a Democrat, did not violate the law. In another case, payment of union salaries to officials engaged in politicking was held legal. . . .

The unions never have been spectacularly successful in putting the bite on members for voluntary political contributions. The response has totaled about $2 million a year in recent elections—a handy packet but not overwhelming either in relation to mass union membership or to totals spent in United States elections.

But to measure union contributions in dollars vastly understates the case, because many union headquarters become virtual political headquarters in the final days before elections. Probably nobody knows how many of some 60,000 union functionaries give their time to the cause—certainly many thousands. . . .

There is no question labor had a role in those Senate races— for example, in marshaling its strength along the Pacific northwest waterfront to help plaster Mr. Eisenhower's two hand-picked candidates, Douglas McKay in Oregon and Arthur B. Langlie in Washington. In Washington labor was effective in licking a "right-to-work" initiative measure that would have outlawed the closed shop; in Oregon it gave the Democrats greater registration than the Republicans in a presidential election for the first time since the Civil War.

In Michigan, it has been easy statistically to show the United Auto Workers-Walter Reuther strength. Reuther-backed Governor Mennen Williams has stayed in power five terms, right through years in which President Eisenhower was sweeping this state. The Michigan legislature has a dozen UAW members, an ex-CIO leader is a state Supreme Court judge and many lower court judges were elected with UAW backing. . . .

It isn't all a victory march for labor. In Ohio and Indiana it has failed these last two years, to the chagrin of Mr. Reuther, and the UAW, to get amendments to the unemployment compensation law which would let the unions gain the advantages won in 1955 contracts with the big auto companies. . . .

But across the board, the unions get good marks for gains they've made in political effectiveness in just a few years. Yet there's reason to think that a basic, inherent American aversion to "bigness"—including union political bigness—will be a restraint on any fancied road to what some fear as union-dominated country.

WHAT LABOR MEANS BY "MORE" [6]

Our goals as trade unionists are modest, for we do not seek to recast American society in any particular doctrinaire or ideological image. We seek an ever rising standard of living. Sam Gompers . . . , when asked what the labor movement wanted, . . . answered "More." If by a better standard of living we mean not only more money, but more leisure and a richer cultural life, the answer remains "More.". . .

We are dedicated to freedom, not only political but also economic, through a system of private enterprise. We believe in the American profit system. We believe in free competition. The American private-enterprise system, despite some defects,

[6] From an article by George Meany, president, AFL-CIO. *Fortune.* 51:92-3+. March 1955. Courtesy *Fortune* Magazine. Copyright 1955 by Time Inc.

has achieved far greater results for wage-earners than any other social system in history. . . .

We are proud, understandably, of the contribution of trade unionism to the changing American private-enterprise system. Certainly we have differed with our employers over the sharing of the benefits—this is the heart of bargaining—and we shall differ again during the next quarter-century. But throughout we have relied upon the judgment of free men, unimpeded by the interference of government, to reach private agreement, and it is certainly the hope and resolve of the AFL that our differences shall continue to be settled in this way. . . .

For the AFL I can say flatly that collective bargaining is not a means of seeking a voice in management. [This was written before Mr. Meany headed the merged AFL-CIO.—Ed.] We do not want so-called "codetermination"—the representation of unions on the board of directors or in the active management of a company. In Germany, where trade unions have endorsed such a plan, codetermination emerges from . . . the political use of corporate power by cartel management. And in that country it has some logic as a means of maintaining economic democracy. Here in the United States, with a different background and tradition, with a different kind of management, with the acceptance of collective bargaining, codetermination has no reality. . . .

There remains the more concrete and difficult question of where a line can be drawn. . . .

While exact answers are hard to give, a general principle can be established: A union exists to protect the livelihood and interests of a worker. Those matters that do not touch a worker directly, a union cannot and will not challenge. These may include investment policy, a decision to make a new product, a desire to erect a new plant so as to be closer to expanding markets, to reinvest out of earnings or seek new equity capital, etc. But where management decisions affect a worker directly, a union will resist. . . .

Merely because management bears the responsibility of managing, it does not acquire the right to pay less than a decent wage as a condition of staying in business. Nor does an effective management allow its plant to become run-down and antiquated. Workers should not bear the price of management's errors. Lincoln once put it: "Labor is prior to and independent of capital. Capital is only the fruit of labor, and could not have existed if labor had not first existed. Labor is the superior of capital and deserves much the higher consideration. . . ."

In the next twenty-five years decentralization probably will be a prime feature of corporate decision-making and corporate management. Inevitably, collective bargaining will have to be adapted to the changing nature of managerial patterns. But collective bargaining is no mere reflex to industrial change. Where firms decentralize in order to move into low-wage areas, or to break up existing wage structures, unions will not acquiesce. . . .

Not only the forms of bargaining, but the range of issues, are subject to change and modification. At the moment, regularity of income or of consuming power is being sought by some unions through a guaranteed annual wage. [See "Guaranteed Annual Wage—Threat or Promise?" in Section III, below.—Ed.] Actually the goal is not new; it is simply one more projection of the basic desire of workers for a decent year-round standard of living. . . . While the guaranteed annual wage is a good objective, the nature of the industry limits its application, and in some industries it is highly impractical. We hope, however, that by 1980 we shall be able to expand our economy in orderly fashion so that the guarantee of year-round incomes for all workers is no longer a problem.

In the next twenty-five years the flexibility of collective bargaining will meet its severest test in the rapid changes in the technological structure of industry and the consequent wholesale changes in the character of the labor force. . . . But we know from experience that progress in technology does not occur in large, magical jumps, but grows out of past advances. Similarly, the attendant problems of adapting to progress do not change basically; they simply appear larger and more complex. Our concern, thus, is less with 1980 than with the road to it. . . .

The answer to technological changes lies in smoothing its transitions and cushioning the shocks that attend it. This means, in the immediate sense, the establishment of severance pay, retraining of skills, reorganization of work schedules. These are social costs that industry will have to bear in order to avoid the wasting of human resources—and to avoid our calling on government to bear these costs if industry fails to do so.

In the longer run we shall press for the time-proved policy of reduction of hours. Through shortened hours, workers not only have more leisure, but we are able to "spread the work." We have set our sights on a thirty-hour week. By 1980 that should be easily attainable for all Americans. . . .

The AFL is primarily an economic organization, seeking its ends in the economic field. In recent years we have been involved wth government. Whether we shall continue to be so depends in large measure on industry. Only when industry has failed to accept responsibility has labor . . . turned to government for help. There is always the danger that concentration of power may whittle away individual freedoms. In fact, the heavy hand of government in the past has throttled freedom for private collective bargaining perhaps more than it throttled freedom for private enterprise. But government has an obligation to help people do what they cannot do for themselves.

The AFL, for example, at one time opposed a government system of social security. . . . But the depression of the 1930's changed our thinking. . . . We still believe that government alone should not be called upon to provide complete social security. . . . Collective bargaining, not government, must ultimately provide the necessary protection against the deficiencies of the economic system. . . .

So long as our relations with employers were wholly in the economic field, political action occupied a small role in the affairs of the AFL. . . . The turning point was reached in 1947 when Congress adopted Taft-Hartley. . . .

Behind this action of Congress was a change in the strategy of antiunion employers and their trade associations—the employers' unions. These employers chose the new battleground—the legislative halls—and forced the trade union movement into the political arena. . . .

But we shall remain in politics. The fact that we do so does not mean that the AFL will be tied to any political party. Nor does it close off any particular road in politics. I do not think the membership of the AFL is thinking now in terms of a national political party sponsored by labor. Yet if the action of the two major parties leaves us no alternative in our efforts to safeguard and raise the living standards of the workers, labor will go as far as it must down that political road. . . .

Our sole principle has been and will be to seek the election—without regard to party labels—of those who believe as we do in an economic system based on prosperity at the lower rungs of the economic ladder, and to oppose those who hold otherwise.

WHAT MANAGEMENT EXPECTS OF LABOR [7]

What industry expects from organized labor breaks down naturally in my mind into three areas:

The area of individual liberty; the area of economic responsibility; and the area of bargaining integrity. . . .

In the area of individual liberty, we hold that every American has the inalienable right to join a labor union and have a voice in its activities, and that this right should not be denied either by employers or unions. We hold that the individual has an equally inalienable right not to join if he doesn't want to join.

Industry expects organized labor to acknowledge and respect this right. It expects the leaders of organized labor—out of their own pride in and respect for American tradition—to refrain from efforts to coerce people into unions against their will. It expects them to cease their unremitting efforts to remove or circumvent the legal protections of this right which are contained in Federal and state laws. . . .

Industry also expects the leaders of organized labor to refrain from coercion and violence. There are instances without number, but I can cite the recent notorious strike against the Perfect Circle Corporation of New Castle, Indiana, to compel the company to sign a union-shop agreement.

[7] From "What Management Expects of Organized Labor," address by George C. Sligh, Jr., executive vice president, National Association of Manufacturers, at the Congress of American Industry, New York, December 1955. National Association of Manufacturers. 2 East 48th St. New York 17. n.d. p 1-19. Reprinted by permission.

This plant of the company employs only about 250 people. Yet a union recruited a mob of 5,000 from all over the state—and many from out of the state—to march on one hundred employees in the plant who refused to join the walkout.

In the ensuing violence, people inside and outside the plant were wounded by gunfire. Some of those inside were women. . . .

Every responsible labor leader should resolve to put an end to such lawless incidents, which deny every tenet of our proud civilization and bring disgrace and shame to every sincere American.

The doctrine that "the end justifies the means" has no place in American life, and it is particularly abhorrent when the means used violate liberty and the right of every law-abiding citizen to be secure in his home and in his person. . . .

We think the union member should have a real voice in all measures affecting his welfare—a voice that is listened to—and that this ought to apply particularly to the calling of a strike. We do not believe a union member should be required to submerge his personal interests unduly or altogether in the interests of the group. We think every man in this country is entitled to advance as far and as fast as his abilities will take him, and that he should not be held down by group interests, as expressed, for example, in the overly rigid seniority rules.

Too often in the constitutions of unions, democracy is all shadow and no substance. The top officers of some internationals control elections and conventions. In some situations they can remove local officials who disagree with them and then appoint their own men as trustees. On the other hand, there often is no effective method by which arrogant or selfish officials may be removed by the rank-and-file. In too many cases the right of dissent is denied and insurgency is dealt with in summary fashion. . . .

It is necessary . . . for union leadership to place some faith in management's judgment as to what wage scale and other labor cost provisions will best promote a thriving, growing business. Pattern bargaining often is harmful to an industry, and the calling of a strike to force what, in the final analysis, is an economic impossibility imposes hardship, suffering and loss on all concerned.

By the same token, contract agreements which limit the amount of work which may be performed, or which require more people on the job than are necessary to perform the work, are destructive of labor's interest, as well as of management's. The cost of featherbedding must show up in the price of the product and cut down its market among consumers. . . .

Management spends about $12,000 to provide plant and tools for each industrial worker. Limiting the use of these tools by slow-downs is an economic waste which can do no one any good. . . .

In its own interests, organized labor should join with management in demanding that our present tax system be modified— so that people who have increased their earnings to the point where they can save a little—this includes the vast majority of workers today—may be able to hold on to and invest more of these savings instead of having a progressively greater part grabbed by the tax collector.

A lively, expanding, growing economy, with ample opportunities for people to get better jobs and increase their earnings offers far more benefits to those in the lower income groups than the few dollars a year they might save in taxes by getting their exemptions increased. . . .

In the political area—where such proposals eventually stand or fall—industry calls upon organized labor to show economic responsibility. Industry urges labor to forgo threats of political retaliation against public officials who fail to follow labor's demands that they support one segment of the population against all others. Industry urges labor to refrain from the preparation of arbitrary black lists as a means of exerting political pressure. Industry decries the unjustifiable and sometimes illegal use of union funds to promote candidates and causes to which many of the members may be opposed.

In spite of this opposition, these members are forced through compulsory union membership to contribute a portion of their dues to political candidates to whom they are opposed. . . .

Organized labor [has] formed itself into one gigantic federation, with our guest, Mr. Meany, at its head. A careful reading of the constitution of this new body—and the publicly expressed views as to its aims and objectives—has caused considerable misgivings. . . .

A proclaimed purpose of the organization is vastly stepped up activity in the political field. The men who control the new federation will have vast funds and manpower and means of communication at their disposal. This sheer weight of concentrated power may enable them to exercise effective control over either or both political parties. . . .

Will the new organization become in effect a labor monopoly? Union leaders point out that their organization still represents only about one fourth of the total labor force and hence cannot be accused of being a labor monopoly. This it seems to me is begging the question. A monopoly exists wherever the entire labor supply of an industry is under the control of one union—and the new federation has announced its intention of organizing industry to the greatest possible extent. When the unions which control the labor supply of a number of major industries are gathered together in a body like the new federation—where they can be made to wheel and turn in response to the voice of the high command—the entire economy of the country is threatened with monopoly control.

Will this new organization become in effect a "ghost government?" Will a handful of men, not elected, not authorized by the American people, pull strings behind the scenes to direct the destinies of the nation? It is the potentials of this situation which worry industry—and many other thoughtful citizens as well.

Organized labor and industry will be able to work together in far greater harmony if the leaders of labor will be guided more by economic reality and abandon efforts to achieve by political means what cannot be justified economically at the bargaining table.

Things also will improve, I believe, if we can come to a better understanding in the area of bargaining integrity. If bargaining is to be harmonious and mutually satisfactory, it must be done in good faith.

Applying pressure during negotiations, either openly or behind the scenes, is hardly good-faith bargaining. In a recent case, the Textile Workers claimed the moral and legal right to call intermittent work stoppages and engage in other pressure tactics while it was supposed to be bargaining in good faith with an employer. . . .

When a bargaining agreement has been concluded, good faith demands that we live up to its spirit as well as its letter. Let us forgo efforts to take advantage of trick clauses or to read into the agreement more than it contains. Let us make it a document to live by and not to fight over.

Let us, above all, place our signatures to it in all intellectual honesty and accept without reservation our full obligations under it. With responsible people, their word is their bond, and responsible agreements are possible only between responsible people. . . .

I would like to propose a Code of Conduct under which both organized labor and industry can serve the nation better and more efficiently. This Code of Conduct would have five points:

1. A recognition of the right of every individual to join a union or to refrain from joining, as he chooses.

2. No interference with this right through violence, retaliation, subterfuge or coercion of any sort.

3. A striving for the utmost efficiency and productivity and the elimination of economic waste of every type.

4. An end to monopoly, whether on the part of organized labor or of industry.

5. Keep politics out of labor-management relations and avoid trying to obtain by political pressure that which cannot be justified economically.

If both organized labor and industry subcribe to this Code and respect their pledged word, we can work together to benefit the entire nation, and in doing so achieve our own goals.

III. SOME BASIC PROBLEMS

EDITOR'S INTRODUCTION

As a background to discussion of current issues between labor and management, this section opens with a study of the role of collective bargaining and an analysis of the "work stoppage" record, both by Federal bureau officials.

A national magazine writer tells the story of a long and bitter strike. A newspaper dispatch provides a footnote, reporting a National Labor Relations Board ruling on one of the key issues in this strike.

The research departments of a labor organization and of a manufacturers' group present their respective arguments on the relationship between wages, profits and prices. A university professor asks whether the proposal for a "guaranteed annual wage" in the automobile industry represents "a threat or a promise"—and offers his opinion. A labor reporter notes the effect of unemployment benefit funds during a business recession.

A former director of the CIO's Political Action Committee gives the reasons why labor has assumed a political role. A management consultant weighs the responsibilities resting on organized labor by reason of its great and growing influence in the nation's affairs.

COLLECTIVE BARGAINING [1]

The cement that binds the ordinary worker to a union is mixed in the work place itself and is compounded of two things: a sense of having participated, even though remotely, in decisions affecting the terms under which he is employed; and the knowledge, which usually is not remote at all, that he enjoys protection against arbitrary day-to-day decisions relating to his employment status. . . .

[1] From "Labor Status and Collective Bargaining," article by H. M. Douty, Chief of Division of Wages and Industrial Relations, Bureau of Labor Statistics. *Monthly Labor Review.* 79:647-53. June 1956.

Collective bargaining is a process through which decisions affecting the employment status of workers are arrived at by negotiation between employers or their representatives and the representatives of organized groups of employees. Failure to reach agreement on the substantive terms of the employment relationship may result in an agreement to arbitrate differences, although the arbitration of the terms of a contract, as distinguished from the arbitration of grievances arising under a contract, is not widespread in the United States. Failure to agree may result in a work stoppage, with the result that one of the parties may capitulate or both parties may decide to compromise differences. The strike or lockout is the ultimate sanction in collective bargaining.

The employing unit to which bargaining relates may be a single plant, several plants of the same employer, or a number of establishments of different employers organized into an association. A 1950 study suggests that multiplant (same employer) and multiemployer bargaining units account for a substantial majority of the workers under union agreements. . . .

It is possible for a union to destroy itself, and employers as well, by attempting to achieve wages or other standards that are not feasible in the specific economic situation in which the bargaining occurs. This has happened, but it is obviously not typical. Most bargaining is "realistic" in the sense that the parties have shrewd estimates of the limitations within which a settlement must be made. That this is so is indicated in part by the fact that the overwhelming proportion of collective agreements are arrived at without recourse to work stoppages. Employers perform a highly significant social function in resisting union demands that threaten the existence of the company or even any significant curtailment in the company's scale of operation. On the other hand, widespread collective bargaining tends to keep management alert and aggressive, conscious of cost, and responsive to opportunities for technical innovation in the broadest sense of that term. . . .

Historically, the content of the collective agreement unquestionably has tended to expand. The familiar expression "wages, hours, and conditions of work" is generally descriptive of the scope of agreements. But the items comprehended under this term are not fixed. Until recently, for example, private pension plans were not generally considered a bargainable issue. It has been observed that "issues over the scope of collective bargaining constitute the management-security counterpart of the union-security issue," and that, in terms of long-run constructive industrial relations, significant extension of the scope of bargaining should be achieved through negotiation and not by strike action or political power. . . .

Decisions relating to wage levels are obviously vital to management because of the importance of wages as cost. They are vital also to employees, since wages in many cases represent their only source of income. What unions do, in effect, is afford workers, through their representatives, an opportunity to explore directly with management their claims on the revenue of the enterprise. Organization makes possible the presentation of claims buttressed by analysis, argument, and persuasion, and by the possibility of collective withdrawal of labor from the enterprise. . . .

The concept of "wages" has lost its original simplicity, as unions have attempted through actions affecting employer expenditures for labor to increase the quantity of goods and services available to workers (through wage rate and premium pay increases); their leisure for the enjoyment of higher real incomes (paid holidays and more liberal vacation arrangements); and their security against social hazards (e.g., dependent old age). The extent to which these several objectives have been advanced in the past decade provides testimony to the extraordinary productivity of the economic system in the United States. Even if we assume that unionism has not increased employer outlays on "wages," considered as a proportion of national income, the allocation of these outlays as between rates and benefits seems plainly to have been affected by labor's participation in decision-making through collective bargaining. . . .

Historically, the question of what constitutes working time has been, next to wages, the major concern of unions and employers in collective bargaining. The two, of course, are intimately related and are often considered together. Working time is not a simple concept in modern industry; it involves not only definition of the length of the scheduled work-day and -week and the fixing of starting and stopping times, but such matters as the scheduling of overtime, late shifts, Sunday or holiday work, and lunch periods, together with questions of what activities, other than direct production, should be included in working time (e.g., rest periods, washup, cleanup, clothes changing and travel).

Another broad range of problems relates to rules affecting the security of workers on the job. Among the rules in this group are those governing the layoff of workers and their recall to duty, promotions, discipline and discharge, and transfer to other jobs within the enterprise. These are matters of concern to workers once they become attached to a particular firm. Rules or policy on these matters are clearly necessary for plant operating purposes; moreover, in terms of plant morale the rules (and their administration) should appeal to ordinary concepts of fairness and equity.

For example, it is a function of management to discipline workers for shirking on the job, disregard of safety regulations, abusive conduct toward supervisors or fellow workers, and other behavior that cannot be tolerated in any organization. But discipline, to be salutary, must be imposed under generally accepted rules. Again, from time to time, layoffs may be necessary at a plant. . . . Some of the most difficult problems of collective bargaining arise as unions and management attempt to reach agreement on day-to-day working rules. . . .

Many matters relating to the administration of wages (rates for new jobs, rates to reflect changes in job content, method of advancement within rate ranges, the setting of incentive standards and rates, and much more) tend to become subject to joint rule making under collective bargaining. In fact, a union literature is beginning to develop on such problems, and a few unions maintain staff technicians in time study and related arts. . . .

Good personnel practice requires that provision be made for the orderly resolution of grievances. Collective bargaining contracts almost always provide a mechanism through which grievances arising under their terms can be considered and settled directly by the parties; the vast majority of grievances are disposed of in this way. In the event of failure of the parties to reach agreement, however, most contracts now provide for arbitration as the final step in the grievance procedure. Grievance arbitration tends to prevent stubborn disputes from erupting into work stoppages, and has facilitated the widespread adoption of no-strike clauses for the duration of agreements.

Collective bargaining has given workers a voice in the determination of the wages and conditions under which they work, and a part also, through grievance procedures, in the day-to-day administration of working rules. . . .

The historical achievement of trade unionism is its enhancement of the status of the worker as an individual. It is not a paradox that this should have been done through organization and collective action. Men as individuals lost status as units in the labor force of the enterprises produced by the industrial revolution; they regained status as individuals through self-organization. For through organization, they won a voice in formulating the rules of their employment, and protection against arbitrary action affecting their role as employees. . . .

Although collective bargaining is an important factor in determining the status of labor in the United States, it would clearly be incorrect to infer that management, whether in union or nonunion firms, has no positive role to play. In fact, the recent studies of dual loyalty (to firm and union) show the continued significance of management attitudes and policies to the work force, even in strongly unionized situations.

A final point: trade unionism and collective bargaining are means, not ends. They are designed to afford wage earners a voice in decision-making in matters relating to their status and welfare in industry. As with other institutions, trade unions can fail to meet their responsibilities. It is clearly important for unions to be responsive to the views of their constituencies, to provide channels for the expression of those views, and to refrain from arbitrary disciplinary actions against members. It is equally important, in terms of the underlying interests of workers, that union power in collective bargaining be used to establish economic standards and working rules that provide room for reasonable operating flexibility and economic growth.

WORK STOPPAGES [2]

Government mediation and conciliation services helped terminate about three out of ten of the year's stoppages—proportion-
ately the same as most years since 1951. These strikes, however,
idled three fifths of all strikers for more than four fifths of the
total idleness—significant increases over the previous year. The
proportion of stoppages settled by direct negotiations between
representatives of the workers and employers was slightly higher
in 1956 than the previous year, and involved 30 per cent of the
workers for 10 per cent of the total idleness.

Situations in which workers returned to their jobs or were
replaced by new employees without an agreement or settlement
being negotiated accounted for 19 per cent of the year's total,
9 per cent of the workers, and 7 per cent of the idleness.

One per cent of the year's strikes ended with the employers
discontinuing business. Nongovernment mediators or agencies
either alone or with the aid of governmental agencies assisted
in the final settlement of an additional 1 per cent of the stoppages, accounting for about 0.5 per cent of the workers and
idleness.

All issues were settled or otherwise resolved at the termination of almost 90 per cent of the strikes occurring in 1956, equal
to the postwar high recorded in the previous year. More than
90 per cent of the workers and more than 95 per cent of the
idleness were involved in these stoppages. Such situations include
those resolved by agreement to use the company's grievance
procedure and those in which the workers returned without a
formal agreement or settlement. . . .

Typically, strike idleness has amounted to from one fifth to
one half of 1 per cent of total time worked by all workers in the
United States. . . . Prior to 1933, work stoppages involved
fewer than 2 per cent of all workers employed. Since that time,
they have generally idled from 5 to 9 per cent. . . .

Despite the large volume of unemployment that characterized
the 1930's unionization grew rapidly, with government policies

[2] From "Analysis of Work Stoppages, 1956," by Ann James Herlihy and
Herbert H. Moede of the staff of the Division of Wages and Industrial Relations,
Bureau of Labor Statistics. (Bulletin no 1218) United States Department of Labor.
Bureau of Labor Statistics. Washington 25, D.C. 1957. p 1-35.

of encouraging collective bargaining expressed in the Norris-LaGuardia Act of 1932, the National Industrial Recovery Act of 1933, and the National Labor Relations Act of 1935. . . .

Labor's attempts to organize, gain recognition, and bargain collectively were reflected in the sharp increase in the proportion of stoppages that centered about these issues from 1933 to 1941. . . . . Interspersed with these attempts were occasional sitdown strikes, notably from 1935 to 1937, and clashes, sometimes fatal, on picket lines.

The period since the 1930's has experienced full or practically full employment, dominated by high levels of defense production, by actual hostilities, or by postwar recovery and adjustment to a peacetime economy. As these events occurred, economic issues became the single most important cause of work stoppages. In most years since 1940, these issues accounted for a majority of the workers and idleness in all work stoppages. . . .

During the period of the United States' participation in World War II, strike idleness declined as emphasis on maximum war production led to labor-management pledges to avoid strikes and lockouts. . . .

In late 1945 and 1946, strike activity, measured in terms of workers involved and man-days of idleness, increased sharply as workers attempted to maintain their weekly earnings in the face of the postwar decline in hours of work. . . .

In 1946, strike activity reached its all-time high as measured in terms of workers involved or man-days idle. In that year, 4.6 million workers (14.5 per cent of all those employed) were directly involved for a total of 116 million man-days (1.43 per cent of all time worked). Stoppages, a number lasting more than fifty calendar days, occurred during the first year after V-J Day in many major industries. . . .

From 1947 to 1956, the number of workers involved in strikes ranged from 1.5 million to 3.5 million a year and generally remained below 2.7 million. Man-days of idleness fluctuated between 22.6 million and 59.1 million a year (0.2 to 0.6 of 1 per cent of total time worked) but were below 35 million in most years. In 1951, with Korean hostilities and wage controls, and again from 1953 to 1956, total idleness in strikes declined somewhat compared with other postwar years.

A STRIKE PATTERN [3]

On April 5, 1954, Local 833 of the United Automobile Workers called a strike against the Kohler Company, which manufactures bathroom fixtures and other products near Sheboygan, Wisconsin. . . . [Thus began] America's longest strike.

Some 700 of Kohler's 3300 production and maintenance workers wanted to keep on working that morning, but when they arrived at the plant gates they found them choked by a dense picket line of about 1500. . . . The union had brought in, from Detroit, Milwaukee and Racine, squads of special strike organizers. Paid $12 to $16 a day plus hotel expenses, they were called "special representatives" and "administrative assistants" by the union, "goons" by the nonstriking Kohler workers. And they were prepared to meet all comers.

When Mrs. Alice Tracey, who started working at Kohler when her husband died in 1927, and who since has educated her four children, came to the plant one morning early in the strike she found the gate blocked. "I don't believe anyone has the right to keep you from a job you're satisfied with," she says. "We were pushed and shoved. A man trod on my feet and asked me if I was afraid. Then he called for women. They kicked my shins, kneed me, and called me all sorts of foul names."

"On the third day," says Harold Jacobs, "we made a real try to get in, but couldn't. They pushed and kicked us. One morning we asked the sheriff to deputize fifty of us who were willing to help open up the lines. He wouldn't. 'There must be no bloodshed,' he said."

Harold Curtiss, thirty-three years with Kohler, says: "There was absolutely no law enforcement. When we told the sheriff that, according to law, he had to open up the picket line and take us through, he walked away."

The "strike kitchen" which the UAW rolled in for Kohler strikers was a twenty-four-karat social welfare program. "We have two thousand men on our relief rolls," stated Allan Graskamp, president of Local 833. The UAW was "pouring

[3] From "Strike Without End—The Kohler Story," by W. L. White, roving editor, *Reader's Digest*. *Reader's Digest*. 71:91-8. October 1957. Reprinted by permission.

$100,000 a week into strike relief." This included house rent, interest payments on home and car mortgages, food vouchers according to family size, hospital and life insurance, utility bills, new and used clothing, $25 in weekly "jingling money" for each striker. In return, the strikers served on the picket line and performed other strike duties.

Yet the company estimated that the strikers were losing $200,000 per week in wages.

The Kohler Company says that in this strange strike, wages are not the real issue; its figures show that they had averaged $2.02 per hour. Including overtime, this was 15 per cent above the average for the plumbing-fixture industry and 33.5 per cent above the average for nearby Sheboygan, where a Kohler job had become a valued prize. The strike was really a death struggle between two forms of "paternalism," old and new.

The late John Michael Kohler, who founded the company, had come from Austria in 1873 to make first farm machinery and then bathtubs. In 1912, to help the workers build a happier life, his son, the late Walter Kohler, Sr., bought two thousand acres of land and hired city planners, architects and landscape gardeners to lay out a model town, with community buildings and a recreation area. He helped set up a loan association through which employees borrowed money to buy individualized homes from the Kohler Company at cost. Kohler Village was no dreary "company town"; it would pass muster as a smart residential suburb for any city. Its dwellers owned their own land, elected their own town officers.

When depression struck in 1929, the Kohlers stuck by their workers. As other firms tapered production, Kohler operated at capacity, stock-piling its unsalable bathtubs. The proudly paternalistic Kohlers took a million-dollar yearly loss. . . .

Challenging the old-fashioned Kohler paternalism with the new union paternalism, Walter Reuther's UAW-CIO in 1952— in an NLRB voting competition with other unions—won the confidence of 52 per cent of Kohler employees. In the next two years the union twice threatened strikes over contract negotiations, but both times settlement was achieved. At the outset it asked for a union shop, which would have forced all of Kohler's 3318 employees in the bargaining unit to join the UAW.

Although Kohler has had its own funded pension plan since 1948, the UAW wanted one whose cost would be borne by the company alone. . . .

The union also asked a 20-cent-an-hour general wage increase and an additional 10 cents for the skilled trades, a 4 per cent lunch time allowance for the enamel shop, plus improvements in the plan for hospital, surgical, disability and life insurance. . . .

According to Harvey Kitzman, Director of Region 10, United Auto Workers, the real causes of the strike were differences over "arbitration and seniority procedures" because "no union could live with what the company offered."

The original contract, which Kohler had offered to renew, provided that in slack periods, men should be laid off in order of seniority, except that the company was granted the right, in 10 per cent of such cases, to lay off those it considered the least efficient and, when rehiring, to select ten per cent at will. This, according to Kitzman, "made it dead murder because any time they wanted to move in on the local union leadership, they could," and therefore it was "a question."

The company's version is that the union was demanding "super-seniority for union officials and shop stewards: in the event of a layoff, they were to have preference, no matter for how short a time employed."

The union, according to Kitzman, also "wanted transfers according to seniority, in order to do away with the evil of the company being able to shift anyone at will. . . . A guy would be working on a clean, well-paid job. Then he'd look at someone the wrong way, and next day he'd be doing shake-down work in the foundry—the dirtiest job in the plant."

Local President Graskamp felt that the union's seniority demands would "eliminate some of the plums the company now gives to nonunion employees." But the Kohler Company contends that the union wanted to strip it of all power to reward "capability, efficiency and reliability" and, according to Lyman C. Conger, its chief negotiator, "the real issue is whether the union or the company will run the plant. For seventeen years we haven't laid off a permanent employee. But we don't feel we should promote a man who doesn't do good work."

The union also wanted veto-power over subcontracting by Kohler—"a naked denial," said Conger, "of our right to run our own business."

In the matter of arbitration, Kitzman charges that the Kohler Company wanted a clause that would "spell out every type of grievance that was not arbitrable, taking practically everything out of the arbitration procedure. But, more than that, they wanted a double-barreled proposition, under which the arbitrator would first decide whether the issue was arbitrable. Then, they wanted the arbitrator's decision not to be final. They wanted to be able to go to the courts, to get decisions they didn't like reversed."

The company side is that it would agree to "arbitration on the interpretation of the contract, and whether or not it has been violated. We do not accept arbitration which permits an arbitrator to write a new contract." . . .

In May 1954 the Wisconsin Employment Relations Board ordered the union to "cease and desist" from blocking Kohler's gates to those who wanted to work. Pickets were limited to twenty-five per plant gate, and ordered to leave a twenty-foot throughway. The flow of men seeking work now began, led by the seven hundred who had never joined the union. Others were from Wisconsin farms and villages.

"A strikebreaker is a job thief," the union stormed. "If a man tries to rob a bank, he is put in jail. Yet for robbing an honest man of his job, the scab is not punished.". . .

"I'm fifty-four" says Fred Arndt, . . . "and I've never had a job as good as this one. I don't think I took a job away from those pickets. They *gave* it to me."

The union warned that "when the strike ends, every striker must have his job back." [See next article in this section for determination of this issue.—Ed.] Kohler countered by promising that "new employees will not be laid off to make room for strikers." Obviously *both* Walter Reuther and Herbert Kohler, president of the company, could not possibly keep their word. That now became the biggest bargaining obstacle. . . .

After the plant's gates had been freed by WERB order, reprisals against the workers took new forms.

More than eight hundred cases of vandalism and violence were reported, most of them against nonstriking employees' cars and houses. The union denied all responsibility, and in most cases the company paid the damage bills.

Harold Curtiss was one who received a "home demonstration." Says Curtiss: "One night at eleven o'clock when we were sleeping, we heard first a blast, louder than a backfire, and then a shower of glass in our living room. Next morning we found shotgun pellets lodged in the wall." In the dead of night paint bombs (mason jars or electric light bulbs filled with red paint) crashed through picture windows into dozens of homes, splattering wallpaper, rugs, furniture.

Workers were pestered by anonymous phone calls, and intimidation took even uglier, more direct forms. In June, Willard Van Ouwerkerk, a Kohler worker, stopped at a tavern with his wife for a glass of beer. Van Ouwerkerk was fifty and weighs 125 pounds. Up came William P. Vinson, age twenty-seven, six feet three and weighing 240 pounds, brought from Detroit to help the strike. He felled Van Ouwerkerk with a blow from behind, then kicked and trampled him. At the hospital Van Ouwerkerk was treated for a crushed chest, four fractured ribs, pierced right lung, bruises and later pneumonia. It was two and a half months before he could go back to work.

When Circuit Court Judge Ferdinand Schlichting sentenced Vinson to one to two years in the penitentiary, the UAW had a counter-blow ready. The judge owned an interest in three food markets which had been cashing about $13,000 per week in strikers' food vouchers. Emil Mazey, the UAW's secretary-treasurer, discouraged strikers from trading at the stores by announcing that the union would no longer issue vouchers redeemable at them because of the judge's "obvious bias" against organized labor.

Earlier Kohler had announced that it would discontinue bargaining until the union stopped "illegal coercion" of employees who wanted to work. This included "welcoming committees" which patrolled nonstrikers' homes—"riotous mobs of

two hundred to three hundred, shouting epithets and threats."
Coercive practices did cease, following a second court injunction.

The union had lost its picket-line battle at the plant gate,
and bathroom fixtures were rolling from the production lines.

The UAW now announced that it would "try to keep materials from moving into the factory." To do this, Local 833
would need help from other unions.

Kohler molds toilet bowls from a special vitreous clay
brought from Cornwall, England. On July 2 a freighter carrying
this clay tied up at Sheboygan. But when a truck towing a
Kohler Company crane arrived at the docks, the driver was
halted by a mob of five hundred to six hundred. In charge of
police was then Mayor Rudolph Ploetz, elected with the help of
Local 833 by a "Farm-Labor League." He later denounced
Herbert Kohler as a "stubborn bathtub baron who lives in the
feudal age." The mob prevented the crane from moving in to
unload the ship, and, later, a Sheboygan county truck hauled it
and the truck away.

The ship moved to Milwaukee, where the Municipal Port
Director had said the clay could be unloaded. But the dock
workers and crane operators said it would not be unloaded, in
Milwaukee or in *any* Great Lakes port. Finally the clay was
unloaded in Montreal, where Canadian Mounted Police, strictly
enforcing Canada's labor laws, blocked the pickets off the docks.
But after the clay had reentered the United States by rail, union
train crews obediently halted before Local 833's new picket line,
stationed across the switching spur which ran into the Kohler
plant. The railroad's white-collar supervisors finally brought the
train in.

As the strike entered its third year in April 1956, Local 833
insisted that 2060 were "still active" in it. Some, however, had
quietly gone back to Kohler, and others had left to seek jobs
elsewhere. The picket line was now reduced to a handful who
showed up irregularly. Some $8,250,000 in dues from other
UAW members had been poured down the bottomless
rathole. . . .

The union had promised that the strike would be won by
legal action before the National Labor Relations Board, which it

said would force Kohler to take back all its strikers. But it also had another weapon: a "legal primary boycott." In a nationwide publicity campaign the union shouted, "Tell your friends, tell contractors you know, tell everyone, 'Don't buy Kohler!' ". . . .

If the nation's 15 million AFL-CIO members joined, this "strike against a product" could cripple Kohler. AFL-CIO plumbers alone, by refusing to install Kohler fixtures, could force the company out of business. True, the Taft-Hartley Act (like many state enactments) prohibits most "secondary" strikes or boycotts, but the company had ample reason to worry. . . .

Peter T. Schoemann, general president of the AFL-CIO Plumbers, . . . sent out UAW's literature to his 200,000 members with his personal appeal to "help the Kohler workers by requesting master plumbers, your employers, your friends, not to purchase Kohler wares." But, with an eye on the law, he discreetly added that *refusal to handle and install* Kohler products would be a "secondary boycott in violation of the Taft-Hartley Act and state laws. . . ."

Meanwhile, the UAW divided the nation into fourteen districts (a rough copy of Kohler's sales organization) and established a boycott committee for each. All were under Donald Rand, who once said, "It is almost sinful to have any labor dispute degenerate to the point where this one has, where we are actually trying to wreck the company.". . .

Over the nation, only seven political bodies have, at the urging of the AFL-CIO groups, passed resolutions denouncing the use of Kohler products on public construction jobs, and none of these is in Wisconsin, where the strike issues are best known. A survey by the Milwaukee *Journal* of twenty-one major cities found the boycott ineffective or unknown in thirteen. . . . Only in Kansas City, which recently had been host to a Plumbers Union national convention, were Kohler sales reported "greatly off."

Early . . . [in the fall of 1957] as the strike ground toward the end of its fourth year, Kohler had all the men it needed, and was not hiring except to replace normal turnover. Its production and maintenance force stood at an estimated 2300— down from the 1954 peak largely because of a national fall-off in residential building. Of these, about 700 had never been on strike, another 600 had gradually deserted the picket lines, and 1000 were new workers. Of the remaining 2000 strikers, the union said that 400 were still receiving "varying degrees" of home relief, and 1600 had found new jobs. . . .

In Sheboygan the hatred sown by the strike is bearing fruit. Churches have had to cancel picnics after fist fights broke out. Following services, Kohler strikers have stood outside church holding their noses as Kohler workers passed. Families have been broken up: when two brothers, one a striker and the other a worker, met at their mother's funeral, the striker turned his back; a striker stopped seeing his sister because her husband works at Kohler. . . .

Whatever the outcome, the once peaceful community has suffered wounds which will take a long, long time to heal. . . .

RULING IN KOHLER CASE [4]

A National Labor Relations Board examiner ruled . . . that the strike-bound Kohler Company, of Kohler, Wisconsin, was guilty of unfair labor practices. . . .

The trial examiner, George A. Downing, . . . based his ruling on his findings that the company prolonged the strike by unfair labor practices in violation of the Taft-Hartley Act. . . .

Mr. Downing said that strikers whose jobs had not been filled before June 1, 1954, were entitled to get them back on request or when the strike ends. If necessary, he said, the company should discharge employees hired since that date to make room for returning strikers.

The June 1 date, Mr. Downing said, marked the first of several actions by Kohler which were unfair and converted the walkout from an economic strike to one over unfair practices. Under the law, a firm may fire strikers during an economic strike but not during one over alleged unfair practices. . . .

Mr. Downing also held that Kohler acted within the law in discharging thirteen members of the union's strike committee for directing mass picketing of the bath-fixtures plant. Mass picket-

[4] From "Kohler Co. Ruled Unfair to Labor," Associated Press dispatch. New York *Herald Tribune*. p 14. October 11, 1957. Reprinted by permission.

ing is illegal under the Taft-Hartley Act. The thirteen do not have to be reinstated. [For a further reference to the Kohler strike see the Editor's Introduction in Section VI below.—Ed.]

LABOR VIEW OF WAGE-PRICE SPIRAL [5]

America's prosperity depends on constant improvement in the living standards of all Americans. With improved income levels, living standards rise and millions of customers have money to buy the products our mass production economy can create.

Three out of four customers in America are people who work for wages and salaries. Their paychecks make up most of America's consumer purchasing power. Their higher wages, which are possible without higher prices, are the basis of growing markets for the output of an expanding economy. . . .

America has learned how to produce more and more goods per worker every year—almost twice as much as in 1929. As the amount of production per worker per hour (productivity) goes up, the labor cost of each item goes down. This rising productivity allows the producer, with lower wage costs per item and more items to sell, to get good profits without raising prices.

Here is a simple explanation of how this works: If a worker earning $2 an hour can make 10 gadgets an hour, the wage cost of each gadget is 20 cents. Later on, with more efficient machines and methods, that same worker can make 20 gadgets an hour. The wage cost for each gadget becomes 10 cents because the worker is turning out twice as many.

With a lower wage cost for each gadget and more gadgets for sale, the producer does not have to raise his price on each gadget when wages go up, because he has reduced his labor cost for each gadget.

A "gadget"—in economic terms—is a unit of production because many producers make only a part of a total item. So the labor cost per gadget—in economic terms—is a labor unit cost.

[5] From pamphlet. *25 Questions and Answers About Wages, Prices, Profits.* (Publication 58) AFL-CIO. 815 Sixteenth Street. Washington 6, D.C. 1957. p 1-17. Reprinted by permission.

In the lumber industry, for example, wages have gone up 25 cents an hour in the last five years—a $3.50 rise in labor costs per 1,000 board feet of lumber. But because of rising output per man-hour of labor (productivity) in the last five years, production costs of 1,000 board feet of lumber have gone down 63 cents. . . .

In the last five years, hourly wages of factory workers went up about 20 per cent. But the rise in production per hour of work has kept labor costs for each production unit almost stationary—up only 2 per cent according to official figures of the United States Department of Labor. . . .

Wholesale industrial prices have risen 11 per cent in the last five years—a mighty big jump to be blamed on a 2 per cent rise in unit labor costs.

The cost of living went up 5 per cent—over twice as much as unit labor costs. These increases can't be blamed on wage gains, especially since some of the wage increases were won to make up for the higher cost of living. . . .

Labor Department experts recently reported price rises in the last ten lears—with just one exception—have exceeded the rise in unit labor costs. The July 1 [1957] issue of *Business Week,* commenting on this report, told the real story: ". . . unit labor costs seem to have followed prices uphill through most of the postwar years—and particularly in those years when the inflationary heat was the most intense."

In the Labor Department's own language, "The index for unit labor costs was lower than the price index for every year prior to 1956, although the difference was very slight and probably insignificant in 1953 and 1954.". . .

Despite high profits and rising output for each hour worked, business leaders in such important industries as steel, oil, auto, cement have boosted prices. The cause, they say, is higher labor costs. But look at the facts:

In 1955, despite the fact General Motors made $2.93 in profits for every hour worked by hourly employees, GM used that year's wage-package increase of 20 cents an hour as an excuse to raise prices.

In 1956, the US Steel corporation used a wage increase of $94 million as an excuse for raising prices to bring the company $340 million greater income—over three times the amount of the wage rise. US Steel's game of "three-for-us-and-one-for-them" has been going on for ten years. And since 1939, US Steel has raised its hourly profits by over 1200 per cent for each employee—from 13 cents to $1.80 per man-hour. . . .

Products of basic industries like cement, steel, and oil are used to build the plants, and make the machinery for competitive industries. If these basic products rise in price, the competitive industries are forced to raise their prices to maintain their profits, and prices therefore pyramid before they reach the consumer. Only if prices in basic industries stay down can we stop this vicious cycle.

We need healthy—not exorbitant—profits. With rising output per hour worked, corporations can afford to share their profits with workers and consumers by granting wage increases and keeping prices low. Only by sharing benefits of productivity can the economy continue to expand. But in the first quarter of 1957 profits were so high that after-tax returns on net assets averaged almost 12 per cent for all manufacturing corporations. The giant corporations in 1956, each with assets over $1 billion, were getting returns of 16 per cent on their net assets. . . .

With rising output and plenty of consumer buying power, corporations can make higher total profits by selling more and more products at a low profit for each unit. Such shared profits are healthy. They give the corporation a fair return, they help to keep production up, they give the consumers more buying power, and they allow the economy to expand. . . .

Since the end of 1956, industrial output has gone down 3 per cent, but prices have continued to go up. This is true at a time when we can produce much more than before because so many new plants have been built. But companies aren't making all they can or lowering prices so they can sell more. Instead, they are producing less and charging more for each unit of production. That means they are getting higher profits—not by sharing the gains of productivity with workers and consumers—but by producing less and charging more for what they produce. . . .

If the basic industries—with declining labor unit costs and other costs of production—lower their prices, the over-all price level can keep steady, despite some price rises. The facts show that US Steel could have cut its prices $6 per ton of steel in June 1957 and still made higher profits than ever before. The cost of living can remain level by balancing the lower prices made possible by higher productivity with the slightly higher prices where productivity rises less rapidly. . . .

Increasingly, corporations want consumers through higher prices to pay the cost of new factories and new equipment. The economic books on economic theory say that new plant and equipment should be paid for by "risk capital." That is, corporations sell new stock to investors who risk their money in the hope of getting dividends on it. Corporations spend this risk capital to pay for new factories.

But American corporations have found they can protect themselves from depending on risk capital by raising prices and getting high enough profits to pay most of the cost of new factories and equipment. For example, between 1946 and 1956, all United States corporations spent $226 billion on new plant and equipment, but floated only $23 billion worth of new stock. Only 10 per cent of plant expansion in ten years came from stock issues, one kind of risk capital.

We have a growing population—a growing number of people who will need jobs to earn a living. Each year about 800,000 more people enter the labor market and look for jobs. Each year automation finds ways for new machines to replace men. Unless we can use our ability to produce more and more, we cannot keep employment high. Without jobs, customers can buy nothing, production drops, and disaster follows.

An expert American economist, Sumner Slichter, recently answered this question by saying that we have to have more buying in America or production will not keep on rising. In Slichter's words: "The . . . figures show that the weak spot in the economy is now consumption, especially of durable consumer goods, and that this weakness exists in spite of a fairly good increase in personal income. . . ."

What have we been trying to say in this pamphlet? Simply this: business sets prices, workers don't.

Rising prices for basic products are not caused by higher wages, but by the desire of corporation managements for greater profits—in part, to finance new industrial construction.

INDUSTRY VIEW OF WAGE-PRICE SPIRAL [6]

Underlying the current rising price level is a picture of important changes in wage-price-profit trends in manufacturing industry, which pose a choice between additional inflation and some degree of unemployment. With costs of production rising in excess of productivity increases, more money is required to keep goods moving.

This study . . . by making clear why prices are rising . . . serves to indicate what must be done if we are to avoid continuing inflation on the one hand or serious unemployment on the other.

The post-World-War-II history of manufacturing has been one of rising costs per unit of output—particularly labor costs and taxes. Compensation of employees rose 23 per cent per unit of output between 1948 and 1956. Corporate taxes rose 32 per cent on the same basis.

These cost increases have been reflected partially—but only partially—in higher prices for manufactured goods, which rose only 10 per cent during the same period. The result has been a drastic reduction in profit per unit of output, which dropped 25 per cent from 1948 to 1956. . . .

The years 1948 through 1956 are selected because both are years of fairly normal and undistorted peacetime prosperity and the eight-year span is long enough to reflect significant post-World-War-II trends. . . .

While manufacturing does not represent the entire economy by any means, it largely sets the pace, particularly in the im-

[6] From pamphlet, *Wages . . . Prices . . . Profits . . . and Inflation.* National Association of Manufacturers. 2 East 48th Street. New York 17. 1957. p 1-10. Reprinted by permission.

portant area of employee compensation. Increases in industrial wage rates swiftly spread to the distributive and service trades, and thus the over-all price level of both goods and services rises.

The post-World-War-II era has been one of dynamic growth in manufacturing. Total physical output increased by 40 per cent in the eight years between 1948 and 1956. The increase in dollar sales was even greater, 56 per cent.

Wages and profits might have been expected to increase in about the same proportion as production and sales over this period—if they had simply kept up with the growth in industrial activity. Instead we find that the increase in total compensation of manufacturing employees rose 72 per cent between 1948 and 1956, while aggregate manufacturing profits lagged far behind.

Because total labor costs are about 3.5 times as great as before-tax profits in manufacturing, a relatively small percentage increase in labor's dollar share, if taken from profits, will cause a substantial percentage drop in the profit figure. . . .

The increase since 1948 in unit labor costs is, of course, due to the ability of giant unions to exact increases in wage rates and fringe benefits which go far beyond gains in output per man-hour, and the tendency of salary scales to follow closely behind. Between 1948 and 1956, the amount paid in compensation for each hour of labor increased twice as fast as the amount produced by each hour of labor.

The impact of rising corporate taxes was added on top of this wage squeeze. The 85 per cent increase in the amount of taxes levied on profits was far greater—percentagewise—than the increase in the profits on which they were imposed. It was greater in proportion than the increase in dollar sales of manufacturing corporations and it even exceeded the increase in the compensation paid to employees.

The net result was that manufacturers' aggregate profits *after tax* showed very little growth in the 1948-1956 period—a mere 5 per cent which did not even compensate for the shrinkage in the value of the dollar, much less keep up with economic growth. . . .

To some degree, the increase in labor costs and taxes was passed on in the form of higher prices for finished goods. But no automatic process exists whereby higher costs are always recouped by higher market prices. The market may or may not yield a higher price to offset the higher cost. On the average, however, prices of manufactured goods rose by 10 per cent from 1948 to 1956—an increase far less than the rise in unit labor costs or unit tax costs. . . .

Profits as a per cent of sales dropped from 4.9 per cent in 1948 to 3.1 per cent in 1956. By way of comparison, the figure for 1921 was 6.4 per cent; for 1937, 4.7 per cent; for 1940, 5.5 per cent. Thus, 1948 was not an abnormally high profit year. . . .

By contrast, the 1956 profit margin appears to be in line with prewar years which were well below a level of full prosperity: 1956, 3.1 per cent; 1935, 3.2 per cent; 1938, 3.5 per cent. . . .

Not a single industry group showed any improvement in its after-tax profit margin on sales between 1948 and 1956. In fact, not a single industry group even held its own in that respect. . . .

Why have profit margins declined by more than 60 per cent in some industries, and only 5 or 10 per cent in others? Can the cost-price squeeze explain these differences, as it has explained the "big picture" for manufacturing generally?. . .

Some industries use a great deal of labor compared with the amount of capital they have invested. These are the *labor-intensive* industries. Others use a great deal of capital combined with a relatively small amount of labor and these are the *capital-intensive* industries. These differences can be measured in terms of number of workers per million dollars of capital invested. . . .

The industries which have been hit most severely—textiles, lumber, clothing, etc.—are the labor-intensive industries. The industries . . . which have suffered less reduction of their profit margin on sales are those which use less labor in proportion to their capital. . . .

With regard to taxes, however, the other factor in the cost-price squeeze, the impact on profit margins has been quite consistent from one industry to another. The record reveals that industries which have suffered worst on an after-tax basis are those which have suffered worst on a before-tax basis and vice versa. . . .

The added costs of labor and taxes have forced the prices of many manufactured goods upward, and this in turn has partially relieved the squeeze on some profit margins. However, no industry group has been rescued by price rises, and some have cut prices. . . .

The conclusion is inescapable that the current inflationary push is due to the rising costs of labor and the continuing heavy tax burden, and not to the "greed" of manufacturers for exorbitant profits, as some people claim.

Profit margins on sales have suffered, just as the American consumer has suffered, from the power of monopolistic unions to exact wage gains unrelated to productivity.

The remedy would seem to lie in strict government economy so that the tax load may be put on a fair and square basis, and a restoration of equality at the collective bargaining table so that individual producers can make wage settlements which are economically sound, instead of being forced to accept increasingly higher unit labor costs in conformity with an industry-wide "pattern" set by union bosses without regard to the public welfare.

GUARANTEED ANNUAL WAGE—THREAT OR PROMISE? [7]

Supporters of the [1955] agreements [of the United Automobile Workers with Ford and General Motors] stress their influence in encouraging managements to work out more stable year-round production schedules, and argue that additional unemployment compensation, by helping to maintain the demand for goods in periods of business recession, will strengthen the resistance of the economy to contraction. [See the next article in this section.—Ed.]

Both the critics and the supporters of the . . . agreements assume that provision for supplementary unemployment benefits will be added to many union-employer contracts during the next few years—just as supplementary pension schemes spread rapidly

    [7] From "Labor's New Victory: Threat or Promise?" article by Sumner H. Slichter, Lamont University Professor, Harvard University. *Atlantic Monthly*. 196: 63-6. September 1955. Reprinted by permission.

after the precedent-setting agreements in the steel industry in 1949. This assumption is correct, subject to the important qualification that these unemployment benefits will meet far more resistance from employers than supplementary pensions and will thus spread more slowly. . . .

In essence, both Ford and General Motors have agreed to contribute 5 cents for each hour worked by hourly-rated employees to a trust fund from which supplementary unemployment compensation shall be paid. No matter how small the amount in the trust funds, the obligation of the companies to make contributions shall not exceed 5 cents an hour. Furthermore, when the funds exceed a certain size in relation to the number of employees, the contributions of the employer are to cease.

After . . . [June 1, 1956] employees with at least one year's seniority who are laid off will be paid supplementary benefits sufficient, when added to state unemployment compensation, to give them 65 per cent of their weekly after-tax straight-time wage for the first four weeks of unemployment, usually after a one-week waiting period, and 60 per cent for the next twenty-two weeks, but in no event less than $25 a week. After twenty-six weeks the employees shall cease to draw supplementary unemployment benefits. Since the average benefits under state unemployment compensation schemes have been only about 35 per cent of average straight-time earnings after taxes, the Ford and General Motors schemes nearly double the unemployment compensation received by the employees of those companies. . . .

The very fact that the Ford and General Motors agreements provide only for *supplementary* unemployment benefits shows that they were not setting up a new principle. The new principle that employers have the duty to provide income for laid-off employees was established first by the state of Wisconsin in 1932 when it set up a state scheme of employer-financed unemployment compensation, and later by the Federal Government in 1935 when Congress, through a special payroll tax, virtually forced the states to set up unemployment compensation schemes. The Ford and General Motors agreements simply attempt to make up for the inadequacy of benefits under the state laws. . . .

The charge [that spread of agreements of this type will put small and less successful employers out of business] naïvely assumes that large concerns are better able to keep down layoffs than small concerns. The spread of the Ford-General Motors type of agreement would obviously help those companies which are best at keeping the number of layoffs low in relation to the number of workers on the payroll. This means that the Ford-General Motors type of agreement, if widely adopted, would confer advantages (1) on those companies which are growing rapidly and (2) on those which are good at limiting the seasonal and cyclical fluctuations in their output. The agreements would add to the difficulties of the enterprises which for any reason are not able to keep layoffs low—firms in declining industries or high-cost and inefficient companies.

In short, the spread of unemployment compensation agreements would help the most efficient companies (large or small) and all enterprises in expanding industries and would hurt the less efficient concerns and all firms in contracting industries. . . .

The extent to which the spread of supplementary unemployment compensation tends to concentrate production and employment in the hands of those firms (large or small) that are best at keeping down layoffs will depend upon the bargaining policy of unions. Unions must decide whether to insist on different rates of contribution to the trust funds by different employers in order to make possible the same scale and duration of supplementary benefits regardless of the employer's layoff rate, or whether to accept differences in the scale and duration of unemployment pay in order to keep uniform the contribution rates of different employers.

Long experience has taught unions that they get into trouble both with employers and with their own members if they go very far in imposing more onerous terms on some concerns among a group of competitors than on other enterprises in the group. Hence, one is reasonably safe in predicting that unions will not vary the rate of contributions made by various competing employers. It follows that the spread of the Ford-General Motors type of agreement would have only a moderate tendency to concentrate production in the hands of firms that are best at keeping down layoffs. . . .

The tendency for the spread of the Ford-General Motors type of agreement to concentrate production in the firms with the lowest layoff rates will be limited by the fact that unions will not be able to negotiate such agreements with the very weakest firms and in the declining industries where the shrinkage of employment has been greatest. Thus the failure of supplementary unemployment compensation to extend to some of the weakest and least efficient firms will help these firms to survive.

Will the spread of the Ford-General Motors type of agreement encourage the use of machines to run machines—so-called automation? The answer to this question is "Yes." Hand methods have the advantage over machine methods, from the standpoint of employers, that they entail fewer fixed costs. When business falls off, the employer who uses hand methods can get rid of a considerable part of his payroll by dropping men, but most machine costs (interest on the investment, depreciation, obsolescence, insurance) go on whether or not the machine is running. Unemployment pay makes hand-method costs more like machine-method costs because it lessens the savings that employers achieve in slack times by making layoffs. To that extent, supplementary unemployment compensation will encourage the shift to machine methods.

But so strong are the present incentives for employers to shift to machine methods that the practical effect of the spread of supplementary unemployment compensation will be small.

Will the spread of the Ford-General Motors type of agreement add substantially to the stability of the economy by increasing the incomes of unemployed workers during recessions? A moderate gain in stability may be expected. Obviously, the laid-off workers who receive supplementary unemployment compensation will be greatly helped in maintaining their demand for goods since . . . their unemployment benefits will be almost doubled. But the effect of the supplementary unemployment compensation will be limited by the fact that, even after it has spread to the fullest practicable extent, it will reach only a small fraction of all employees. It will not extend to any important degree beyond union members, of whom there are about 16 million in private industry. But many union members are in industries in which for one reason or another it is either not necessary or not feasible to negotiate supplementary unemployment benefits. Hence, unless union membership grows quite rapidly in the next few years, supplementary unemployment compensation is not likely to cover more than about 10 million workers, less than one fourth of the nonagricultural employees in American industry and only about one fourth the number covered by the various government unemployment compensation schemes.

On the other hand, supplementary unemployment compensation agreements are likely to be concentrated in manufacturing, mining, transportation, and construction—the industries in which the cyclical ups and downs of employment are greatest. Hence, even if supplementary unemployment compensation covers less than one fourth of the nonfarm employees, it will raise the incomes of a much higher proportion of the unemployed. . . .

Paying men unemployment benefits of 60 per cent or 65 per cent (or even 75 per cent) of their straight-time earnings after taxes is not likely to deter many men from working. In the first place, wives do not care to have idle husbands around the house when jobs are available, and the influence of the wives is not to be overlooked.

In the second place, consumption in the United States is rather competitive, and the family with only 65 per cent of its usual income after taxes cannot live in the way that it has been accustomed to live and in the way that the neighbors are living. . . .

To the extent that unemployment pay sustains incomes in periods of recession and thus limits the drop in the demand for goods that accompanies recessions, it will be an inflationary influence. In fact, *any* arrangement that limits the severity of recessions is inflationary because such arrangements tend to prevent prices from falling sufficiently during recessions to offset the rise in prices that accompanies most booms. But supplementary unemployment compensation will not be a *major* influence determining the long-run movement of the price level in the United States.

Since various antirecession measures (of which supplementary unemployment compensation is only one) will prevent much of a drop in the price level during recessions, the long-run movement of prices will depend upon how much prices rise during booms. The principal determinants of the movement of prices during booms will be (1) the strength of trade unions, (2) the willingness and ability of employers to resist the demands of unions, and (3) the rate of technological change. These three conditions will determine the movement of labor costs to which the price level must adjust itself.

A widely expressed fear is that unemployment pay will weaken the spirit of adventure that has always characterized American industry. If adding new employees to the payroll imposes heavy obligations on the employer, will not enterprises be reluctant to expand?

The argument is without merit. Employers who have orders or who expect orders are going to hire enough employees to fill them. Failure to receive good service would cause customers to take their business elsewhere. It would take a very high rate of unemployment benefits to make employers prefer to lose customers rather than to add workers who may be needed only temporarily.

In two ways the spread of more liberal unemployment pay will encourage industry to expand. In the first place . . . the broad adoption of the scheme will confer advantages on the firms that through expansion and other means are able to keep down the rate of layoffs. In the second place, to the extent that supplementary unemployment benefits limit the severity of recessions they reduce the risks of expansion. On the whole, one must conclude that the widespread adoption of supplementary unemployment compensation would strengthen rather than weaken the dynamic influence in the American economy. . . .

The most important criticism . . . is that supplementary unemployment compensation, even if widely adopted, is not a satisfactory substitute for adequate normal unemployment benefits. In other words, it does not give the country what it needs— an adequate system of unemployment compensation. . . .

At the best, supplementary unemployment compensation agreements could be expected to reach only about one out of four of the workers now covered by government unemployment compensation schemes. Furthermore, in the very spots where unemployment is most serious, in declining industries and among weak firms, unions will have the greatest difficulty in negotiating agreements of the Ford-General Motors type. . . .

An important characteristic of an adequate scheme of unemployment compensation is that it costs less than nothing— it is an asset to the community, not a burden. The test of whether any economic or political arrangment is a burden or an asset is whether it tends to add to or to subtract from production— whether it makes for a higher or a lower standard of consumption. Adequate unemployment compensation, if properly managed, does not subtract from production and consumption in times of boom, and it does help check the drop in production and employment in times of recession. Hence, over the entire business cycle it tends to increase production and consumption.

An adequate system of unemployment compensation would not only add to the security of workers—it would also add to the security of business enterprises and would enhance the value of the investment in American industry and the value of every farm. It is amazing that the businessmen and farmers have not sought to stabilize their markets by insisting that the government provide an adequate system of unemployment compensation.

A TEST FOR UNEMPLOYMENT BENEFITS [8]

Union-management unemployment benefit funds are helping thousands of jobless workers weather the recession.

The funds, financed by employers in the steel, auto, rubber, glass, maritime and allied industries, have reached their first real test as the business slump has put a mounting strain on their reserves.

For employees of the United States Steel Corporation alone, the program is adding roughly $1 million a month to the state unemployment insurance payments drawn by laid-off workers.

[8] From "Recession Testing Jobless Aid Plans," by A. H. Raskin, labor reporter. New York *Times*. p 16. January 27, 1958. Reprinted by permission.

No accurate estimate is available of the sum being pumped into the economy by all the union-management plans, but it probably will exceed $7.5 million this month.

The private benefits bulk is small when compared with the national total of $250 million that idle workers will receive in January through the operation of state job insurance systems. However, the supplementary payments have enabled many workers to maintain their purchasing power at nearly two thirds of normal take-home standards, instead of the one third possible through sole reliance on their state checks.

Thus far all of the industry funds have been able to meet their full benefit obligations. However, in the steel industry particularly, there is fear that a continuation of the present high lay-off rate may force a cut in benefits in accordance with built-in safety factors designed to assure a maximum spread of the fund's protection.

Fund experts in most industries are hopeful that an upturn will prevent any compulsory halt or reduction in payments. Auto union leaders are so confident of the adequacy of their industry reserves that they are seeking an increase in both the amount and duration of benefits with no rise in employer contributions.

The general attitude of company executives is a good deal more hospitable to the unemployment programs than it was when labor was making its big push for such benefits three years ago under the slogan of the "guaranteed annual wage."

In place of wage guarantees, the Ford Motor Company agreed in 1955 to a program under which it put 5 cents an hour for each worker into a trust fund designed to supplement state unemployment insurance checks. This became the model for most of the programs, now covering 2 million workers.

The American Can Company, which started paying benefits to its idle employees October 1, 1956, has notified the United Steelworkers of America that it feels the program has helped promote greater job stability.

In a report to the union on the first year of benefit distribution, the company set forth its belief that the plan could be considered a success "because the objective of reducing layoffs and not the payment of benefits was met to a considerable degree."

The industrial relations chief of a major steel producer said: "We feel that these payments have become a valuable economic bulwark in steel-making communities. We consider it a sound diversion of money that might otherwise have gone into direct wages.". . .

The most dramatic community dividends have been registered in localities affected by plant closings. United States Steel had two experiences of this kind, one with a zinc plant in Donora, Pennsylvania, where 460 workers were made idle, and the other with a coke plant at Joliet, Illinois, where 350 lost their jobs.

Reports from Donora indicated that mortgage payments were being made on time, installment loans being met and savings bank deposits holding firm weeks after the zinc works had been shut. The Pennsylvania Department of Assistance said few displaced workers had applied for public relief. Local merchants were pleased with the steadiness of sales.

Because payment records are kept on a company-by-company basis, reliable estimates of the number of workers now receiving supplementary benefits are impossible. Guesses at the current total range from 100,000 to 200,000, wth the average worker getting an industry payment of $15 to $25 a week. This is on top of state benefits averaging $30 a week.

Reserves in trust funds and in contingent liabilities total at least $250 million. In the steel industry employers pay 3 cents an hour directly into a trust fund and assume liability for paying another 2 cents an hour if needed to satisfy benefit requirements. In other industries the full employer contribution is put into the fund until stipulated reserve ceilings are met.

In two principal industrial states, Ohio and Indiana, authorities have put legal obstacles in the way of simultaneous collection of public and private benefits by the jobless. In Ohio, a coalition of union and company attorneys is fighting a state administrator's ruling against dual payments. The case is on trial in Youngstown.

In Indiana, where a law was passed prohibiting workers from getting two checks, unions have had to resort to various strategems to permit payments. Many employers in both states have put benefits in escrow rather than risk legal complications. Other industrial states have sanctioned the dual benefit system.

The United Steelworkers, with 763,500 members in basic steel, aluminum, can and fabricating plants covered by the program, feels it has been godsend in an industry that is operating at less than 60 per cent of capacity.

John F. Tomayko, director of the union's insurance, pension and unemployment benefit department, noted that the maximum benefit under the Pennsylvania unemployment insurance law was $35 a week for thirty weeks.

Under the union program a Pittsburgh steel worker with four dependents would get $33 on top of this, bringing his total lay-off pay to $68 a week. When he exhausted his state benefits at the end of thirty weeks, the worker would still qualify for twenty-two more weeks under the industry-financed plan at a weekly rate of $55.50.

Mr. Tomayko warned that the volume of unemployment in recent weeks had brought some company funds down to a level that might require a reduction in weekly payments in the next three or four months. However, an industry spokesman said the major producers believed it would be possible to continue without curtailment of benefits until employment picked up.

At the end of October 1957, the thirteen biggest steel companies had $60 million in trust funds and contingent liabilities. However, Mr. Tomayko reported that some companies were now paying out more in benefits than they were putting in, thus straining reserves.

In the auto industry, General Motors has reserves totaling $85 million and has distributed $5.5 million in benefits since payments started a year and a half ago. For Ford the figures are $36,898,000 in reserves and $2,058,000 in benefits, and for Chrysler $22 million and $3.4 million.

The Studebaker-Packard fund totals $2,056,818, with payments reported at $298,394. American Motors has a $1,213,000 fund and $62,500 in benefits to idle workers. The average payment is $15 a week, compared with $23 in steel. The union wants higher benefits and a fifty-two-week payment plan, in place of the present twenty-six-week ceiling.

LABOR'S POLITICAL ROLE [9]

Unions, except for those on the extreme fringes, do not seek to "take over" established political parties, nor do they seek to use political parties as the instruments for the propagation of strange and new social doctrines. The notion that they do has been useful to those who oppose labor's participation in politics in any degree. . . .

It was the Taft-Hartley Act, against the background of previous legislative assaults on labor organization, that made the trade union member, the secondary leadership of the trade union movement, and the more conservative old-line trade union officials conscious of the necessity for political action.

A second basic assumption generally made and in need of correction is the notion that labor seeks through politics to attain a dominant role in the life of the nation and to mold society along preconceived lines. . . .

In politics, labor is conscious of the fact that it is a minority group. Although the United tSates is perhaps the most highly industrialized country in the world, its working population is the least organized, with only about a third of the nonagricultural working force belonging to trade unions. In addition, there are large groups of professional and semiprofessional people, rural workers and agriculturalists, small business proprietors and white collar workers who belong to no trade union and who, in most instances, are not reached by trade unions.

To enlist the support of these groups for its political program, labor must conciliate and engage in coalitions the essence of which is considerably less than 100 per cent of labor's requests. . . .

[9] From an article by Jack Kroll, former director, CIO Political Action Committee. *Annals of the American Academy of Political and Social Science.* 274:118-22. March 1951. Reprinted by permission.

A third basic assumption generally made is that there is a "labor vote" and that this vote is rigidly controlled by the few elected leaders of American trade unions. . . .

"Blocs" and "controlled votes" are concepts that belong to the machine politicians. But machine politicians are powerful only when the general public is apathetic and stays away from the polls. The small groups that they are able to "deliver" are swamped when large numbers of people are moved to vote. The major purpose of labor's political action is the achievement of a maximum vote, and this concept is the antithesis of machine politics. . . .

Its [labor's] most important functions, as I see it, are the stimulation of voter interest in the records and platforms of candidates and the increasing of the size of the total vote. The achievement of either one of these objectives can have a profound influence on the kind of people elected to pubic office and on the program which they will pursue. . . .

Labor has sought to place stress on the voting record of the candidate rather than on the more usual political attributes. This has involved the selection of important issues and the presentation of these issues to our membership so that the background of the voting record may be understood. . . .

I do not urge that we have yet reached the point where voters are selecting candidates entirely on the basis of their records, but I do argue that voters today are more conscious of the records of their candidates than ever before, and that they have a greater knowledge of the issues than they ever had before.

The effects of this development upon party organization are obvious. Political parties tend to become more homogeneous, and party discipline and responsibility assume greater importance. This places greater emphasis on the work of the party's national committee and results in a tightening of the entire party structure. Candidates selected in the primary become more truly representative of the national party, and the national organization must assume more responsibility for them and, consequently, greater control over them.

The net result is that the distinctions in political philosophy between the two major political parties become more clearcut, and the voter is more certain that the candidate for whom he votes will fulfill the pledges and platform upon which he sought election. This, I think, is one major change taking place in the political life of the nation which has been brought about by labor's political activity—specifically, by labor's insistence that the voting record of the candidate be examined and that the issues at stake be understood.

The second major change is the increased emphasis on voter participation in elections. The basic premise of labor is that the United States is inherently a progressive nation, that in a fair test the liberal philosophy of government with its emphasis on the human welfare of the nation's citizens will always win out over the conservative or reactionary philosophy of government which relies upon the welfare of the business community to take care of the welfare of the whole community. . . .

Labor's political activity, therefore, is conducted on a year-round basis of making sure that its members, their wives, and the adult members of their families are registered. . . . It is estimated that about 55 to 60 per cent of labor union members in the country are registered, which represents only a slight edge on the general population. In coming years this edge is expected to increase, and the ultimate goal is the registration as a voter of every eligible trade union member. . . .

The basic structure of labor's political organization is the trade union, a continuing organization in which members are held closely together by economic self-interest, by mutual employment, and, in many cases, by mutual social activity. It is a much stronger basis than that of the usual political organization, which holds a few people together by means of patronage but which is, for the most part, inactive except in an election period.

Trade union political activity is financed by the voluntary contributions of the members rather than by donations from interested parties or corporations. Most of the work done on election day is volunteer work. This, again, is a reversal of the usual political party pattern, in which the worker is paid for his efforts and in which his efforts are seldom more than commensurate with his compensation, and frequently less.

Labor political activity is highly decentralized. Endorsements of candidates are made by the organization in the area in which the candidate solicits votes. . . .

Labor is engaged in political action as a matter of principle. We feel that we are making a distinct contribution to the life of our nation, not only in supporting the only philosophy which offers a true alternative to totalitarianism, but in heightening the interest and concern of the citizens of the United States in their democratic government. Labor will, I am sure, continue to be active in politics and will continue to seek to mobilize the strength of our people on behalf of genuine self-government. The direction it takes will be, to a certain extent, dictated by the direction the opponents of labor take, by the methods they use and the appeals they make to gain support.

LABOR'S RESPONSIBILITIES [10]

Never before, it seems, has organized labor been as strong, as powerful, and as accepted in this country as today. Yet the American labor movement faces its most serious crisis. It is a crisis of success, not of failure—but that may make it all the more severe. Our union leaders still live in the days when they had to fight for recognition, if not existence. But the problems they really face are those of labor's power and responsibility as a ruling group in industrial society.

True to the traditions of this country—and they are good traditions, in this case at least—the problems will not be solved on the theoretical or abstract level, but pragmatically and case by case. But it is quite clear what the areas are in which the decisions will have to be found. They are: (1) wage policy, (2) the "right to strike," (3) union control over the citizen's access to a livelihood, and (4) internal union organization.

It is no exaggeration to say that today practically the entire wage and salary structure of the United States is determined by union-negotiated wages. . . . Even those industries which are not unionized . . . set their wage and salary rates largely in

[10] From "Labor in Industrial Society," article by Peter F. Drucker, management consultant. *Annals of the American Academy of Political and Social Science.* 274: 145-51. March 1951. Reprinted by permission.

accordance with the wages obtained by the strong unions of the community. . . .

In fact, this total dependence of the wage and salary structure on union wage rates may be one of the greatest obstacles to the expansion of unionism. In the textile industry, for instance, where only one third of the workers are organized in the Textile Workers Union (CIO), the other two thirds can be fairly certain of receiving union wage rates or better; and I have heard repeatedly from workers in the industry that under these conditions they see no reason for joining a union.

At the same time, wages and salaries take two thirds of the total national income—that is about as much as they can possibly take. Of the remaining 33 per cent or so, 10 per cent goes to the farmers; the rest is split between the small businessmen and professionals, the payments on interest and bank and funded debts, the host of transfer payments, and profits, with each category probably as low as it can go. . . . During a depression, the shares of the nonwage recipients would drop very sharply, and wages and salaries would rise to 80 to 85 per cent of the national income.

As far as union wage policy is concerned, this means concretely:

1. It is no longer possible for one group of workers to increase their wages at the expense of another group—usually an unorganized group—of workers. This method—certainly one by which the early American Federation of Labor obtained its gains—becomes totally unusable when there is one wage pattern throughout the whole national economy, as there is today.

2. An increase in labor's *real* wage is no longer possible—certainly not to any appreciable extent—through an increase in labor's share in the national income. In other words, increases in wage rates will be purely inflationary unless accompanied by a corresponding expansion in the national production.

How complete a change in basic policy this involves can be easily seen if we spell out concretely the resulting requirements for union wage policy. These include an acceptance of the existing distribution of national income as fair and equitable—or at least as given. Secondly . . . they imply acceptance of "rational" wage criteria: that is, of factors outside and beyond the existing power situation as the factors which actually decide the wage rate. . . .

It will certainly be difficult for any union leadership to accept the new concepts, whatever they may be, and even more difficult to obtain their acceptance and understanding on the part of the membership.

Union cohesion and union power rest primarily on the right to strike. Without the ability to call a strike and bar the employer's access to the means of production, no union could discharge its functions, let alone remain strong. But at the same time the right to strike is the right to paralyze the national economy; and no society can give such a right to a private group without abdicating.

In this country, we have curtailed the right to strike—and this during a period of very great union power inside and outside the government. It has always been considered unlawful . . . to strike against the Federal Government. . . . It has been made unlawful in many states . . . to strike against any governmental body. . . .

Actually, we have gone far beyond this. In a good many states strikes against "essential" industries have become forbidden. The Federal Government so far has no similar law on its statute books; but it has become increasingly clear that it will not tolerate strikes against such industries as the railroads or the power companies—in short, strikes that are at all likely to have a marked adverse effect on the national economy or on national preparedness. . . .

The important thing is not that the area in which strikes are permitted has been narrowed and that a long state of international crisis is bound to narrow it even more. The important thing is that we have come increasingly to regard the strike as an extraordinary and abnormal phenomenon which can be allowed only under definitely prescribed conditions: (1) if it does not interfere with national preparedness; (2) if it does not interfere with the national economy, the welfare, the health, or even the comfort of the citizens; (3) if it is not directed against a governmental body. In other words, we have begun to question the right to strike. . . .

From the union point of view, union security is a necessity. Without it, the union can never be certain of its position in the enterprise. Above all, it can never be certain that it can actually call out the men on strike, or that it can enforce observance of an agreement it has signed. But union security is also in the social interest. Without it, no union can be expected to accept the responsibility for labor relations and for contract observance which our society must demand of a successful union movement.

But union security also means that the union acquires control over the citizen's access to work. Union membership becomes a condition of employment. . . .

Union security also gives the union power over the individual's civic rights—over his political convictions, his political activity, even his political opinion. Already, union members have been expelled for political opinions or activity. And finally, union security, unless controlled by society, makes its possible for union leadership to perpetuate itself in power indefinitely. . . .

Hitherto we have considered all these problems to be private problems of the union, on the legal assumption of the union as a purely private and voluntary association. But it is becoming obvious that this assumption is no longer tenable. No society can give to a purely private and voluntary association the powers over the civic and political rights and the economic opportunities of the individual citizen which the unions enjoy today. . . .

It is unrealistic to expect that union leaders can solve these problems. Few groups in history have been able to make voluntarily and through their own leadership the adjustments to the needs of society which their own power and success demand. The record of American business management in the last seventy years is only one illustration. Yet these problems will have to be tackled—and very soon. Without the cooperation of union leadership, they will be very difficult to solve; and it is almost certain that they will not be solved very successfully, and that we will again, as so often in our history, confuse regulation with restrictive and punitive measures.

But even if union leadership totally refuses to face the realities created by its own power and success, the coming decades will make tremendous demands on it. . . . Both the labor movement and society need a union leadership of exceptional intellectual ability, of exceptional emotional maturity, of exceptional experience, and of exceptional integrity. . . .

There are two central problems of internal constitution which the labor movement will have to solve to be able to survive. There is a basic problem of the relationship between the local organization of the union and its central government—the international president, the policy boards of the union, and so forth. A union needs both—and both have to be strong. . . . But today, with very few exceptions, our unions have only the one or the other: either the strong, if not dictatorial, central power, or the strong local.

Equally serious is the other problem: the conflict between the functional and the political requirements of union leadership. The problem is analogous to that faced by every free society in respect of the control of foreign affairs. Foreign affairs . . . demand a permanent body of experts working out and following a long-range policy, uncontrolled, except in the broadest possible manner, by the constituents and by the passions of the political arena. At the same time, the basic beliefs of a free society demand that foreign affairs be conducted in the open, that they be under the immediate and day-to-day control of the electorate, and that they be in the hands of people elected by the electorate and changing with every change in the political climate.

Functionally, a great deal of the union leader's work is "foreign relations"; the relations with management and with society. But the political necessities of the union movement demand that the union leader be elected and be answerable to the constituents. Today we either have a union leadership which is in effect removed from any control by the electorate and responsible to no one but itself, or we have what is misleadingly called "democratic" unionism in which union leaders have to subordinate their entire conduct to immediate expediency in order to be reelected, if indeed they are not being thrown out of office every year. . . .

The internal organization of the union is thus of major importance to the solution of the problems of labor in an industrial society. So far, however, only a mere handful of union leaders have even realized that there is a problem of union organization which it is their responsibility to tackle.

In the final analysis, the problem of labor's role in our industrial society is one of conflict between the position of the labor union in the individual enterprise and the position of the labor union in modern society. In the individual enterprise, the union is first and foremost a permanent opposition, an "antibody." There are many areas within this relationship where the interests of enterprise and union go together; and the more cooperation there can be in these areas the more effective, and the stronger, will both enterprise and union be. But the union can never subordinate itself to the enterprise's rationale of profitable and efficient production as the final yardstick of decisions, behavior and policy. Its major function will always be to set against the purely economic goals of the enterprise the economic, social, and political goals of the employee.

Society, however, must demand of the union movement that it take positive responsibility for the strength and success of society and economy. It is not possible for the union movement to claim exemption from this responsibility on the ground that the labor union is just another pressure group. . . . No other pressure group . . . has ever been able to control either the citizen or society. The labor union, inevitably, can do both. And this means that the labor union, rather than being a pressure group, that is, an economic organization, inevitably has political and social powers. . . .

Society must demand that the labor movement subordinate its own aims and beliefs to the aims and beliefs of society, to the productivity of the economy and the profitability of the enterprise system. But at the same time, society demands that the union act as a permanent opposition within the individual enterprise.

IV. THE TAFT-HARTLEY ACT

EDITOR'S INTRODUCTION

The National Labor Relations Act of 1947, or the Taft-Hartley Act, as it is more generally known, is the subject of the articles in this section.

A professor of law summarizes the provisions of the law. After tracing the development of labor legislation in the United States and its effect on workers, a university economist comments adversely on the law's restrictions on union activities. A selection from a national business magazine shows the trend of recent decisions by the National Labor Relations Board in interpreting the Taft-Hartley Act. Dean Roscoe Pound's recent book, *Legal Immunities of Labor Unions,* is next discussed. A monograph on the monopoly power of labor unions sets forth the views of a management organization on our present labor laws, with suggestions for their revision.

A labor spokesman finds that the Taft-Hartley Act has proved "ineffective and frequently inept" in achieving its ostensible objectives, that its administration has been marked by "many departures from fair treatment," and that its procedures are time-consuming and sometimes frustrating.

PROVISIONS OF TAFT-HARTLEY LAW [1]

In 1933 . . . the NRA [National Recovery Act] . . . guaranteed to workers in industries under the NRA the right of self-organization and collective bargaining. NRA . . . was declared unconstitutional by the Supreme Court in 1935. . . . The labor sections of the NRA were succeeded by the Wagner Act. In the Wagner Act, at long last, labor achieved recognition . . . of its right to organize, to bargain collectively and to carry on other activities. The Wagner Act undertook to guarantee

---

[1] From "Provisions of the Taft-Hartley Law," by William P. Murphy, professor of law, University of Mississippi, in *Proceedings of the Taft-Hartley Forum, December 5-6, 1954.* University of Mississippi. Department of Conferences and Institutes. University, Mississippi. 1954. p2-29. Reprinted by permission.

that right to employees by proscribing certain unfair labor practices of employers. It also provided broadly for employees a method . . . by which the employees could organize and get their organization recognized and certified as a collective bargaining agency. . . .

The Supreme Court upheld the constitutionality of the Wagner Act in 1937. . . .

The Taft-Hartley sponsors [in 1947] stated that their primary purpose was the equalization of the labor law. They said the Wagner Act was one-sided; it benefited only the employees; proscribed unfair labor practices only against employers. . . . The two broad purposes of the [Taft-Hartley] Act, as stated in Section I, . . . were first, to promote industrial peace in America, and second, to encourage equality of bargaining power between employees and employers. . . .

Section 7 . . . sets forth the rights [of employees] to form, to join, to assist labor organizations, to bargain collectively with employers and to engage in other concerted activties for their mutual aid and protection. . . . Taft-Hartley added this language: and the employees "shall also have the right to refrain from any or all of these activities" except to the extent that there might be a union shop contract which operated in these situations. . . . Employees still have their same rights as they had under the Wagner Act, but Taft-Hartley adds that they also have a right to refrain from them.

Wagner and Taft-Hartley both undertook to protect these rights of employees . . . by setting forth certain things which employers could not do in derogation of those rights. . . . These are carried over almost verbatim from the Wagner Act into the Taft-Hartley Act. . . .

It . . . [is] an unfair labor practice for employers to dominate or interfere with the formation or administration of any labor organization or contribute financial or other support to it. . . .

It . . . [is] an unfair labor practice for an employer by discrimination in regard to hire or tenure of employment or any term or condition of employment to encourage or discourage membership in labor organizations. . . .

The main way in which an employer could discriminate in favor of a union would be through what is called a union security provision. A closed shop, for example, or a union shop . . . would obviously be a discrimination in favor of a union . . . unless the law made a special provision, and the law does make . . . the union shop proviso. It permits employers and unions to enter into a union shop contract . . . .

If an employee reports to the Labor Board that his employer is engaging in unfair labor practices or if he makes a charge against his employer or if, when there is a hearing, he testifies as a witness to that effect, . . . then the employer cannot discriminate against him because of his having reported the matter to the Board or appearing as a witness. . . .

Refusal to bargain collectively . . . is the fifth unfair labor practice which employers can commit. . . .

Those were the only unfair labor practices that the Wagner Act had, and Taft-Hartley . . . sought to equalize the situation. Taft-Hartley therefore included unfair labor practices which can be committed by unions. . . . [There are] six of them, and one of them is broken down into four parts, so we really have nine. . . .

It is an unfair labor practice for a labor organization or its agents . . . acting with apparent authority from the union, . . . to restrain or coerce employees in the exercise of rights guaranteed in Section 7 [to refrain from union activities]. . . .

Another violation [of this section] would be mass picketing, for example, which completely prohibits access to a plant. . . .

It . . . [is] an unfair labor practice for a labor organization or its agents to cause or attempt to cause an employer to discriminate against an employee in violation [of this section]. . . .

It . . . [is] an unfair labor practice for a labor organization or its agents to refuse to bargain collectively with an employer, provided it is the representative of the employees.

It . . . [is] an unfair labor practice for a labor organization or its agents

. . . to engage in, or to induce or encourage the employees of any employer to engage in, a strike or a concerted refusal in the course of their employment to use, manufacture, process, transport, or otherwise handle or

work on any goods, articles, materials or commodities or to perform any
services, where an object thereof is: forcing or requiring any employer or
other person to cease using, selling, handling, transporting, or otherwise
dealing in the products of any other producer, processor, or manufacturer,
or to cease doing business with any other person. . . . [This is the
"secondary boycott" provision.—Ed.]

In jurisdictional disputes . . . a strike to force the employer
to assign the work to one of the unions is an unfair labor
practice on the part of the union calling the strike. . . The Act
gives the Labor Board authority to hear and decide the dispute. . . .

Where there is a union shop situation, it's an unfair labor
practice for the union to charge an excessive or a discriminatory
initiation fee as a condition of membership. Here the Board has
the duty of determining whether the fee . . . is excessive or
discriminatory.

It's an unfair labor practice under [the] "featherbedding"
provision to "cause or attempt to cause an employer to pay or
deliver or agree to pay or deliver any money or other things of
value, in the nature of an exaction, for services which are not
performed or not to be performed." . . . Linotype operators, . . .
put out of a lot of work due to the development of new type
machinery, . . . rather than lose the pay which they would
normally get, require their employers to have them set "bogus"
type . . . which will never be used for printing anything and is
immediately thrown away upon being set. . . . That's pretty
clearly the sort of thing this section was aiming at, and yet the
Supreme Court has held that it is not prohibited by this section,
because it specifically refers to services "which are not performed"
or "not to be performed," and here the union is actually performing service, even though it is an unwanted service and
even though economically the work is useless. . . .

There's a proviso in . . . [the] collective bargaining section
which provides for a sixty-day notice, a "cooling off" period
. . . where there is a collective bargaining contract in effect
. . . and either party wants to terminate or modify that contract. . . . First, you've got to serve written notice on the other
party at least sixty days prior to the expiration date of the
contract, or, if there is no expiration date, sixty days before the

time you want the modification or termination to take effect. . . .
Second, you've got to offer to meet and confer with the other
party with respect to the new contract. Third, at the end of
thirty of those sixty days, if you have not reached an agreement
as to the new contract, you've got to give notice to the Federal
Mediation and Conciliation Service so they will have opportunity,
if they deem it important enough, to send one of their conciliators
or mediators down to try and help the two parties to reach an
agreement. The fourth thing required is that the party has got
to continue "in full force and effect, without resorting to strike
or lockout, all the terms and conditions of the existing contract
for a period of sixty days after the notice is given or until the
expiration date of the contract, whichever occurs later." . . .

Any employee who engages in a strike within this sixty-day
period shall lose his status as an employee for purposes of this
Act. . . . Does it matter if it's an unfair labor practice strike . . .
or an economic strike? . . . This section doesn't specifically
answer it, but the Board says if it's an unfair labor practice strike
you don't lose your status as an employee; if it's an economic
strike, you do. [See "Ruling in Kohler Case," in Section III,
above.—Ed.]

Taft-Hartley prohibits by implication the closed shop [where
union membership is required for employment] and permits the
union shop [where new employees must join a union within a
specified period]. . . . [But it] permits states to pass laws which
ban all forms of union security. Put it this way: Taft-Hartley
undertakes to permit the union shop, but says that a state law
prohibiting the union shop will, however, prevail over Taft-
Hartley. . . .

Taft-Hartley also provides for the national emergency situation. When the President comes to the conclusion that a strike
or lockout is of sufficient importance to imperil the national
health or safety . . . [he] appoints a board of inquiry which
makes a quick report to him, and then he may authorize the
attorney general to get an injunction from the Federal courts
restraining the strike for the duration of the injunction. After
sixty days, if it is still unsettled, the Board reports back to the
President what the last position of the two parties was. Within

fifteen days after that, the National Labor Relations Board holds an election in which the employees get the opportunity to accept or reject the last offer made by the employer. Then within five days after that the NLRB reports the results of the election. You've heard about your eighty-day injunction; there it is: sixty, fifteen, and five. . . . At the end of eighty days, Taft-Hartley provides that the attorney general has got to go into court to get the injunction dissolved. Then, if the dispute is still unsettled, he throws it into the lap of Congress for them to do what they will with it. . . .

In Section 301 of Taft-Hartley unions are recognized as entities, and suits against [them] for breach of contract are specifically recognized, provided, however, that . . . you can only collect your damages out of the union treasury—you can't go against the assets of any of the individual officers of the union. . . .

Secondary boycott situations, jurisdictional dispute situations, etc., are unfair labor practices. . . . The mandatory injunction provision applies with respect to them. . . . Any person who is damaged monetarily when the union engages in those practices may bring a damage suit against the union for having engaged in them.

So there are three ways Taft-Hartley operates against these practices: they are unfair labor practices, they are subject to mandatory injunction, and they subject the union to damage suits. . . .

Section 304 of Taft-Hartley sought, by amending the Federal Corrupt Practices Act, to restrict financial contributions by unions to political campaigns for Federal office . . . and also the expenditure of any money in connection with the election. The CIO in its newspaper . . . took positions for and against certain candidates. They were prosecuted, . . . and the lower court found that this provision of Taft-Hartley was unconstitutional, a deprivation of the right of freedom of press. . . . The Supreme Court didn't meet the constitutional question and decided it on another ground. . . .

Title V . . . has a few more definitions, including one of "strike," and a saving provision which seeks to make plain that nothing in this law is to be construed to make the individual quitting of work by any employee an illegal act. Courts cannot compel employees to work where they don't want to. Finally, a separability clause. The Supreme Court used to have a habit, if any part of a law was unconstitutional, of knocking down the entire law. Congress, in order to meet that propensity of the Court, put a separability clause in: that is, if any part of the law was declared invalid, the rest of it would still stand.

PROS AND CONS OF THE ACT [2]

There are provisions of the Taft-Hartley Act of which I approve. Organized labor has taken a position, ever since the Taft-Hartley Act was enacted, that this law should be repealed and the Wagner Act restored. It has also stated that in the reenactment of the Wagner Act amendments incorporating some features of the Taft-Hartley Act might well be included. The bill favored by labor in the . . . [82d] session [of Congress] included some provisions from the Taft-Hartley Act. . . .

But there are also many provisions of the Taft-Hartley Act which are bad in every respect, and, as I see it, many more that have more of the bad than of the good. President Eisenhower has referred to the Act as including provisions which are unfair to labor and has spoken of these provisions as "union-busting." The late Senator Taft, one of the authors of the Taft-Hartley Act, in 1949 put through the Senate the Taft bill, which made no less than twenty-eight changes in the present law, nearly all of them in the direction of easing restrictions now imposed on unions. . . .

The Taft-Hartley Act at the time of passage was represented as an equalizing act. But it is an equalizing act only in the sense that, as the Wagner Act imposed restrictions upon employers, so the Taft-Hartley Act imposes restrictions on unions. Supporters of the Taft-Hartley Act say that it incorporated the Wagner Act,

[2] From "The Development of Labor Legislation and Its Effect upon the Welfare of the American Workman," address by Edwin E. Witte, professor of economics, University of Wisconsin, at Conference on Government and Public Affairs of the University of Illinois and Twin City Federation of Labor, October 31, 1954, at the University of Illinois, Urbana. (Lecture Series no 11) Mimeographed. Institute of Labor and Industrial Relations. 704 South Sixth St. Champaign, Ill. 1954. p 1-24. Reprinted by permission.

leaving intact the restrictions on employers but supplementing them with like restrictions on unions. While it is true that the Taft-Hartley Act reenacted much of the Wagner Act, although weakening many of its provisions, the restrictions on employers are not nearly as extensive as are those on unions.

This is a matter, not merely that there are more restrictions on unions, but also that the most drastic restrictions on unions have no parallel in any restrictions on employers. The so-called "secondary boycott" provision is a good illustration. In this provision the words "secondary boycott" or "boycott" do not even occur. The so-called prohibition of secondary boycotts is really one directed against all or nearly all sympathetic action by unions or union members in support of other unions in difficulties with employers. Unions may still contribute money to support workers of other unions who are on strike. But the law forbids unions from pressing an employer to cease dealing with another employer and also prohibits all pressure to compel an employer to recognize other than a certified union. It is spelled out that the prohibited pressure may take the form of refusing to work for such an employer or to buy, transport, or handle any unfair products. What the "secondary boycott" provision of the Taft-Hartley Act principally prohibits are strikes—strikes in sympathy with other unions, strikes against unfair materials, and strikes to compel recognition of other than certified unions. It also prohibits refusal to handle unfair products. Some of these strikes involve elements of boycotts, but the provisions go much further than boycotts, prohibiting any sort of action, other than money contributions, to help workers not employed by the same employer who are involved in strike action or any other dispute with their own employer.

These provisions directed against "secondary boycotts" have no counterpart in restrictions upon employers. Employers can give any sort of help they wish to other employers in disputes with unions. They can refrain from trying to take over their customers while a strike is on against another employer, or, if the latter employer so desires, fulfill his contracts. Under recent decisions they may even lock out their own employees to help employers engaged in strikes.

The restrictions upon "secondary boycotts" do not end with declaring them to be an unfair labor practice when engaged in by unions but not when practiced by employers. Secondary boycotts by unions are expressly stated to afford a legal basis for damage suits against unions, and many such damage suits have in fact been instituted. In the case of secondary boycotts, also, the Taft-Hartley Act expressly provides that when the regional director of the NLRB finds, after an ex parte investigation and before any hearing has been held, that an act of "secondary boycott" has been committed, he shall issue a complaint against the union charging it with an unfair labor practice. The law further requires that at the same time when the regional director files charges of unfair labor practices against a union, to be later tried on its merits before the NLRB, he *must* apply to a United States District Court for an injunction prohibiting the union from continuing the acts complained of until the NLRB hears the cases and determines whether the charges are valid or not.

It is this provision for mandatory injunctions against unions in cases of strikes and other "secondary boycott" action, of strikes to gain union contracts where the union has not been certified, and in jurisdictional disputes, which is one of the worst features of the Taft-Hartley Act. Not only has this revived "injunctions in labor disputes," but it has revived them in their worst form. It is mandatory for the regional director to apply for an injunction in such cases, prior to any hearing before the NLRB on the unfair labor practice charge on which the injunction is based. Further, the Taft-Hartley Act provides that the safeguards of the Norris-LaGuardia Act against the abuse of injunctions shall not apply to the mandatory injunctions provided for in this act. These injunctions are to be issued before the unions have had a chance to present their side of the case or before there has been any hearing on the merits of the charges against them. In numerous cases, mandatory injunctions have been issued on charges which the NLRB found unwarranted after a full hearing—months after the injunction had been issued. The old evil of injunctions without affording the accused a hearing on the merits of the case has been revived.

The Taft-Hartley Act has no similar provisions for mandatory injunctions against employers who are charged with unfair labor practices. The law provides that the NLRB *may* (not *must*) apply for an injunction against the employer to stop a continuing unfair labor practice, until the charges are tried on their merits. In the six and one half years of the Truman Administration after enactment of the Taft-Hartley Act, two injunctions of this kind were sought by the NLRB against employers; none in the present Administration. I do not believe that injunctions should be issued against employers before they have had a chance to refute the charges against them. That the Taft-Hartley Act requires the NLRB to seek mandatory injunctions in many cases against unions before they have had a trial on the merits of the charges is an abuse of fundamental principles of justice. Several hundred such mandatory injunctions have been issued under this law. . . .

Other provisions of the Taft-Hartley Act which have hurt organized labor include those relating to union security and to the organizational efforts of unions. The union security provisions not only outlaw closed and preferential shop agreements, but make it unlawful to ask for such agreements. Unions have in numerous cases been forced to pay damages to nonunion men denied employment or who were discharged on the union's demand, except where a union shop agreement of the type sanctioned by the statute was in effect. Even when a union shop agreement is in effect, the union may seek the discharge of any employee only for the nonpayment of dues or initiation fees. The disloyal union member, the trouble-maker, even the Communist agitator, are all protected against discharge on the demand of the union, so long as they pay or tender the union dues. If discharged, in accordance with a union shop agreement, such people can recover damages alike from the employer and the union.

Restrictions on organizational efforts are not spelled out in the Taft-Hartley Act, but by interpretation they become very drastic and are in the process of becoming more drastic. Picketing for organizational purposes has been held to violate the Taft-Hartley Act. In restricting picketing, NLRB proceedings and orders have largely replaced injunctions issued by the courts and are equally restrictive. Even asking the employer to do something which the Taft-Hartley Act frowns upon is an actionable offense. All threats, however veiled, when made by union men are unlawful. Threats of any kind to keep employees out of unions made by employers, theoretically, are also unlawful. The Taft-Hartley Act, however, includes a specific guarantee of the right of free speech to employers and no corresponding provision guaranteeing a right of free speech to union men; and, as now interpreted, almost anything that the employer may say or publish to keep out or defeat a union seems to be OK. . . .

The Act includes the absurd restriction that watchmen may not belong to the same unions as the production workers. Foremen are denied all protection of the law when they organize even when their unions are independent from those of the production workers. The Act allows injunctions against strikes producing national emergencies, but only after a board, named by the President because he thinks a national emergency exists, has reported to him that there is in fact an emergency. Then the President can direct the Attorney General to get an injunction against the strike, which is to be effective for eighty days. Before the end of the eighty-day period, the workers must vote on the last offer to settle the dispute made by the employer. As is the case in so many other provisions of the Taft-Hartley Act, there is no corresponding provision for a vote of the stockholders on the last proposal of the union. After the eighty days during which the injunction is effective have expired, it must be dissolved. Thereafter the workers are free to strike, and the law is silent on what is to be done in that event.

With all its absurdities and its provisions unfair to labor, I repeat that the Taft-Hartley Act is not the most restrictive labor relations law that could be framed. Some provisions in some state labor relations laws are now more restrictive. . . .

The Taft-Hartley Act has not hindered unions as much as its proponents, probably, expected or hoped for. In a time of a high level of employment such as has prevailed during most of the time this law has been in effect, unions have somewhat increased their membership, although at a somewhat slower rate than earlier. During this period labor has also suffered some setbacks, particularly in its efforts to organize the South. Very certainly, the unions have not been destroyed, and, on the whole, are stronger today than ever before. And I do not believe that the unions will be wiped out, even if further restrictions upon organized labor should be put into effect, either by way of amendment or through further unfriendly interpretations of the Taft-Hartley Act.

It must be remembered, however, that the Taft-Hartley Act has not been tested in a period of prolonged depression. In a long, severe depression, more employers can be expected to invoke the restrictive provisions of the law, and with much greater prospects of seriously hurting the union. It needs to be kept in mind also that because a particular union has not to date experienced the harshness of the Taft-Hartley Act is not to say that it will never have such an experience in the future. Many unions, and particularly AFL unions, have had such experiences, and many more doubtless will have them. . . .

It is clear that the American unions need to continue to interest themselves in the restrictive labor relations legislation we now have on the statute books and to fight all efforts to make it worse. Though restrictive legislation the efforts of workers to improve conditions of employment through economic action can be all but nullified. Unless labor has freedom to combine and to use its economic power, if necessary, it cannot make headway in the economic sphere. I believe also that organized labor in this country should revive its interest in protective legislation. Government does matter to American labor, although it prefers to determine conditions of employment through collective bargaining. What government does or does not do needs to be watched closely by labor. Who is elected to executive and legislative offices determines whether labor will be helped or harmed by governmental action.

AS NLRB INTERPRETS THE LAW [3]

Judge Leedom, now that the Taft-Hartley Act is ten years old, how would you say it has worked?

The answer to that would depend on the viewpoint of the person answering. A labor leader might have one view and

[3] From "What the Labor Board is Saying," interview with Boyd Leedom, chairman, National Labor Relations Board. *Nation's Business.* 45:38-9+. August 1957. Reprinted by permission.

many have been very critical. A businessman might have another
view and some businessmen have been critical. I think that it
has worked pretty well.

What do businessmen complain about?

Businessmen complain chiefly about secondary boycotts and
the Board's interpretation of law in this area. They also complain of Board decisions as to bargainable issues, particularly
with respect to pension plans, stock purchase plans, and other
so-called management prerogatives.

Notwithstanding the management complaints, I think the
secondary boycott is pretty well under control. This vice, in the
main, has been substantially diminished by the operation of the
Taft-Hartley Act.

What is the rule on secondary boycotts?

The subject is complicated, but the law seems to be pretty
well settled in all except a few areas. One important contro-
versial area is the so-called "hot cargo" clause, and we appear
to be nearing a final answer on that. This is a clause by which
an employer agrees that his employees may refuse to handle
goods the union considers "hot" because they are being trans-
ported to or from an employer whom the union considers unfair.

The majority view of the Board is that, under the law, such
a clause cannot authorize the union to go to the employees and
ask them to take part in such a secondary boycott.

This position of the Board has been affirmed in some courts,
reversed in others. I think the Supreme Court will decide the
question reasonably soon.

What about unions putting pressure on secondary employers?

That remains a question of policy to be decided by Congress.
As the Taft-Hartley Act is written, it does not prohibit a union
from inducing a secondary employer not to handle hot goods.
Therefore, the Board can do nothing about that under the Act.
The Act forbids only inducement of employees of a neutral
employer.

What do unions complain about most?

Mostly their criticism is general. However, one specific criticism goes to the free speech provision in Taft-Hartley. It was not in the Wagner Act.

There is also a good deal of complaint about Section 14 (b), which permits states to pass right-to-work laws. [See Section V, below.—Ed.]

What are the legal limitations on free speech by employers?

Under the law as presently interpreted, neither the company nor the union may make a speech to employees on company time for or against organization during the twenty-four hours immediately before a union election.

Generally speaking, an employer or a union can advise the employees that it is for or against their interests to vote for a union so long as the statement does not involve a promise of benefit or a threat of reprisal, and is not otherwise coercive. . . .

What other policy questions are pending in the courts?

Another important issue now before the Supreme Court . . . is the question of whether an employer has a right to insist that a contract include a provision that the employee must vote to strike before the union can call a strike. The employer in this case also insisted that the contract provide that any last offer the employer made must be submitted to a vote of the employees for acceptance or rejection.

The Board held (another member and I dissented) that the company had no right to insist upon such conditions. The Court of Appeals reversed the Board, and the Supreme Court has consented to review it. . . .

Are you getting more cases than you are deciding?

Over the years we have taken in from 13,000 to 14,000 cases a year. Our output is within the same range.

In the approximately twelve years of the Wagner Act, the Board decided about 13,800 cases.

One significant thing under Taft-Hartley is the tremendous number of cases which have required a Board decision—about 27,000.

What caused this increase?

The Wagner Act dealt with unfair labor practices by employers only. The Taft-Hartley amendments added unfair labor practices on the part of unions. This broadened the area for unfair labor practice cases. Under the Wagner Act the individual could file charges against an employer. Under Taft-Hartley he can file against the union as well.

What proportion of cases are filed by individuals?

Individual employees today are filing about 42 per cent of all the unfair labor practice cases. This is only 2 per cent less than are coming from labor organizations. Employers are filing about 17 per cent of the charges.

About 60 per cent of the charges filed by individual workers are against employers, the other 40 per cent against unions. . . .

What unfair acts do individuals complain about?

The major charge made by individuals involves illegal discrimination against them in the course of their employment. This would include the outright discharge of an individual by his employer because of his union activities, or a discharge at the union's request because of some disagreement with the employee. Or, it might mean the loss of seniority by an individual as a result of union pressure upon the employer. In the main, the most frequent complaint by individuals involves job rights.

What relief do individuals get?

In the past decade, more than 15,000 employees have been reinstated to jobs from which they have been illegally separated due to discrimination by the employer, the union, or both. In addition, workers who had suffered one form of discrimination or another received a total of more than $11 million in back pay.

Who paid this?

About $10 million was paid by employers and the remaining $1 million by unions.

Under what circumstances would a union pay back pay?

This would happen in a case where the Board found that the union had caused the employer to discharge a worker or refuse to hire him through an illegal arrangement.

What happened under the Wagner Act?

Under the Wagner Act about 41,000 employees received about $12.5 million in back pay. . . .

Will you comment on the union charges that the law is antiunion?

Some union leaders may believe the Taft-Hartley Act is slanted against labor. However, I think the position of many union leaders is the natural result of the imposition of regulations on unions. They, like everyone else in our society, dislike regulation.

The Taft-Hartley Act was the first effort of government to restrict organized labor in its dealing with management. This was almost certain to provoke resistance and criticism, just as the Wagner Act provoked resistance and criticism from management. . . .

What about corrupt union officials?

We have had cases where there were intimations of corruption in unions and collusion between management and union officials, but that problem is outside the scope of our authority. It, therefore, cannot be a significant factor in our decisions except to the extent that corruption or collusion interferes with a worker's right either to join or not to join a union. . . .

LABOR UNION IMMUNITIES [4]

The Wagner Act of 1935 went a long way to establish practically complete immunity of labor organizations for torts,

[4] From article in *Economic Intelligence* (published by the Economic Research Department of the Chamber of Commerce of the United States). no 107:1-2. June 1957. Reprinted by permission.

restraints of trade, coercion and other anti-social acts committed by their leaders, their members or the union in cases of union promotion, bargaining and strikes. Section 7 (rights of employees) guaranteed to employees the right to "engage in concerted activities for the purpose of collective bargaining or other mutual aid or protection." No limit was imposed upon the measures employed or the effects of these concerted actions. Five "unfair labor practices" on the part of employers were listed and elaborate provision was made to prevent those employer practices. Unfair practices by employees or unions were not mentioned and no means of prevention or securing against them were provided.

This almost complete immunity was offset somewhat by the Taft-Hartley Act of 1947 by listing six unfair labor practices of labor organizations or their agents and placing some limitations on secondary boycotts.

In an important new study, *Legal Immunities of Labor Unions,* Roscoe Pound, formerly Dean of the Harvard Law School, shows the degree to which government itself is responsible for the build-up of labor leader power and the abuses which have resulted.

In an interesting fashion, he traces the history of immunities of numerous groups. There was a time when "the king could do no wrong." Special immunities not available to ordinary mortals formerly were available to public officials, legislators, diplomats, clergymen and many others. Most of these immunities have been abolished or diminished. Meantime, labor leaders are still free from most of the restraints applied to other people.

While the Wagner Act is by no means the only culprit building up excessive labor-leader power, it was the keystone in the arch.

Dean Pound states that the immunities of labor unions rest upon four features of American labor law as it has developed through legislation within a generation:

(1) Substantial elimination, as against labor organization, of what in practical effect is the assured method of enforcing the law applicable to everyone else.

(2) Refusal of labor organizations to be treated as legally responsible organizations by becoming incorporated and so legally tangible entities.

(3) Not distinguishing unlawful action by labor organizations, their leaders and their members, done outside of the employer-employee relation, from practices in that relation.

(4) Committing all matters affecting labor organizations to an administrative agency instead of confining its jurisdiction to matters involved in the employer-employee relations.

The resulting immunities have been fortified by the abuse of the constitutional concept of interstate commerce so as to take purely local conditions and situations largely out of control of the states. Congress established the Interstate Commerce Commission, the Federal Trade Commission and others to protect the citizen, to protect the consumer. On the other hand, the National Labor Relations Board and similar administrative agencies in the states (along with the legitimate function of assuring equality in collective bargaining between employer and employee) acquired a function of upholding immunities of labor organizations and their leaders at the expense of the public. Pound categorically says, "They do not protect the public." His study unquestionably points in the direction in which we could move in the period ahead.

Compulsory unionism should be outlawed. [See Section V, below.—Ed.] Strict enforcement at the community level against the private use of force and violence is increasingly becoming an essential feature for attracting and holding employers. Many people believe that the Taft-Hartley law ought to be amended to require that the employer need only deal with union representatives chosen by secret ballot from among the individual employer's own employees.

These steps would pave the way for a little more democracy in unions and reduce union racketeering. They would go a long way to make labor organizations truly voluntary associations. Antisocial wage inflation would be mitigated and a sense of community between the employer and his own workers could again be restored.

LABOR'S MONOPOLY POWERS [5]

Monopoly power may be described as the possession of power by an individual or a group to control the supply and fix the price of needed goods and services. . . . Certain international unions . . . virtually control the labor supply of [some basic American] industries and have proved on many occasions their ability to dictate the terms on which the services of labor are available to produce the goods and services the nation needs. . . .

A principal cause of union monopoly power is the immunity of labor unions from the legal liabilities to which every one else is subject. . . .

The exemption of labor unions from legal liability as defined by the antitrust laws was reached by judicial and administrative decisions after passage of the 1932 Norris-LaGuardia Act, even though Congress specifically refused to declare labor unions exempt. We, therefore, have new substantive law by interpretation under a procedural statute (the Norris-LaGuardia Act) and under statutes having entirely different objectives (the antitrust laws and the labor laws). . . .

To summarize certain of these aspects of union abuses and immunities (i.e. the "double standard" of antitrust application):

1. While group boycotts or concerted refusals by businessmen to deal with other businessmen are deemed undue restraints of trade, whatever their purpose, and are condemned under the antitrust laws, unions may freely engage in similar activities. Unions demand and obtain contracts under which nonunion employers are boycotted, as well as other employers and products which the union chooses to designate as "unfair." It is clear that such agreements to boycott would violate the antitrust laws except for the immunity of unions.

2. Unions continuously impose unreasonable restrictions on the use of modern innovations, and thus retard production and increase costs. But, in cases where businessmen have combined to suppress patented inventions or new technologies, their conduct has been held unlawful under the antitrust statutes.

[5] From *Monopoly Power as Exercised by Labor Unions*, monograph by the National Association of Manufacturers Study Group on Monopoly Power Exercised by Labor Unions. The Association. 2 East 48th Street New York 17. n.d. p 1-31. Reprinted by permission.

3. Agreements between businessmen, either actual or potential competitors, not to compete in specified territories violate the antitrust laws. However, unions freely divide territories and restrict business competition.

4. Businessmen violate the antitrust laws when they enter into agreements which restrict production and increase prices. However, the unions arbitrarily restrict production with impunity. For example, the United Mine Workers, in 1949, arbitrarily curtailed all coal production to three days a week in order to "stabilize" production and prices. . . .

5. The Supreme Court has held that Section 2 of the Sherman Act is violated if a single business firm, or group of firms, possesses sufficient economic power to exclude new competitors, or fix market prices. Unions, however, may and do possess and exercise the same monopolistic power with impunity, arbitrarily dividing up and allocating industries, territories and jurisdictions among themselves, to the exclusion of competitors and without regard to the wishes of the employees they are supposed to represent.

6. Finally, the monopolistic powers of some labor unions have been used to force business enterprises in some areas to use only products manufactured in plants employing members of a certain local union. This conduct has created artificially high prices to the consumer and has excluded competing products. Some unions have even gone so far as to use their power for the purpose of revenge against some employer by seeking to exclude his products from competition. Yet it is fundamental that the exercise of monopoly power by a businessman—or group of businessmen—to exclude a competitor violates the antitrust laws. . . .

The Federal law, *as interpreted*, not only permits restraints of trade by unions, but also prevents the states from regulating them. Thus, in a 1955 case . . . the Supreme Court held that the state of Missouri could not enjoin union picketing designed to force an employer to agree to deal only with unionized contractors, even though this would violate the state's antitrust law. The court reasoned that the Federal Labor-Management Relations Act has preempted the field and precluded the states from regulating conduct touched upon in any way by the Federal law. . . .

The most far-reaching trend toward monopoly power is to be found in the centralization of authority in national and international unions.

The fact-finding board appointed by President Truman to deal with the steel dispute and strike of 1949 . . . said:

> In collective bargaining in the steel industry, the practice has developed by which almost the entire industry generally follows the pattern set by United States Steel Corporation and perhaps a few of the other large companies in their contracts with the union.
>
> As a result, there is frequently little or no serious bargaining or discussion between most of the individual employers and the union.
>
> This practice is clearly a variation from the accepted concept of collective bargaining as defined in the statutes and interpretations; it tends to promote a feeling of dissatisfaction and disharmony between the parties which makes cooperation difficult.
>
> Now that the organizational phase of union activities has been passed, the field ought to be reexamined to see whether the public interest requires any modification in the definition and theories of collective bargaining in accordance with the new situation faced, not only in the steel industry but in other industries where varying kinds of industry-wide rather than individual collective bargaining have grown up. . . .

The lines drawn in the law and public policy today between restraints of trade and price-fixing practiced by business (which are presumably illegal and against public policy), and practically identical conduct by unions (which is presumably legal and in accord with public policy as the Supreme Court interprets the intent of Congress), is the root of the growth of monopoly power in unions. . . .

The dividing up of territory which is illegal for businessmen under the antitrust laws, is a standard monopolistic device of unions. Unions can and do tell employers where they may operate and where they may not enter. . . .

Probably the best known example of the practice of regional monopoly is found in the electrical industry of New York City. In this case, the Brotherhood of Electrical Workers, AFL, in an agreement with New York manufacturers of electrical equipment, refused to install in New York City fixtures made by manufacturers not parties to the agreement, thus effectively excluding from the New York market competitive electrical equipment. After long litigation, the United States Supreme Court in 1945 found this practice illegal, but only because the union acted in collusion with the employers. If the union bars equipment on its own, as it has done since the Supreme Court decision, what was hitherto illegal is again legal. . . .

Under the Taft-Hartley Law, employers cannot be forced to pay for services "which are not performed" [the practice known as "featherbedding"]. However, the Supreme Court has ruled that an employer can be forced to pay for services that are not wanted or not needed. . . .

Trucks coming into New York City may be required to take on a "helper" who is not needed and not wanted. However, warehousemen may not enter trucks to remove merchandise and the driver of the truck may not touch a box or a crate. Therefore, the helper must be hired, at the ever-increasing union scale, to move the merchandise a few feet from the truck to the platform.

Should the truck be driven by a union driver from a "foreign" local, it may be forced to take aboard an extra New York driver before it enters the city. Local 807 of the Teamsters does not permit members of foreign locals to drive in New York unless one of its own men is aboard. The latter does no work, but he gets a full day's pay. Under the Supreme Court ruling he is available for work, even though his presence is entirely superfluous. . . .

Unions in the skilled trades severely restrict their membership rolls and thus maintain a permanent "sellers' market" for the skills of those lucky enough to hold cards. Some unions will admit as apprentices only the sons of members, or other relative if the member has no son. . . . It is perfectly legal for unions to "keep the supply short" by refusing membership to otherwise qualified applicants.

The law provides that employees shall be entitled to select their own bargaining representative by secret ballot. But the law offers little protection to the employees, the employer or the public when a union which fails to win a representation election chooses to disregard the verdict of the ballot box.

In one case, a maker of electric signs, Neo Products of Lima, Ohio, had to build a whole new plant it didn't need when its employees selected a CIO union to represent them. The AFL electrical union, which controlled installations all over the country, told its men not to work on signs with the CIO label. The company's only way out was to build another plant employing AFL members. . . .

The ability of the Teamsters Union to paralyze the movement of supplies and goods makes it virtually a law unto itself. It can bring almost any company into line if it wishes to get tough —and it does get tough at the slightest provocation. By playing ball with other unions, it can help them get what they want also.

In Los Angeles, the employees of the Danish Maid Bakery had voted 3.5 to 1 against joining the AFL Bakers Union. The Bakers called on the Teamsters for help. The Teamsters picketed the back entrances of the bakery's best customers, the chain stores and supermarkets, where the supplies were delivered. If they wanted anything else to sell, the stores had to stop carrying Danish Maid products.

The law as it is interpreted and enforced today has very little restraining influence on the unions. They are well aware of the powers they wield and of how difficult it is for employers, the government or their own members to curb their actions.

The most shocking aspect of uncurbed union power—and its misuse—involves the arbitrary domination exercised over the lives of both union and nonunion employees. In a case arising out of the Kohler strike, the Wisconsin Employment Relations Board in a decision sustained by the Wisconsin State Supreme Court found that officers, members and agents of the UAW-CIO

(1) engage in mass picketing . . . , (2) attempted to prevent the lawful work or employment of persons desiring to work . . . by force, threats and intimidation and by massing pickets at the plant entrances, (3) the large numbers and mass formations round the entrances obstruct and interfere with the free use of public streets, and (4) the officers, members and agents of the union have forcefully taken into custody persons attempting to enter the plant of the Kohler Company, forced them to accompany such officers, members, and agents to the strike headquarters of

the . . . union and prevented them from pursuing their lawful work and employment. [In addition] officers, members and agents of the union have followed the cars of persons attempting to enter or leave . . . the plant and picketed their homes and have threatened [them] with physical injury. [See "A Strike Pattern," in Section III, above.—Ed.]. . .

While it is not the purpose of this report to propose specific amendments to our complex labor legislation, Federal and local, the facts presented herein indicate that the following objectives must be sought in order to protect the interests of the public and of union as well as nonunion employees:

Real bargaining at the local level and an end to the domination of bargaining by international unions;

An end to compulsory union membership in any form;

An end to organizational picketing to force people into unions;

A ban on boycotts and on clauses in contracts which provide for boycotts against other employers;

A ban on economic waste in the form of "featherbedding," restrictions on output, unneeded employees, and refusal to allow new machines or processes to be used;

A modification of the doctrine of Federal preemption so that state and local authorities can reassume their responsibilities in labor-management matters;

A prohibition against the use of union funds and union staff employees for partisan political purposes.

CRITICISM OF TAFT-HARTLEY ACT [6]

There are three central criticisms of the Taft-Hartley Act in action. The first major criticism is that it has been ineffective and frequently inept in achieving the ostensible purposes of many of its provisions. The second major criticism stems from the many serious departures from fair treatment found in the legislation. The third large criticism is the excessive time consumed in the processing of cases.

[6] From *Taft-Hartley Act in Action*, pamphlet by Jack Barbash, professor of economics, University of Wisconsin. 51p. League for Industrial Democracy. 112 East 19th Street. New York 3, 1956. Reprinted by permission.

The most glaring example of ineptness has been the provisions dealing with emergency disputes which could be enjoined during an eighty-day period. The provision for the eighty-day injunction used in seven disputes generally deterred rather than encouraged the settlement of such emergency disputes. . . .

An examination of the disputes in which the emergency disputes procedures of Taft-Hartley were invoked . . . adds up to this: first, settlements were rarely made during the period of the injunction; second, in the cases in which settlements came during the injunction, it is a real question whether the settlement came because of, or in spite of, the injunction; third, in the majority of cases the injunction made settlement more difficult.

The provision that the union members must vote on the last offer made by an employer during an eighty-day injunction period was similarly ineffective. . . .

Generally, the emergency disputes provision set up a rigid timetable of procedures which left no discretion to the government to tailor its procedures to meet the peculiar characteristics of each dispute. . . .

Another fault with the . . . Act is that its ban on the closed shop has worked injury on the industries which are generally characterized by casual employment. . . .

A construction contractor and his associated subcontractors who need several hundred steamfitters, bricklayers, iron workers, would soon find it impossible to function if they had to go out in the open market and hire these complements of workers on short notice for the short terms of employment typical of the construction industry. The development of relationships between the union and the employers in this industry have made the union hiring hall the only place where a construction contractor can get a required number of competent craftsmen on short notice and for short term employment. . . .

The attempt to eliminate Communist control of certain unions via the Taft-Hartley affidavit route has been generally recognized as a failure. . . . It is questionable whether a ritual like the affidavit is suited for the purposes of ridding unions of Communist leadership. The proof is that it has not. In the first six years of the Act, only one union officer was convicted of false swearing on a non-Communist affidavit. In point of fact, the non-Communist affidavit provision was responsible for considerable delay in the processing of cases of unions which are not Communist-dominated.

Another of the criticisms of the . . . Act is that many of its provisions were offensive to any concept of equal treatment, while failing to contribute to the achievement of a useful public purpose. . . . The law contains a provision for an eighty-day injunction restraining an emergency strike. The injunction operates only to restrain the workers. It applies no sanction against the employer. The effect of the injunction is to resolve by statute all of the issues in the dispute which caused the strike in favor of the employer for at least eighty days. During this eighty-day period, the employer has no strategic incentive for yielding to union pressure, because the most potent weapon in the union's bargaining arsenal—namely the strike—has been banned. . . .

The law provides for another type of injunction against secondary activities of unions. There are two significant characteristics of this injunction. In the first place, it *must* be requested by the General Counsel [of the National Labor Relations Board] if he has reason to believe that the allegations of the employer are true. Second, it is confined to the restraint of unfair labor practices of unions. No unfair labor practice against the union is subject to this type of injunction. . . .

Now it can be argued that there are many unfair labor practices against unions which are in this category, . . . for example, the employer's failure to comply with an order of the Board directing him to bargain in good faith. . . . If the employer refuses for any length of time to bargain, the Board's order, when it is issued, becomes ineffective, as a union cannot survive indefinitely in the face of an employer's refusal to bargain. . . .

The sweeping ban . . . on secondary activity unfairly impairs union solidarity. Many students of labor, myself included, contend that secondary boycotts carried out by labor are not offensive to the public interest when secondary activity is used in a peaceful way to protect union standards from being undermined by sweatshop competition. . . .

Another section which has failed to protect the rights of labor . . . provides that

the expressing of any views, argument, or opinion, or the dissemination thereof, whether in written, printed, graphic, or visual form, shall not constitute or be evidence of, an unfair labor practice under any of the provisions of this Act if such expression contains no threat of reprisal or force or promise of benefit. . . .

Now, there can be no objection to safeguarding free speech for both the employer and the union. . . . But this purpose is achieved by the first amendment to the Constitution. As a matter of fact, the courts ruled in several cases that the Board had overstepped constitutional bounds in finding employers guilty of an unfair labor practice based solely upon speech. This provision, however, does something more than enact constitutional doctrines. It prevents the Board from appraising the effect of the expression *in all of the circumstances.* And we should realize that the circumstances surrounding speech or statements are critical in determining whether or not it has a coercive effect. . . .

Apparently . . . the free speech license works only one way. Thus, the National Labor Relations Board found that the unfair list issued by a central labor union declaring certain employers unfair was not privileged free speech in a secondary boycott situation. . . .

An economic striker [one striking for wages, hours or working conditions] . . . loses his status as an employee and, therefore, his right to vote in a subsequent representation election if he is replaced. . . .

A Senate Labor subcommittee concluded that

The effect of that doctrine . . . is obviously that, since the back-to-work movement had replaced the strikers, the old union would be ousted, and the competing union which had no valid interest in the plant prior to the dispute would emerge victorious from any election. Under such circumstances as these, the doctrine would convert the ultimate exercise of economic strength by the unions to strike into a suicidal weapon.

The Taft-Hartley law makes it an unfair labor practice for a union to require an employer "to pay or deliver any money or other thing of value in the nature of an exaction for services which are not performed or not to be performed." The short-hand term of opprobrium for this is "featherbedding."

In principle, "featherbedding" amounts to an attempt of the union to inject certain human and welfare considerations as the employer goes about trying to cut labor costs. If held within reasonable tolerance, the union's attempt to protect its members' jobs and earnings, and the employer's attempt to cut costs, are both necessary parts of collective bargaining in a free enterprise economy. I must hasten to add that I know of no way of enforcing these reasonable tolerances, except that it is not a job for government.

In any case, it appears that the "featherbedding" problem was grossly exaggerated if one is to judge by the fact that the NLRB has not, as this is written, upheld a single complaint on this point. . . .

A further case of unfairness is the provision . . . which instructs the Board not to give controlling weight to the extent of union organization in determining the appropriate unit in a representation proceeding. . . . [For example] the Board finds that a unit of two plants is the appropriate unit for collective bargaining. But the union has organized only one of the plants. The Board may not . . . direct an election on the one-plant basis solely because it is the extent of union organization. . . . The effect . . . is to force the union to hold back its demand for recognition until it has been able to organize the whole unit. . . .

The . . . law . . . authorizes several types of damage suits in Federal courts. A union can be sued for engaging in an illegal secondary boycott. Thus, the law provides an arsenal of weapons that can be used against this union activity; it can be restrained through injunction; it is a cause of action in an unfair labor practice determination, and in addition to all of these the employer can sue for damages. It is worth noting that an unfair labor practice against the union can be proceeded against only through the long-drawn-out unfair labor practice act. . . .

In . . . [one] case, the NLRB found that certain picketing activities . . . did not constitute an illegal secondary boycott. On the same facts a jury found that the union had engaged in an illegal secondary boycott and awarded damages. . . . The Circuit Court of Appeals upheld both decisions. . . .

The Taft-Hartley law tries to outlaw jurisdictional strikes. But it does no such thing if a jurisdictional strike means what it is supposed to mean, namely a dispute between two unions as to whose members are entitled to work on a specific job.

First of all, the Board makes no attempt (whether it should, or could, is another matter) to make a finding as between the claims of two unions. Rather, it confirms the employer's original assignment of work to one or another of the contending unions. In effect, this provision underwrites the employer's choice in a work assignment dispute.

Second, it is doubtful whether the Board has the competence to decide a *jurisdictional* dispute on its merits.

Third, the Board has, in at least one case, found a jurisdictional dispute to exist when a union and an employer contest whether it (the union) or an unorganized group of employees shall be assigned certain work. The employer assigns the work to the unorganized employees. What the Board then says is that it is possible to have a jurisdictional dispute where only *one* union is involved, which is absurd. . . .

It is clear that the government has no sensible answer to the jurisdictional strike, and that it best be left to the internal procedures of the labor movement. . . .

Under the act, certain groups of workers are disqualified from coverage. These include supervisors and foremen, who are not recognized as employees. . . .

No showing has been made that the foremen who were in the printers' union, for example, were not able to exercise their supervisory responsibility in good conscience, even though they were members of the union.

But the unfairness of this exemption exists independently of the issue of conflicting loyalty. It still would have been possible to safeguard the rights of union organization and collective bargaining for foremen and supervisors by specifying that super-visors' unions could not be a part of a plantwide unit or affiliated with a union which admits other than supervisory employees. . . .

Excessive delay . . . has existed in the processing of cases that have come before the NLRB. . . .

On the average, it takes the National Labor Relations Board more than a year to process an unfair labor practice charge through the full course of the Board's procedure. The Board order has no compulsive effect in and of itself until it is enforced by a circuit court decree. It may take as much as a year to get enforcement in the circuit court.

V. "RIGHT TO WORK" LAWS

EDITOR'S INTRODUCTION

The requirement of union membership as a condition of employment is discussed in this section. Proponents of the closed shop and the union shop refer to these as "union security" arrangements; opponents call them "compulsory unionism."

Three articles from the United States Department of Labor publications survey legislation and labor contracts affecting union security provisions and state "right to work" legislation.

A union railway worker, in a pamphlet distributed by a group advocating "right to work" laws, gives his reasons for supporting such legislation. Management's position in favor of these laws is set forth in a monograph by an industrial employers' group and an address by one of its executive officers.

An article in the AFL-CIO's monthly economic publication assails legislation restricting the closed or union shop as "right to wreck" laws. The Secretary of Labor pledges the Administration's opposition to similar national legislation. The Governor of New York brands such state laws as "a fraud." A national magazine surveys the effect of such laws in states that have them.

LAWS ON UNION SECURITY [1]

Federal law dealing with the authority of employers and labor unions to contract on the subject of union membership (union security agreements) is contained in two statutes: the Taft-Hartley Act and the Railway Labor Act. Generally speaking, contract provisions on this subject fall into two categories: provisions for a closed shop, where employers may hire only members of the contracting union, and provisions for a union shop, where the employee is not required to be a member of the unon when he is hired but must join after a certain period of employment.

[1] From "Federal Provisions Affecting Union Security." Mimeographed. Department of Labor. Washington 25, D.C. n.d. p 1-3.

The provisions of the National Labor Relations Act, as amended by the Taft-Hartley Act, define certain "unfair labor practices" by employers and by organizations of employees in business enterprises affecting interstate commerce, and prescribe remedies for these practices. Under these provisions, in any employment subject to the Act, employers and representatives of employees may not provide in their agreements for closed shop or other similar arrangements, such as hiring halls, which restrict employment to individuals holding membership in a union at the time of hiring. On the other hand, the Act permits employers and qualified unions to execute union shop agreements requiring employees to join the union thirty days after employment or the date of the agreement, whichever is later, except in states where such agreements are forbidden by state law. However, under a valid union shop agreement, an employee may be discharged for lack of union membership only when it results in his failure to tender on time "the periodic dues and the initiation fees uniformly required." If a majority of employees wish to revoke a union shop they may do so through a secret ballot deauthorization referendum conducted by the National Labor Relations Board. The Act provides for the Board to conduct such a referendum whenever a petition is filed by 30 per cent or more of the employees in the bargaining unit covered by the agreement and certify the results to the employer and the labor organization.

For a union security agreement to be valid, all of the following requirements must be met:

1. The contracting union must be free from employer domination or assistance as proscribed by the Act.

2. The agreement must cover employees in an appropriate unit who have legally designated the contracting union as their representative.

3. The contracting union must have complied with the filing and non-Communist affidavit requirements of the Act.

4. The union's authority to make the agreement must not have been revoked by the employees voting in a union shop deauthorization poll within the preceding year.

5. The agreement must contain an appropriate thirty-day grace period for all employees who are not members of the union when it takes effect.

The Taft-Hartley Act originally required an election before a union could be authorized to execute this type of agreement. It was found, however, that union shop authorization polls placed an unnecessary administrative burden and expense upon the Board. In fiscal [year] 1949, 93.9 per cent of employees eligible to vote in such elections cast ballots in favor of union shop conditions and authorized the negotiation of union shop contracts in 96.7 per cent of the elections held. The law was amended in 1951 to eliminate these pre-contract polls, but continuing the provisions for elections to rescind authority after a union shop had been negotiated.

The Railway Labor Act governs the labor relations of railroads and airlines engaged in interstate commerce and their employees. The Act was amended in 1951 to permit employers and labor organizations to make union shop agreements requiring employees to join such an organization within sixty days, notwithstanding any other law of the United States or of any state or territory. The Supreme Court has upheld the constitutionality of this amendment as coming within the commerce power of Congress and ruled that it expressly permits union shop agreements in employment covered by the Act despite the provisions of any state law to the contrary.

UNION SECURITY CONTRACTS [2]

Federal labor legislation since 1935 has safeguarded the right of a majority of the employees in a given unit to choose representatives for collective bargaining purposes who would speak for all employees. Through collective bargaining union members have traditionally sought more specific guarantees of the status of their unions by the negotiation of clauses requiring that all employees should be or become union members. Federal and some state statutes currently in effect, however, restrict the

[2] From "Union-Security Provisions in Agreements, 1954," by Rose Theodore, Division of Wages and Industrial Relations, Bureau of Labor Statistics. The Bureau. United States Department of Labor. Washington 25, D.C. 1955. p 1-10.

degree to which union membership may be established by employers and unions as a condition of employment.

The union-shop clause usually requires employees already on the payroll to become union members and new employees to join within a specified time after hiring. It is the principal type of union-security provision now found in labor-management contracts, according to an analysis made by the Bureau of Labor Statistics of 1,716 collective bargaining agreements in . . . 1954. Nearly two thirds contained union-shop clauses. Of the 7,405,000 workers covered by the agreements studied, 64 per cent were employed under union-shop provisions.

Maintenance-of-membership clauses, which do not require employees to join the union but to maintain membership once acquired, appeared in 14 per cent of the agreements. The remainder of the agreements studied (21 per cent) contained sole-bargaining clauses which recognize the union as the exclusive bargaining agent, but do not specify membership requirements. . . .

When an employer negotiates a union-shop provision, he agrees to require, as one of the conditions of employment, that all, or nearly all, employees must join the union within a specified time and must remain members in good standing. The development of harmonious relationships between management and labor is often advanced as one of the benefits to be gained from such arrangements. . . .

The type most common (60 per cent of the union-shop agreements) required that all present employees be or become union members within a specified time and that all newly hired employees join within a specified time after starting work. Under such agreements there is no limitation on the employer in the selection of new workers, either in terms of hiring only union members or of giving preference or consideration to union members. . . .

Exemption from the membership requirement was granted to certain groups in the bargaining unit (commonly designated as a modified union shop) in . . . 18 per cent of the . . . contracts. In most instances, employees who were not union members when the agreements became effective were not required to join the union. A few contracts exempted only employees with relatively long service; a few others required a specific proportion of new employees (e.g., nine out of every ten) to become union members within a specified time.

An escape period after one year, during which new employees were permitted to withdraw from the union, was provided in forty-two agreements. These covered about one half of the workers under all modified union-shop contracts, including a large segment of the automobile industry. . . .

In thirty company-wide or association agreements which covered some plants in states banning union-shop arrangements, provision was made for a union shop but workers in these states were exempted. . . .

Union-shop provisions in sixty-nine agreements stipulated some degree of preference in hiring for union members. Usually the union was permitted to refer union members for job vacancies who would be considered with other applicants on the basis of their qualifications. . . .

The closed shop, which is the strongest form of union security agreed to by employers in collective bargaining, usually requires that only union members may be hired; however, if no union members are available, other workers may be taken on provided that they join the union prior to or shortly after starting work. The closed shop is forbidden in industries subject to the LMRA [Labor Management Relations Act of 1947—i.e., the Taft-Hartley Act], but it is still found in establishments not covered by the act or by state bans. In the present study, eighty-seven agreements, concentrated largely in local trade and service industries, contained closed-shop provisions. These accounted for less than 8 per cent of the union-shop agreements. . . . Union-status provisions are negotiated within a framework of Federal and state legislation and are affected by decisions of the National Labor Relations Board . . . and court rulings. The Labor Management Relations Act of 1947, applicable to industries affecting interstate commerce, bans the closed shop but permits union-shop and maintenance of membership provisions. . . .

State legislation prohibiting the requirement of union membership as a condition of employment, thereby outlawing the negotiation of closed- and union-shops and maintenance-of-membership provisions, is given precedence over provisions of the LMRA under section 14(b) of the act, which reads:

Nothing in this act shall be construed as authorizing the execution or application of agreements requiring membership in a labor organization as a condition of employment in any state or territory in which such execution or application is prohibited by state or territorial law. . . .

The most significant impact of the LMRA of 1947 on union-security provisions occurred during the years immediately after its passage, when union-shop provisions replaced the closed shop as the predominant form of union security. . . . In 1946 . . . it was estimated that 33 per cent of all workers under agreement were covered by closed-shop provisions and 17 per cent were covered by union-shop agreements, a total of 50 per cent. According to the Bureau's study of agreements effective in 1949-1950, the importance of union shops and closed shops combined had shifted only slightly. However, less than one tenth of the agreements in this combined group required union membership at the time of employment. . . .

Under a maintenance-of-membership provision, the employee is not required to join the union, but if he is a member when the clause becomes effective or later chooses to become a member, he must thereafter maintain his membership as a condition of employment. Usually, however, such provisions provide for an escape period immediately after signing of the agreement to permit withdrawals from the union. After this period, maintenance of membership is generally required for the duration of the contract. . . .

A variation of membership-maintenance clause, introduced in major steel agreements in 1952 and found in other industries, requires each new employee to sign an application for membership in the union, with the option of canceling the application between the fifteenth and thirtieth day of employment. If not canceled during that period, the application becomes effective and the employee is required to maintain his membership for the duration of the contract. . . .

Frequently, the negotiation of a maintenance-of-membership provision represents a compromise between the union's demand for a union-shop clause and management's objection to such a provision. During World War II, membership maintenance was granted by the National War Labor Board in a number of cases. Under such arrangements, the employee's individual choice is protected because membership is voluntary; the union's security is guaranteed to some extent because membership, once acquired, must be maintained. In comparison with the union shop, however, membership maintenance increases the union's organizing job in recruiting members and in retaining them if an escape clause is provided. . . .

The prevalence of membership-maintenance clauses has declined since World War II. The Bureau estimated in 1946 that 25 per cent of all workers under agreement were covered by such clauses; by contrast, 17 per cent of the workers under the agreements examined in 1954 were similarly covered. . . .

All agreements, by their nature, assure sole-bargaining rights to the union. In most agreements, as already indicated, the union's status is further protected by requirements that employees acquire or retain union membership as a condition of employment. However, in 21 per cent of the agreements in this study, covering 19 per cent of the workers . . . the union had only the exclusive right to bargain for all employees in the unit, union and nonunion alike. . . .

Under six contracts, hiring was to be done through a union hiring hall. The union hiring hall, traditionally operated prior to passage of the LMRA for the benefit of union members, is permitted now only if it functions as a nondiscriminatory "employment agency" for union and nonunion workers.

Under the terms of thirty-six sole-bargaining agreements in states prohibiting union-security clauses, some provision was made for union security if the law should be changed. . . .

Checkoff is a dues-collection method whereby the employer agrees to deduct from the employee's pay his union dues, and in some instances, initiation fee, fines, and assessments, for transmittal to the union at regular intervals. . . .

Checkoff is permissible under the LMRA only on written authorization of the individual employee. A few of the state "right to work" laws incorporate similar checkoff regulations.

Under LMRA, the employee's authorization may be irrevocable for a maximum of one year, or the duration of the agreement, whichever is shorter.

Almost three fourths of the contracts studied, covering a slightly higher proportion of workers, contained checkoff provisions. . . . Dues as the sole deduction were stipulated in over one fourth of the 1,275 agreements with checkoff; dues and initiation fees in a similar proportion; dues, initiation fees, and assessments in less than one fifth. . . .

Checkoff provisions may be negotiated in connection with the union shop, membership maintenance, or sole bargaining. . . . Virtually all agreements providing for membership maintenance and 88 per cent of those with only sole-bargaining rights provided for checkoff, in contrast to 66 per cent of union-shop agreements. Since all employees working under a union-shop arrangement are subject to discharge for nonpayment of dues, the checkoff in these circumstances is not essential in assuring that dues payments do not fall in arrears. However, the checkoff is a convenient method of collecting dues where large numbers of workers are employed in a single plant.

Slightly over 40 per cent of the workers under agreement in 1946 were estimated by the Bureau to be covered by checkoff arrangements, compared with almost 80 per cent of the workers under the 1950-1951 contracts examined. The Bureau's study of agreements effective in 1952, as well as the present study, showed a slight increase since 1950-1951 in the number of agreements with checkoff provisions, with virtually no change in the proportion of workers under such arrangements.

STATE "RIGHT-TO-WORK" LAWS [3]

"Right-to-work" is the label used to describe a group of state laws that make null and void, or unlawful, contracts requiring membership in a labor union as a condition of employment, or excluding from employment any person because of nonmembership in a union.

[3] From State "Right-to-Work" Laws, processed pamphlet issued by the Bureau of Labor Standards of the United States Department of Labor. Washington 25, D.C. 1957. p 1-8.

These laws, in essence, usually provide that as a condition of employment:

(a) No person shall be required to be (or become) a member of a union or to abstain from membership;
or

(b) No person shall be denied, or excluded from, employment on account of membership or nonmembership in a union.

The effect of these laws is to ban all union-security agreements. They prohibit not only the closed shop, where employers may hire only members of the contracting union, but also the union shop, where the employee not a member of the union must join after a certain period of employment. They also prohibit "maintenance of membership" which requires that those persons who are union members at the beginning of a contract period must remain members during the period of the contract.

Eighteen states now have "right-to-work" laws of general application: Alabama, Arizona, Arkansas, Florida, Georgia, Indiana, Iowa, Mississippi, Nebraska, Nevada, North Carolina, North Dakota, South Carolina, South Dakota, Tennessee, Texas, Utah, and Virginia.

A nineteenth state, Louisiana, has a right-to-work law limited to agricultural laborers and workers engaged in the processing of certain agricultural products. This law was passed in 1956, after a right-to-work law, general in application, which had been enacted in 1954, was repealed.

Over half of the right-to-work laws were enacted in 1947. The earliest enactments were the Arkansas and Florida constitutional amendments adopted in 1944; the most recent, the Indiana law in 1957. . . .

In Florida the state Supreme Court, in a 1950 case, stated that . . . [a] constitutional amendment . . . set forth the public policy of the state of Florida with respect to labor activities and labor opportunities The Court pointed out that these provisions guaranteed complete freedom of decision in whether to join or refrain from joining any labor organization.

During 1957, right-to-work measures were before the legislatures of fifteen states. These measures were divided about
equally between bills to adopt right-to-work laws or submit
right-to-work proposals to a referendum vote, and bills to repeal existing right-to-work laws. Eight of the fifteen state
legislatures (Connecticut, Delaware, Idaho, Illinois, Indiana,
Kansas, Louisiana, and Maryland) had before them measures
to adopt right-to-work bills or proposed constitutional amendments. Two of these passed. Indiana enacted a right-to-work
law, and the Kansas legislature adopted a resolution to submit
a right-to-work constitutional amendment to the voters at the
1958 general election. A bill is still pending in the Delaware
legislature. . . .

In Idaho, where a right-to-work bill failed in one house this
year, initiative petitions are being circulated to have the question submitted to the voters at the 1958 general election.

In the seven other states (Alabama, Iowa, Nebraska, Nevada,
North Dakota, South Dakota, and Utah) measures to repeal
existing right-to-work laws were introduced. Six of these failed
to pass.

A UNION WORKER'S VIEW [4]

Almost everyone will agree that a worker should have the
right to join a union if he so desires. Offhand, it would seem
that almost everyone would also agree that a worker should have
the right not to join a union or to quit being a member if he
no longer believes in its leadership or objectives. . . .

When we get down to cases, we find almost all labor
union officials arguing that it is wrong to force a man to stay
out of a union, but right to force him to join a union. Many
labor leaders support the principle of voluntarism where it
concerns a choice for the union. (For example, shall it join
the new AFL-CIO federation or not?) At the same time, they
deny voluntarism for the workers and support forced individual
membership in the union. . . .

[4] From *Forced Union Membership,* pamphlet by W. T. Harrison, railroad clerk
and member of the board of the National Right to Work Committee. National
Right to Work Committee. 1025 Connecticut Avenue. Washington 6, D.C. n.d.
p 1-15. Reprinted by permission.

What are the arguments of the big labor spokesmen? They say that the union shop is necessary for union security to protect the unions from being wrecked by the enemies of labor.

They say also that majority rule is a democratic principle and a minority of workers who would not voluntarily support the union should be compelled to do so.

They argue further that as the agreements negotiated apply to all employees, the nonmember gets the benefits without cost, or is a "free rider." They contend the "free rider" should be forced to pay.

The argument that the union shop is needed to prevent the unions from being wrecked is pretty thin. In 1933, there were less than 3 million union members in the United States. Today, there are well over 16 million members and the organized labor movement is something that must be taken into account by industry and government alike. . . .

The history of the union movement shows that the unions do not need compulsion to grow and protect themselves once they have statutory protection for the right to organize and bargain collectively. The big growth in the AFL and CIO after the Wagner Act was passed took place without compulsion. With the exception of the printing and construction industries, there were few closed shop and union shop contracts until World War II. The War Labor Board helped put over compulsory unionism during the war—at a time when the unions already were strong and healthy and did not really need it.

The unions are getting bigger, richer and stronger all the time. They don't need to force men to join their unions in order to protect themselves. . . .

In their argument on majority rule the union spokesmen entirely overlook the fact that under the laws of our land the rights of the minority are protected, which they are not in a union shop contract. . . .

Well, what about this argument that a worker shouldn't be permitted to get benefits from the union free of charge—the "free rider" argument? . . .

Actually the unions themselves have insisted that agreements reached in collective bargaining must apply to all the workers affected, and not just members of the union—and for a good reason. If the employer were free to give nonmembers different rules and rates of pay from the union members, he could quickly destroy the union by merely giving the nonmember better conditions and more pay while holding the union members to the terms of the contract. No union could survive under such circumstances.

Too, if we but stop and think a moment, we'll see that all of us benefit from organizations and movements to which we don't belong and don't contribute directly.

Most of us will agree that the churches do a lot of good and we wouldn't care to live where there are no churches. But would we want to be forced to belong to a particular church and contribute to it?

Obviously, the answer is No! . . .

Whether they admit it or not, advocates of the union shop are advocating dictatorship. They are giving the worker no choice. He must join a union or lose his job, the job upon which he depends for a living. He has lost his freedom, for freedom means a choice and he has no choice. . . .

The labor leaders say that if an individual union member objects to any policy, he can work to have the policy changed and at election time he can vote to change the union officials who have recommended the policy. Those of us who know the way unions are really run get a snicker out of such statements, knowing them to be pure "hogwash.". . .

It has reached the point where many local unions and local union officers often have little or nothing to say about their own affairs. The officers of the national or international decide things for them. . . .

When the members of Cincinnati Union Terminal Lodge 207 of the Brotherhood of Railway Clerks insisted on electing George W. Witt (a member in good standing and of high repute as a citizen) as financial secretary-treasurer, despite the opposition of the Grand Lodge officials, Mr. Witt was expelled and the affairs of the local taken over by the Grand Lodge. (The constitution of this organization gives the Grand President "sole power and authority to interpret the constitution.")

Other union constitutions permit such action during so-called emergencies. It is an emergency when the local opposes the big boys or does something they don't like.

The constitution of the International Typographical Union provides that any individual or local may be kicked out if he or it fails to "comply with the dictates of the International President."

That power has been used in quite a few cases.

Men have been kicked out of the American Federation of Musicians just for criticizing the union boss, J. Caesar Petrillo.

There is on record testimony before a congressional committee that any member of the International Union of Operating Engineers who asked questions about the disbursement or expenditure of funds was not only fired but union strong arm squads beat him up.

Under some union constitutions it is awfully easy for a man to get himself kicked out—for such things, for example, as "causing dissension," for criticizing decisions of union officers and for "conduct unbecoming a member," whatever that may be. . . .

With the union shop in operation, a man has to think before he objects to anything his union officers are doing. For—don't forget—the men who bring the charges against him will try him, too. It's a kangaroo court from beginning to end.

A strike is a mighty serious business to a workingman. He's off the payroll while it is going on and he is losing money which he and his family need badly. Yet a worker often doesn't get a fair chance to express his real views on a strike—the ballot isn't a secret ballot and he knows his bosses are watching. In most cases, he votes as he thinks they want him to vote—for the strike. . . .

All of us know that for a long time the railway unions didn't want a union shop because they were afraid of company unions. Finally, in 1951, they decided they were so strong that the railroads would never be able to have company unions. So George M. Harrison, head of the clerks' union, and the rest went to Congress and managed to pass an amendment to the

Railway Labor Act which permitted the union shop. (This law had expressly forbidden coercion by either party.) They then put the squeeze on the railroads and most of them signed up.

The newspapers have carried stories—never denied—that on the New York Central Railroad alone, 426 employees were fired because they refused to be compelled to join a union. About 130 more quit for the same reason. . . .

It is easy to see why the union bosses want the union shop. Then they don't have to worry about keeping their members satisfied. They can do as they please; the men have to stay in the union if they want to work.

It's also easy to see why some employers want the union shop. If they can reach an understanding with the heads of the union everything is all right. Maybe that understanding isn't good for the workers but that doesn't make any difference. Just so the union leaders and the employers are pleased. Keep in mind that it is a lot easier to please a few men than a lot of them.

A setup like that makes a sellout of the workers easy and there is nothing they can do about it. If a man speaks up to protest mismanagement or corruption his days are numbered. Something is going to happen to him.

Yes, there are reasons why union leaders want the union shop and there are reasons why some employers like that arrangement too. But are there any good reasons why the average worker should want the union shop? Is he any better off with it than he would be without it?

The answer in just about ninety-nine cases out of a hundred is—No.

If the union is strong enough to demand a union shop contract it doesn't need such a contract to protect it from co-called enemies of labor or anybody else. Let the union justify its existence on merit, and it won't need to force members to belong to it. They'll consider it an honor.

It is when the union cannot justify itself; when it does not serve the best interests of the workers that they need protection against its bosses. The only way they can be assured of that protection is to have the right to resign from any union that no longer represents their best interests.

To repeat, if there is a union shop and the union leaders and the employers get together on a sellout, the men are sunk. They have nowhere to go. If they have a legitimate protest, who listens? Their union bosses won't pay any attention to them. Nor will their employers. They are out of luck.

All who have been union men and watched the unions grow strong know how union leaders have increased and abused their power. Gangsters, crooked politicians and a certain type of labor leader are working together more and more. They are victimizing the workers and the general public. The union shop helps such unwholesome alliances. The worker is tied hand and foot; he cannot weaken the power of the unscrupulous labor leader by getting out of the union. He has to go along. His membership and money help these enemies of society. . . .

The right-to-work laws are in the interests of the average worker. They protect his right to join or not to join a union as he sees fit. They protect his freedom and his liberty. They give him a choice. They don't interfere with the right to bargain collectively which is all a union needs for its protection. They are in the best interests of the workingman, of the right kind of union and of our country.

AN OFFICIAL INDUSTRY VIEW [5]

A man's freedom to get and hold a job without regard to the compulsion of union membership is the basic issue in labor relations.

Indeed, it goes to the very heart of the problem because forced union membership is the major contributing cause to union monopoly. It is a ready-made device to extend the tentacles of union power, without any cost or effort on their part, nor any obligation to merit the support of members.

[5] From "A Monograph Discussing the Major Aspects of the Intercollegiate Debate Issue, 'Resolved: That the Requirement of Membership in a Labor Organization as a Condition of Employment Should be Illegal.'" Processed. National Association of Manufacturers. Employee Relations Department. 2 East 48th Street. New York 17. 1957. p 42-4. Reprinted by permission.

The recent revelations before Senator McClellan's committee show one significant pattern—the unconcern of Dave Beck, Frank Brewster, James Hoffa and others for what the membership of their unions would think of the damaging disclosures.

All during the presentation of evidence . . . there was not one indication of concern by the accused men for how the membership would react. . . .

How can high-ranking union leaders afford this disdain for the opinions of union members? Compulsory unionism is the answer. Why bother with what the membership thinks about the manner in which the local or the entire union is run—no matter how flagrantly nefarious it may be—if you hold each member's economic life in the palm of your hand? He cannot work at his trade under a union-shop contract, unless he remains in good standing, and member-critics of labor union regimes usually find themselves ruled in default. This means that their employers must discharge them, no matter how well they are doing their jobs.

That explains why we have had the incredible spectacle of James Hoffa being elected president of an international union of a million and a half members at a time when he stands accused by a senatorial committee of eighty-two separate acts of wrong-doing in the conduct of his own local in Detroit and in the union's central district council. . . .

If union leaders lost the self-perpetuating protection of compulsory unionism, they would be forced to go before their memberships on the basis of their records in office and earn their votes and support. This could result in more attention to the wishes and welfare of the membership and to community responsibilities. They'd be competing for the good will of the members, just as management is required to compete for the favor of its customers and employees alike. Without rigid membership control, union leadership would be less attractive to the racket fringe, and would be safer from involvement in shady dealing.

Everyone in the entire nation is affected by this situation . . . because compulsory unionism is the foundation for the monopoly practices of organized labor, an abuse of privilege that seriously threatens free competitive enterprise. . . .

The rising cost of labor, without a corresponding increase in productivity . . . is providing inflation with its principal upward thrust. . . .

If productivity has failed to keep pace, why have wages gone up? Because of the ability of giant unions, especially those in basic industries, to extract increases in wage rates and fringe benefits which go far beyond gains in output per man hour.

Union leaders are able to get these concessions because they are in control of the source of labor; not a wheel turns unless they have given the green light. Once a basic industry is taken into camp, a chain reaction of price rises is set into motion. A manufacturer, forced to pay more for steel because of wage hikes in that industry, must increase the price of his product. His customers, in turn, must pass the advance on to their outlets, and soon every segment of the economy has been infiltrated. . . .

The revelations of the McClellan committee are a challenge to all believers in freedom, justice and decency and in the dignity of the workingman.

While outwardly everybody is against the corruption and violence that have been revealed, privately union leaders are hardly enthusiastic about the "full cooperation" they promised to Senate investigators. The fact is that the mail received by the committee, far from subsiding, is beginning to mount and is already well past the level of fifty thousand letters mostly from rank-and-file members who are concerned about what is going on in their unions and where their money is going.

There is an unmistakable and rising public demand for an end to the freely practiced abuses of union power. Obviously, forthright action is indicated to assure public policies that truly safeguard human rights and the general welfare.

Our society, dedicated as it is to the freedom and the sanctity of the individual, must decide whether unionism is to be voluntary or compulsory. If compulsory, we are knowingly permitting a single private group to be moved into the position of an authoritarian agency—and thereby jeopardizing the very fundamentals of our American system.

"CHALLENGE TO FREEDOM" [6]

Americans always have been proud of the term "free labor." We consider this one of our strongest assets. We tell ourselves it is the one advantage we possess which, in the long run, is sure to win out over the slave labor of communism. But some of us here in America interpret this phrase differently from others.

The phrase "free labor" can have only one true meaning— freedom for the individual workingman—freedom to work at any trade or calling for which he has the capability; freedom to join a union if he wants to; freedom not to join if he doesn't want to; freedom to get out of a union if he is opposed to its actions; freedom to do his best in his work and to progress to the full extent of his capacities; freedom to support the political party or candidate of his choice.

Many union leaders interpret this phrase differently. They believe it means freedom for the union, not for the people who belong to it. They believe it means freedom for *them* to exercise monopolistic powers—to do as they please, uncontrolled and uncontrollable. And to anyone who challenges their freedom to ride roughshod over the rights of others, including their own members, they cry "union buster" and "labor baiter.". . .

The laws and the decisions of the courts, while not designed to create union monopolies, have provided no definite prohibition against them and in the aggregate effect have encouraged them. And through this loophole the union bosses have driven with all their energy and determination to create monopolies, in fact, in most of our basic industries.

The cornerstone on which union monopoly power rests is compulsion—compulsion on the employer to sign a union-shop agreement; and compulsion on the workingman to join the union if he wants to make a living. And the basic reason for seeking monopoly power is to be able to use compulsion whenever it seems, to the holder of that power, necessary or even just desirable; as an example to others, perhaps.

[6] From "Union Monopoly Power: Challenge to Freedom," address by Cola G. Parker, chairman of the executive committee of the National Association of Manufacturers. The Association. 2 East 48th Street. New York 17. 1957. p 1-10. Reprinted by permission.

Union monopoly power is sustained financially by the compulsory collection of union dues—the checkoff. Members must agree in writing to have dues deducted from their pay, or they will find themselves out of jobs. Whenever the union overlords decide they need extra money for some purpose, the members are assessed. If they don't pay the assessment, there are various direct and indirect ways to compel payment. . . .

There are some in America who think this situation is perfectly all right—some people in high places, in intellectual circles, in government, and even in business. The argument goes that the so-called union shop—which in actual practice becomes the closed shop—should be a matter of contract between an employer and a union; and that any prohibition of such agreements by law is a curtailment of the right of contract.

What happens to the human dignity and rights of the individual craftsman under these circumstances? His representation in the important matter of earning a living is all staked out for him. . . . He must accept it no matter how arrogant or venal it might be; and he must maintain himself in the good graces of the union if he wants to earn a living at his trade. If he opposes the union boss, he won't be certified for a job. . . .

Many who support such forced surrender of individual rights justify it on the ground that it is "practical," that it will encourage labor-management "peace," a matter in which the public has an important stake. . . .

With a captive membership, every head of a union is a law unto himself. He can be thrown off the AFL-CIO Executive Council. His union can be ejected from the big labor combine, as happened in the case of the International Longshoremen's Association in New York several years ago. But the officers of this union were not deposed. The AFL-CIO could not deprive them of access to the financial resources of the union, or of their steady incomes from members' dues, or of their authority over the union's welfare fund. For all of its prestige and authority, neither the AFL nor the AFL-CIO has been able to defeat the ILA in three representation elections. It now has given up trying.

So, in short, these union officials against whom charges of corruption were made could not be shorn of their power—their autocratic power which rests on compulsory unionism.

It is this power which enables union leaders to perpetuate themselves in office; to appoint their own henchmen to the key positions and to the elective bodies which elect the union officials; to remove from office any local official who dares to question the actions of the top man and put a "stooge" in his place as trustee. It is this power which enables them to operate unions as their own private principalities. It is this power which must be curbed.

It is being used to compel many people to join unions against their will and once they are in, to push them around with no regard whatsoever for their rights or their feelings as human beings. The instances which can be cited run into the thousands and tens of thousands. Union members have been beaten, thrown out of the hall, shot, intimidated, fined, suspended, and reduced to whining supplicants because they dared to question the actions of their union leaders. Many unions, from the locals up to the front office of the international, are run by tightly knit cliques, who, like storm troopers, take orders and carry them out ruthlessly. In these, the rank-and-file member has nothing—absolutely nothing to say. He is shouted down if he tries to protest within the union; he is brought up on charges "unbecoming a union member" if he protests outside the union; he cannot resign in protest without forfeiting his job and his livelihood.

The props which gave rise to and now sustain union monopoly power are three in number; the immunities under the law which are available to unions but denied to all other persons and organizations; compulsory union membership in thirty of our forty-eight states, including nearly all of the highly industrialized ones; and the ability of union leaders to tap the funds of union members to support political candidates who will do their bidding and to defeat candidates they fear will curtail their power. . . .

Any supposedly voluntary association which needs compulsory membership in order to survive and thrive is obviously not operating in the best interests of those whose money supports it.

According to union leadership, the union shop is necessary for union security. But they are the only voluntary organizations making claim to the necessity for compulsion; and Samuel Gompers always fought against it. In my opinion the only kind of security they are entitled to is the security which comes voluntarily from a loyal and enthusiastic membership for whose true interest they are always working. The fact that union leaders say they need compulsion for security is positive evidence they are not doing this kind of job in many cases today.

LABOR'S OFFICIAL VIEWS [7]

The record of secret-ballot elections conducted by the National Labor Relations Board indicates that union security is supported by the overwhelming majority of workers in establishments organized by unions. Under the original terms of the Taft-Hartley Act, adopted in 1947, a union could not negotiate union-security provisions in collective bargaining agreements unless a majority of the workers in the unit voted for union security. Up to October 22, 1951, when the Act was amended, the government agency conducted 46,119 polls, with union security winning 97 per cent of them. "Not until government conducted the elections required by the Taft-Hartley Act," states Harvard University economist Sumner Slichter, "did the country realize how strongly workers favor the union shop."

In the union-security elections held during those four years, there were 6,542,564 workers eligible to vote; 5,547,478 valid ballots were cast in the polls, and 91 per cent of them were cast in support of union security. So overwhelming was the support for union security that Congress amended the law to eliminate the necessity for the government to conduct these costly and burdensome elections.

Union security is supported by people from all walks of life. Unions naturally desire it. So do many employers and community leaders. . . .

[7] From "The 'Right-to-Work' Controversy." *Labor's Economic Review* (AFL-CIO). 1:1-8. January 1956. Reprinted by permission.

Paul M. Geary, executive vice president of the National Electrical Contractors' Association, an important employer group, states:

> You cannot expect to have a responsible union unless you give it the means of achieving responsibility. That is, the union must have a measure of security. The closed-shop type of contract which has been in effect between labor and management in an industry assures the union of security and gives it an opportunity to concentrate on helping to improve production—the only road to greater benefits of labor, management and the public alike. . . .

Peter Drucker, the nationally prominent management consultant, states that

> union security is also in the social interest. Without it, no union can be expected to accept the responsibility for labor relations and for contract observance which our society must demand of a successful union movement.

Nevertheless, the age-old antilabor drive for the open shop continues. The campaign to ban all forms of union security has been building up steam since the end of World War II.

The Taft-Hartley Act declares the closed shop to be illegal. This Act also permits the states to bar employers and unions from enforcing all other types of union-security provisions, as well. . . .

The open shop "right-to-work" propagandists always refer to liberty, justice, and free choice which union-security provisions supposedly take away from workers. But underlying their misleading declarations of high principle is the attempt to undermine and destroy trade unionism.

Harry A. Millis and Royal E. Montgomery—one a former chairman of the National Labor Relations Board and the other a university professor—state in their book, *Organized Labor* . . . :

> The typical spokesman for employers opposing the union-closed shop usually reckons with his audience and asserts that the closed shop is un-American, that it keeps the nonunion man out of work or compels him to join the union in order to secure employment. This, he says, deprives the worker of an inalienable right. Of course, this is largely twaddle. Under ordinary circumstances, most employers evidently have not cared about anyone's right to work or about coercion applied to the man they

have not wished to employ. They perhaps have wished to have unlimited right of discharge, and the chances are that, while denouncing union compulsion, they, individually, or in association, have attempted to compel nonunionism or company unionism.

The demand for union security is entwined with the need for strong unions. It is connected with the way people earn their livelihood in industrialized America.

Four out of every five breadwinners depend on employers for their jobs. They cannot determine their own working conditions or set their own work-schedules. . . .

Except for the protection of law and union contracts, most Americans—wage and salary earners—are now subject not only to the forces of the market place, but also to the policies and decisions of business executives and managers.

The individual worker on his own is at a distinct disadvantage in trying to influence the employer's decision regarding his wages, hours and working conditions. Consider the ridiculously unbalanced bargaining relationship between the individual worker and General Motors, US Steel, the Bell Telephone System or the Prudential Insurance Company! Without the strength of the union to assist him, the individual worker is compelled to accept the wages and working conditions that are established by the employer.

Unions attempt to bring about a balance in this employer-employee relationship. Through collective organization and action, the union attempts to give the individual worker the bargaining power he lacks on his own. This function of the trade union was recognized in the Wagner Act. And it was carried over in Section 1 of the Taft-Hartley Act:

Experience has proved that protection by laws of the right of employees to organize and bargain collectively safeguards commerce from injury, impairment, or interruption, and promotes the flow of commerce by removing certain recognized sources of industrial strife and unrest, by encouraging practices fundamental to the friendly adjustment of industrial disputes arising out of differences as to wages, hours, or other working conditions, and by restoring equality of bargaining power between employers and employees.

By joining together with other employees in his industry, trade or craft, the individual worker gains a voice in determining his wages and the conditions under which he works. The union gives meaning to the individual worker's rights in an industrial economy. It brings democracy into the employer-employee relationship. And the union, thereby, strengthens the democratic fabric of society as a whole. . . .

The trade union has certain specific rights and obligations under the law, after selection by a majority of employees in the bargaining unit—such as a craft, department, plant or company. . . .

Section 9 of the Taft-Hartley Act states:

> Representatives designated or selected for the purposes of collective bargaining by the majority of the employees in a unit appropriate for such purposes, shall be the exclusive representatives of all the employees in such unit for the purposes of collective bargaining in respect to rates of pay, wages, hours of employment, or other conditions of employment.

The doctrine of exclusive bargaining rights for the majority union did not spring up suddenly. It developed on the basis of American experience and does not exist in most foreign countries.

Chaotic conditions could easily result if the majority union did not have exclusive bargaining rights—if several unions represented the same group of workers. If an employer had to bargain with minority unions as well as with the majority union, it could lead to multiple contracts for the same group of workers, conflicting seniority provisions and wage rates, conflicts over representation on bargaining committees, and a lack of a sense of responsibility on the part of the unions.

The grant of exclusive bargaining rights to the majority union does away with the possibility of such chaos. It promotes orderly procedures for collective bargaining. It aids the development of responsible unions that aim to keep the support of the majority of workers. And it tends to free the union from continuing battles with numerous competing unions for collective bargaining rights with the employer during the life of the agreement.

Behind the doctrine of exclusive bargaining rights is the simple democratic idea of majority rule. A Republican President

—elected by a majority vote—is the President of the United States, not of Republicans alone. The union selected as the bargaining agent by a majority of employees becomes the sole bargaining agent for all employees in the unit.

The doctrine of exclusive bargaining rights has been upheld in the courts. It is the law of the land. United States Supreme Court Justice Jackson stated in . . . [a] decision in 1944:

> The very purpose of providing by statute for the collective agreement is to supersede the terms of separate agreements of employees with terms which reflect the strength and bargaining power and serve the welfare of the group. . . . The workman is free, if he values his own bargaining position more than that of the group, to vote against representation; but the majority rules, and if it collectivizes the employment bargain, individual advantages or favors will generally in practice go in as a contribution to the collective result.

Unions, therefore, are unlike other types of membership organizations. Their legal rights and obligations are different from those of fraternal organizations, professional associations, or churches. . . .

Veterans may join veterans' organizations if they wish. But no veterans' organization is required by law to represent all veterans. No farm organization is required to perform direct services for farmers who are not members. Yet a union selected as the bargaining agent by a majority of workers in a unit is legally required to represent all the unit's workers.

If the union fails to fairly represent all the employees in the unit, its basic bargaining rights may be challenged. In such a case, the courts may rule that the union has violated the law.

For example, in a case where a union . . . wanted to charge a fee for processing the grievances of nonmembers, the National Labor Relations Board said it could not, that "an organization which is granted exclusive bargaining rights under Section 9 has, in return, assumed the basic responsibility to act as a 'genuine representative of all the employees in the bargaining unit.' ". . .

The burden of exclusive representation is a difficult one. The union must place its strength and finances at the service of all the workers in the unit. . . .

Union representation leads to benefits for all the workers in the unit—for both union members and "free riders," the non-paying, nonmembers who enjoy the benefits of trade unionism. Mrs. Elinore Herrick, the personnel director of the New York *Herald Tribune,* one of the leading Republican newspapers in the nation, stated in 1954:

> Hardly a day passes on my own job that I am not aware of how much trade unionism has done to raise the wage level, to protect workers from unjust discharge, and to improve working conditions. . . . Because so much of the present well-being of the workers is due to the efforts of the unions through collective bargaining, I do not really like "free riders" myself. . . .

Is it unreasonable, then, to ask all workers in the bargaining unit to contribute financially to the support of the union that represents them? Can society properly sanction the nonmember who refuses to assume his share of the burden of citizenship in an industrial community?

Tax payments are one form of obligation that we owe to the organized group to which we belong. They are a price tag for the privilege of living in organized society. Union membership and dues payments are an obligation that workers owe to the unions that serve them.

The nonpaying nonmember who enjoys the benefits of trade unionism is like a member of the community who refuses to pay taxes for the upkeep of the schools, parks, police and fire departments, and refuses to vote in the community's elections. Such a citizen is not merely antisocial; he is a threat to the continued health and safety of the community. If he is permitted to get away with it, others may well follow his example. The finances of the community could be weakened, community service could suffer, and possibly community peace and order could be supplanted by chaotic battles between taxpayers and nontaxpayers.

It is similar in industrial relations. The nonmember refuses to accept his social obligations. His fellow workers view him as a self-appointed person of special privilege. He is a threat to the union and to the continued peace and order of collective-bargaining procedures. Dues-paying union members view nonmembers as an insult. The presence of nonmembers creates a situation that is loaded with danger to peaceful relations and uninterrupted production. . . .

To accept the idea that all workers in the bargaining unit have an obligation to support the exclusive bargaining agent is to accept union security in one form or another. The basis of union security is that simple idea: The union that is the bargaining agent for all the workers in the unit should be supported by all the unit's workers.

Payment of union dues, however, is not enough to qualify wage and salary earners as good citizens of an industrial community. Active participation in the affairs of the union is called for.

Unions are not mere dues-collecting agencies, any more than the state governments are mere tax-collecting agencies. Trade unions require dues payments to maintain the organizations' functions. But they want and need not just dues-payers, but active members who attend meetings, discuss and vote on issues, and vote in union elections. It is through active participation in the affairs of the union by all the workers in the unit that democratic unionism can be assured. . . .

While insisting on the duty of all workers in a union-organized establishment to join the union, most unions have shown sincere willingness to arrive at some compromise arrangement with those few individuals whose religious scruples may forbid membership in a nonchurch organization or the taking of an oath to such an association. . . .

About four fifths of all collective-bargaining agreements in the United States provide for some type of union security. Approximately two thirds of all labor-management agreements provide for the union shop. The vast majority of employers, who have direct relations with trade unions in their own establishments, have negotiated and agreed to union-security provisions in their own contracts with unions. . . .

Union security provides a sound basis for a collective-bargaining relationship that benefits both workers and employers. For that reason, unions seek the right to sit down with employers and try to work out union-security provisions, without **Federal or state government interference.**

SECRETARY OF LABOR'S VIEWS [8]

I believe that when employers and unions representing a majority of their employees agree on a union shop they should have the right to have one.

Seventeen states, twelve of them in the South, have enacted laws which deprive unions and employers from making such agreements. They call these "right-to-work" laws, but that it is not what they really are. Actually, these are laws which make it impossible for an employer to bargain collectively with a majority of his employees about the security of their union. Before I go any further on this subject, I want to make this point crystal clear so that there will be no misunderstanding about it. I am not saying that the states do not have the right and the privilege to legislate in this area. They certainly do.

However, I hope that the states which have these laws will give them further consideration. If they do, I believe, they will find that these laws do more harm than good. In the first place, they do not create any jobs at all. In the second place, they result in undesirable and unnecessary limitations upon the freedom of working men and women and their employers to bargain collectively and agree upon conditions of work. Thirdly, they restrict union security and thereby undermine the basic strength of labor organizations.

I oppose such laws categorically.

Good relations between labor and management must be developed at the plant level. Certainly an organized effort by employers to promote state laws undermining union security is not conducive to harmonious working relations between employers and their employees.

NEW YORK GOVERNOR'S VIEWS [9]

Two conflicting attitudes are evident in the Federal and state laws which deal with labor relations. One policy seeks

[8] From an address by Secretary of Labor James P. Mitchell before the sixteenth convention of the Congress of Industrial Organizations, Los Angeles, California, December 7, 1954. Mimeographed. Office of the Secretary of Labor. Washington 25, D.C. 1954.

[9] From " 'Right-to-Work' Laws Are a Fraud," by Averell Harriman, Governor of New York. *American Federationist.* 64:8-9. February 1957. Reprinted bv permission.

to build up collective bargaining as expressed in the New York State Labor Relations Act. The other policy tends to cut down such activity, as in the misnamed "right-to-work" laws.

The encouragement of collective bargaining as a civilized way to avoid strife between employers and employees is the keystone of our national labor policy. This attitude was written into the 1935 National Labor Relations Act, the original Wagner Act, and has even survived in the Taft-Hartley amendments of 1947, which produced the Labor Management Relations Act. . . .

It is still the national policy to promote industrial peace

by encouraging the practice and procedure of collective bargaining and by protecting the exercise by workers of full freedom of association, self-organization and designation of representatives of their own choosing, for the purpose of negotiating the terms and conditions of their employment or other mutual aid or protection.

The pivotal idea of the original Wagner Act was that collective bargaining would mitigate the economic evils and industrial strife which spring from lack of equality in bargaining power.

The law, therefore, set out to protect the right of employees to organize so that they could engage in effective collective bargaining.

The constructive policy of fostering collective bargaining was accepted by several states shortly after 1935 in the form of baby or little Wagner Acts. In 1937, when the United States Supreme Court upheld the national Wagner Act's constitutionality, Massachusetts, Michigan, Minnesota, New York, Pennsylvania, Utah and Wisconsin created their own images of the 1935 law. Essentially, the state labor relations laws endorsed the main theme of the Wagner Act.

A contrary policy, however, developed in some state laws by 1947, the year of the Taft-Hartley Act. By that time there were seven state statutes which had either changed favorable policies to unfavorable ones, or initiated policies which tended to strait-jacket collective bargaining.

Wisconsin and Pennsylvania, for example, revised their laws in 1939, as did Minnesota and Michigan, which also proceeded to impose controls on union activity. Kansas and Colorado joined the parade in 1943, and Utah, changing her direction in 1947, followed this new line by adding restraints on union behavior.

The heaviest damage to the cause of union security, however, came in the form of a delayed time bomb planted carefully in the Taft-Hartley Act as Section 14-b, reading as follows:

> Nothing in this act shall be construed as authorizing the execution or application of agreements requiring membership in a labor organization as a condition of employment in any state or territory in which such execution or application is prohibited by state or territorial law. . . .

Basically, this section granted states the power to impose harsher restrictions on union security than even the Taft-Hartley Act provided.

By thus abdicating the Federal Government's right to set fair labor standards in interstate commerce, the Taft-Hartley Act invited competition among the states in low labor standards. . . .

The policy of allowing states to pass laws on union security is one that is loaded against organized labor. A state law, for example, which is sympathetic to labor organization and which allows a closed shop contract would be superseded by the Taft-Hartley Act, which bans closed shop contracts in interstate commerce. Similarly, a state law which is unsympathetic to labor organizations and bars a union shop clause in a labor agreement supersedes the Taft-Hartley Act. Thus, a more restrictive policy against unions is fostered by Section 14-b, especially in states with strong antilabor lobbies.

What has been the impact of Section 14-b on labor organization? Within a short time after the passage of the Taft-Hartley Act, eighteen states—more than a third—had enacted laws depriving organized labor of rights which had been won after more than a hundred years of heart-breaking experience and courageous struggle.

Inaccurately called "right-to-work" laws, these statutes have in effect reimposed judicial regulation of union practices on state levels after such regulation had practically vanished from the national scene. One outstanding characteristic of these state acts is the prohibition against union security agreements—even where such provisions are arrived at with the consent of both sides.

An examination of the so-called "right-to-work" laws reveals nothing in any of these statutes which actually guarantees either the getting or holding of a job. Nor do they impose any check on the power of an employer to dismiss any employee, with or without reason.

There are two effective ways to place reasonable limits on the employer's exercise of the power to fire. One way is by statute. The other is by contract. A state law, for example, may prohibit discriminatory dismissal for either racial, religious or union reasons. A union contract may require the employer to go to arbitration in order to prove just cause for the dismissal.

Clearly, in the absence of state laws the union contract is virtually the sole method for controlling capricious discharges. If there is no state law and no collective agreement, then employees obviously work under an employer's ax which could fall at any instant and cut them from their jobs.

The most effective method of overcoming the bargaining inequality of the individual and protecting him in his job is the collective union agreement. Protection of the right to work exists today in nine out of ten collective agreements which contain arbitration clauses. Under these contracts an employee may challenge a dismissal in an impartial arbitration proceeding to test fairness of the employer's action.

Such protection can be assured to workers by unions which have strong membership support. Weak organization of employees, on the other hand, frequently means futile collective bargaining.

This is the crucial issue in the current campaign against the state right-to-work laws. The garden variety of right-to-work law hampers collective bargaining by making individual bargaining paramount. The inevitable effect is to diminish the chances for collective agreements and to arrest the development of fair standards for dismissal. In these circumstances so-called right-to-work laws sustain the power to fire rather than the right to work.

Such laws are thus a hoax. They undermine the very right which they purport to preserve. In the name of protecting the individual employee, he is being deprived of the recognized benefits of union representation. A state that supports this kind of legislation is following a policy of discouraging union organization.

Such a policy ignores the lessons of our national experience as to the industrial facts of life. We have learned that collective bargaining leads to easing industrial strife, to a more equitable sharing of the output of industry and to expanding democracy within industry.

By hindering these goals, right-to-work laws become a road-block to a state's progress.

Their continuance constitutes a menace to free collective bargaining.

SURVEY OF EFFECT OF LAWS [10]

A nation-wide survey of employers and union leaders, re-cently made by *Fortune,* indicated that right-to-work laws have had singularly little effect on labor relations. If the laws are intended to "bust unions" (as the AFL-CIO contends), they have had scant success; in every one of the right-to-work states, membership appears to be as high as it was before the law was passed—in a number of cases membership is higher. In at least one state, ironically enough, a right-to-work law that attracted new industry seems actually to have caused an increase in union membership. Scarcely any union members, whom the laws were intended to "liberate," have in fact resigned. It is, of course, harder to compel new employees to join a union in the right-to-work states than it is elsewhere; yet few of the state laws include any effective enforcement apparatus, so that a worker who feels he is being pressured into joining a union can only resort to expensive injunction proceedings. The worker who doesn't want to join a union seldom gets much comfort from his employer—quite the contrary. Said one union official:

We've found that in the right-to-work states, some of the big nation-wide corporations which have the union shop elsewhere will often cooperate with us in getting new employees to join. The plant super-visor just has a little chat with the man when he's hired, and says a few kind words about the union—and the worker usually gets the point.

[10] From "The Right-to-Work Laws." *Fortune.* 56:235-6+. September 1957. Courtesy *Fortune.* Copyright 1957 by Time Inc.

The role of "big business" in the right-to-work controversy
is indeed, ambiguous. The NAM [National Association of
Manufacturers] and the United States Chamber of Commerce
fervently support the laws, but very few of the largest corporations have taken a position one way or the other. (General
Electric, which says that it prefers right-to-work states as loca-
tions for new plants, is a conspicuous exception.) In steel,
auto, rubber and railroads, big companies have long since given
up the union-shop fight. Lobbying in state legislatures for
right-to-work laws is chiefly being pushed by small business
and farm organizations—particularly the American Farm Bureau
Federation. . . .

Of the twelve states that turned down right-to-work laws
in the latest legislative session, only Idaho saw a really close
battle over the issue. The bills were beaten easily in all the
heavily unionized industrial states where they were offered—
California, Connecticut, Illinois and Ohio. And in such strong
union centers as New York, New Jersey and Michigan, right-
to-work legislation has never even been a serious issue. It may
well be that the right-to-work tide is now at its crest in the
states. What the AFL-CIO fears most is not a steady growth of
state laws, but a right-to-work amendment to Taft-Hartley.
However, this prospect is not imminent; the Administration has
consistently opposed Federal right-to-work legislation.

VI. INSIDE UNIONS

EDITOR'S INTRODUCTION

The Senate Select Committee on Improper Activities in the Labor or Management Field headed by Senator John L. McClellan (Democrat, Arkansas) has focused attention on a minority group of dishonest labor leaders and on undemocratic unions. A widely publicized case history is that of the Teamsters, expelled by the AFL-CIO at its 1957 convention.

Dave Beck, convicted of embezzling union funds, was retired with the title "president emeritus," carrying full salary. His successor, James R. Hoffa, was elected while under indictment on a wire-tapping charge and on call to testify before the McClellan committee. A temporary injunction granted to thirteen rank-and-file Teamster members, who contested the legality of his election, delayed his assuming the presidency. His wire-tapping trial ended with a jury disagreement, and a compromise settlement out of court cleared the way for him to take over the union leadership.

Another crucial labor problem investigated by the McClellan committee was the strike of the United Automobile Workers against the Kohler Company which is still unsettled after four years. (See "A Strike Pattern" and "Ruling in Kohler Case" in Section III.—Ed.) The hearings on the Kohler strike lasted for five weeks, during which there was a parade of witnesses from both sides, closing with the testimony of Herbert V. Kohler, the company's president, and Walter Reuther, the union president. Evidence was presented showing that there had been violence on both sides. Mr. Kohler denied any wrongdoing on the part of the company. Mr. Reuther acknowledged that various acts of violence on the part of the strikers were wrong but blamed the company's "feudal" policies for creating the situation in which these acts occurred. At the time this book went to press it did not appear that the hearings had done anything to hasten the end of the strike.

Background for discussion of union abuses is provided by a history of labor corruption and violence, excerpted from a business weekly. A labor writer for a popular monthly contributes a candid portrait of Hoffa.

Suggestions for legislation to deal with irregularities in administration of union pension and welfare funds are quoted from the final report of a subcommittee headed by Senator Paul H. Douglas (Democrat, Illinois).

A resolution adopted at the 1957 AFL-CIO convention sets forth that organization's view on the McClellan investigations. A labor reporter comments on the likely effects of expulsion of the AFL-CIO's biggest member union.

The last two articles, on the subject of democracy in unions and union ethics, are remarks by the same reporter and by a union lawyer made at a meeting of the National Industrial Conference Board.

AMERICAN LABOR'S CRISIS [1]

There are many today who believe that the unions have run amuck. And it now seems sure that belief is going to produce action—efforts at legislation to restrain the unions.

In Congress, the McClellan committee has produced a long series of revelations of corrupt practices in the Teamsters and other unions. These are inevitably leading toward new, untried efforts to discipline unions and union officials to make them conform to socially set standards of conduct.

Farther in the background, but evident, is a widespread belief that labor costs are a prime cause of inflation. Organized labor, having achieved immunity to inflation's effects through escalator contracts or periodic bargaining rounds, begins to look like an overprivileged class. And that points toward the reprisals usually meted out to any overprivileged class, toward new limitations designed to curb labor's bargaining power. . . .

The problem of dealing with these evils runs deep. For the violence and corruption that have shocked the general public

[1] From "Labor Violence and Corruption" *Business Week.* p76-90. August 31, 1957. Reprinted by permission.

arise directly out of basic union rights—out of the rights to organize, to bargain, to strike. These are rights that the unions have won through long struggles and have finally seen confirmed in law. These are the rights that are often credited as a bulwark of the nation's social stability. They have also been the source of abuses.

It is the right to organize that Johnny Dio used in preying upon ignorant Puerto Rican workers in New York.

It is the right to bargain that many unscrupulous men with union authority have used to write sweetheart contracts with employers for a personal consideration.

It is the right to form voluntary associations that sanctions the establishment of phony "paper locals," used to rig union elections and assure gangster control.

It is the right to strike that, when used and resisted by employers or unwilling workers, means violence, property destruction, and bloodshed.

But it is a very mixed picture. These same rights were used by the coal miners' union to bring a decent standard of living to the coal towns—and also to bring John L. Lewis to near-dictatorial power. The auto workers' union used them to introduce industrial democracy into the world of the assembly line. They also brought Walter Reuther to his seat of power.

These rights enabled the Teamsters to protect truck drivers against the shape-up, the crooked employer who cheated them of their wages, and the twelve-hour driving day. They also gave Frank Brewster, Dave Beck, and Jimmy Hoffa the opportunity for arrogant power and plunder.

Up to a point, all labor has benefited from the unions' strength. It has raised the national wage level, produced fair handling of employee grievances, pushed industry toward private systems of social benefits such as pensions, vacations, and insurance.

Now we seem to be reaching another point, a point where it looks as if the bad outweighs the good. The unions have made the powers they need for the business of protecting labor's welfare appear to be a menace. This the community will not tolerate.

Doubtless, something will be done. But doing it is not going to be easy. For the unions perform a function, and if their powers are taken away entirely, some other institution will have to perform it. It's not clear now what that institution could be. Management itself can hardly be asked to be disinterested in conflicts affecting its interests. And government can hardly take the responsibility without such intervention into economic life as to threaten a free society.

But there will be an effort to create by statute a new kind of unionism. It won't be along for a while. Congress is waiting for the McClellan committee's recommendations, which are not yet being formulated. When they are, it looks as though all the panaceas for labor trouble that have been argued for years will finally get legislative consideration. Among them are proposals such as these:

Antitrust regulation of some sort applying to unions. This would be designed to penalize or curb strikes "in restraint of trade." The problem here is that every strike restrains the trade of the struck employer. Legislation or the courts would have to distinguish between a strike with a legitimate economic purpose and one intended to restrain trade per se. This would require an analysis of the motive—something so complicated to determine that many lawyers are cool toward the proposal. The unions maintain that such legislation could outlaw all strikes.

Antitrust coverage of unions might also be used to break up interstate organizations, the way the old Standard Oil Company was fragmented. Thus, for example, the United Mine Workers might be ordered to split into the UMW of Kentucky, the UMW of Pennsylvania, and so on.

A ban on organizational picketing. This would be intended to prevent a union from trying to put economic pressure on an employer before his workers are organized and represented by a certified union. Organizational picketing is a widely used tactic in recruiting and in jurisdictional disputes.

Full disclosure of union finances. This would not only affect the private financial affairs of such men as Beck and Hoffa. It would also tear the veil of secrecy from expenditures that some unions maintain are vital—but necessarily surreptitious.

For example, it is argued, some local police officers always "have their hand out," and to secure their neutrality in policing a picket line, a payoff is required.

A national right-to-work law. This would make it illegal to require union membership as a condition of employment. Unions oppose this on the ground that workers will—as human nature—take the benefits of unionism if they can without meeting the obligation or paying the dues of union membership. Without members' support, the union cannot live.

A ban on persons with criminal records in union office. Such a measure is now in effect on the Port of New York waterfront, under special bi-state legislation approved by New York and New Jersey. It has been of questionable value in reforming one of the nation's worst labor sinkholes. . . . On the other hand, it would affect hundreds of union officials who have brushed with the law in strikes and organizing campaigns for carrying on what labor calls "routine union responsibilities."

These and a number of other proposals will be receiving very serious consideration from Congress. In its present mood, the test of practicality may not always be applied. Punitive action is in the air. The unions are in for trouble. . . .

From the very beginning labor disputes have been attended by violence. A strike or a lockout is industrial warfare. It is designed to force an unwilling consent through economic coercion. In a strike, the objective of the employees involved is to close the workplace and keep it closed until the employer capitulates. For the employer, the object is to operate the workplace until the employees, in discouragement and defeat, accept the employer's terms. Accordingly, the key to success or failure of such industrial warfare is control of the entrance to the workplace. . . .

The United States has, by legal enactment significantly reduced the occasion for violence in labor disputes. It has done so by making one of the most important issues in union-employer relations soluble without a strike. This issue is union recognition.

The first thing a union must do is to secure recognition from the employer. Then it can deal in collective bargaining as the representative of its members in the company's employ. Once recognition is achieved, it must be retained. A fight for recognition can occur when the union first appears, and it can occur again and again whenever the union's representation right is challenged either by the employer or by a rival union.

In the days when gangsters swaggered through the garment industry, a union's recognition had to be rewon whenever the employer, with muscle to back him up, simply declared that he would no longer deal with the union. In other industries, it was fought over whenever the employer felt himself strong enough to challenge the union.

In 1935, however, there was written into the Wagner Act —and preserved in Taft-Hartley—a way to determine a union's claim for recognition peacefully. This is the election procedure under which a union claiming to represent a majority of the employees in an appropriate bargaining unit submits to a secret ballot conducted by the National Labor Relations Board. If a majority does, indeed, vote to be represented by the union, the union is legally certified by NLRB. It then becomes a statutory obligation for the employer to recognize it and bargain with it. If a majority votes against representation, the employer is protected in his right to refuse recognition of the union for at least a year.

To this extent, the law cut into the employer's freedom in running his business. But once this process came into general usage, violence in United States labor was substantially reduced. The classic example of the law's effectiveness is the CIO's fight to establish itself in the so-called Little Steel companies in 1937 and 1938.

In 1937, the steel union was refused recognition by a group of companies including Bethlehem, Republic, Inland, and Youngstown Sheet & Tube. It struck. The clashes over control of the entrance to the plants—control of which would make the strike a success or failure—were the bitterest and bloodiest in modern labor history. The companies won the battle to keep operating, and the union gave up what was a lost strike.

It was also an historic strike. It was the last of its sort America has seen. During its 1937 term, the United States Supreme Court upheld the constitutionality of the Wagner Act.

Up to that point, management and labor both had been skeptical of whether it would survive the court test, and it had been little used. By 1938, the steel union had regrouped its forces, and it used its legal right to petition for elections in Little Steel. It won the elections handily. Thus it achieved recognition only a year after its galling and costly defeat on the picket line— without a shot being fired, or as Philip Murray, the late president of the steel union and CIO, once characterized it, "without a cross word being spoken.". . .

A second effort to substitute the ballot box for violence proved unsuccessful. When first passed, the Taft-Hartley Act required that in a "national emergency" strike the employer's "final offer" of terms be voted on by the employees in secret ballot.

That proved completely meaningless and has since been repealed. In over a dozen elections held under the act, employees voted overwhelmingly to reject the "final offer." In each case, the union advised a "No" vote, promising that more would be forthcoming if the offer were rejected. And in each case it worked out that way.

During World War II, union-management differences were effectively settled with little recourse to strikes and violence, through processes tantamount to arbitration and fact-finding. Under the brilliantly led, tripartite (labor, management, and the public) National War Labor Board, America achieved a notable record of labor peace. . . .

But by the end of the war a great change had occurred in the anatomy of the strike and counterstrike. When a huge steel mill or giant auto plant was struck, the union and management cooperated in an orderly shutdown. The strikers went home; the employer shut his gates; a few token pickets apppeared, leaned lazily against the fence, exchanged jokes with the company guards. Settlement negotiations were carried on in a de luxe hotel suite, in meetings presided over by federal mediators, in Washington.

The NWLB, wartime habits, and a new unwillingness of employers to take action that would precipitate violence had effected a miracle. The "peaceful" strike became a commonplace.

But to say that labor relations in America had moved to a new and more civilized plane was to take in too much territory.

The old-fashioned strike did not become a thing of the past. Of very recent, lurid memory are the violence-filled strikes of Portsmouth, Ohio, telephone workers, of employees of the Louisville & Nashville Railroad, of employees of Southern Bell. In these cases, employers in public service industries refused to submit quietly to a cessation of their operations. They insisted on running their business, and violence of the traditional, deadly sort was the result.

Nor has the determination to keep operating in the face of a strike been confined to the public service industries. The Perfect Circle Corporation strike in Indiana and the Kohler strike in Wisconsin have been very bad medicine.

In their very nature, unions are unyielding when there is a threat that their strikes may be broken. Violence is predictable whenever an employer decides to exercise his right to operate in the teeth of a strike. The unions believe—and live by the belief—that unless the employer is effectively resisted in such a case, the union will perish.

Thus violence on the labor front is not a random thing. It will occur wherever the employer feels strong enough to resist the union, and the union has the strength to react.

Nor is corruption a random thing. It will be found flourishing in those areas of business where competition is of dreadful intensity—and the individual employer must operate on a margin so narrow that labor trouble will put him out of business. This is where the payoff—sought or tendered—is an evil fact of economic life. . . .

There is also a contagion to corruption. Starting in the small-scale, highly competitive stevedoring industry that rims the waterfront in New York, Boston, and Philadelphia, crooked practices in the longshore unions have fanned in both directions. They have involved some of the world's largest steamship companies at one end and important import and export firms at the other. And the Teamsters Union has carried the plague of corruption into widely scattered industries. . . .

American labor unions, as Professor John T. Dunlop of Harvard noted in a recent address to the American Bar Association,

are probably the only labor movement in the world—outside the Communist orbit—not dedicated to altering the basic features of the economic system of the society in which they operate . . . . The American community today would reject outright a labor movement which was radical toward our business institutions; the labor movement has increasingly adopted the forms of business.

It was not always thus. And the profound change that has occurred has a lot to do with American labor's problems today. . . .

Zealous and fanatical, the early labor leaders were dedicated men. They had a vision of a new and better world they would create by organizing labor's latent power. These men did not hesitate to call strikes and use violence, but it always had the "pure" purpose of building the union, stopping exploitation, or winning some improvement in the harsh standard of living suffered by their followers. These men took little or no pay from the organizations they built. To ask or take money from an employer was unthinkable.

It's no accident that the Becks and Hoffas and others of that ilk have become heirs to the empires built by men prepared to sacrifice themselves in labor's cause. These contemporary figures are able, audacious, resourceful, too. They have built the unions further and increased their power. But more importantly, they have understood the times and sensed what Professor Dunlop has said about the American community's rejection of radicalism. They pattern their unions on business enterprises, pride themselves on seeing industry's point of view and being responsible men.

Dave Beck was, after all, the darling of Seattle business and a vehement spokesman for the enterprise system. For the employer who dealt with Beck on his terms, life was singularly free of labor problems; violence never came close.

At the other end of the contemporary labor spectrum stands Walter Reuther. Just as Beck and the Teamsters Union have come, in the public mind, to symbolize get-rich-quick labor leadership and racketeering, so Reuther and the auto union symbolize political ambition, labor violence, and special interest unionism that exacerbates the wage-price spiral.

At first glance, Reuther seems to bear a remarkable resemblance to the early, vanished labor pioneers. But he came to the top through making deals with Communists and other unsavory elements within and outside the auto workers' union. He has used his position to build himself personally as the top leader of American labor both at home and abroad. Reuther commanded the forces that loosed the terrible violence in the recent Perfect Circle and Kohler strikes. And more of that violence lies just barely below the surface, to be unleashed should the auto industry ever challenge him.

The habits of both the Becks and the Reuthers arouse a public reaction and legislative attacks that may transform, if not destroy, our unions.

There is more to American unionism than organizations of the Beck and Reuther type. They stand at the polar extremes. The labor movement has not lost all of its integrity.

The great majority of its officials are decent, uncorrupted men. They do their job for a salary and take pride in their work. Their sense of honor is no more deficient than it is in any other occupational or professional group. And they are as shocked as the general public at the revelations of how men in positions like their own have wantonly abused their trust.

AFL-CIO President George Meany is now trying to speak and act for these men. Without power to enforce them, he has nevertheless had codes of ethical practice written, and he wants every union and union officer to accept and live by them. The movement for self-reform within the union is gathering strength.

But there is a real question as to how much can be done by voluntary means. And another, sharper question: Is labor's own cleanup too late to avert action from outside? And can it go far enough?

The AFL-CIO can conceivably throw out affiliates in which corruption nests—and so become a simon-pure federation. But the expelled unions will still operate, and little will really be changed.

John L. Lewis voluntarily took the mine workers' union out of the AFL, but the powers, functions, and jurisdiction of the union never changed.

The AFL expelled the International Longshoremen's Association for refusing to move against the racketeers who ran it. But the ILA still controls the East Coast waterfront.

The CIO kicked Harry Bridges' union out for being Communist-dominated, but Bridges' power is just as great as ever.

It may give honest labor leaders in the AFL-CIO great satisfaction to expel the Teamsters Union under Jimmy Hoffa, but it will not be a staggering blow to the union. Nor will it affect corruption in that union.

The AFL-CIO has no police powers. It can dissociate itself from unions that do not meet decent standards. But it cannot make them meet such standards.

When the nefarious exploits of the robber barons of the nineteenth century were exposed, all industry suffered in consequence. When the shady dealings of some Wall Street speculators came to light in the 1930's, the financial community was subjected to Federal Government supervision—despite the fact that the majority of industry and finance was honest and abhorred the evils being practiced. Now the turning wheel brings labor unions public scorn and contempt. More feared in the public mind now than big business, or even big government, is big—and rotten—unionism. The kind of reform job labor can do will simply not be good enough to satisfy the public. The signs seem to read that America is no longer "pro-union."

Thus, new laws to cover unions can be forecast. The public wants racketeers and plug-uglies driven out of labor organizations. It wants full disclosure of union finances, and an end to violence. Can that be done without making the unions incapable of performing their economic functions? The public—apprehensive about inflation as well as corruption—may not really care.

That is why labor in America is in crisis.

HOFFA'S PERSONAL POWER [2]

There have been kings who wielded less power than a labor leader whose name . . . [is] James R. Hoffa. The R stands for Riddle, and about this man swirl some of the most perplexing questions in labor today.

Hoffa is a vice president of the International Brotherhood of Teamsters. [He was elected president at the 1957 convention but was enjoined from assuming that office until an out-of-court settlement ended a suit brought by thirteen rank-and-file members. He was at that time under indictment on wire-tapping charges, on which a jury was unable to agree, and under investigation by the Senate committee inquiring into improper labor and management practices.—Ed.] His union, 1.4 million strong, is America's most powerful, for it is in the driver's seat of industries—trucking, warehousing, retailing—on which all others depend. Through this union, Hoffa can keep the food from the tables of millions of Americans; he can withhold the fuel that warms their homes and runs their cars; he can keep them from work by shutting off supplies from factories and stores. These things he can do simply by halting the truck wheels in twenty-three states [Hoffa's jurisdiction at the time this article was written.]. . .

He has put the union label on a cynical brand of labor activity in which leaders use unions as road to riches. He is in many businesses: he has owned pieces of a brewery, race track, oil-prospecting company, investment firm. His aides sport stables of race horses, drive Cadillacs. He suppresses members' rights, so rank-and-filers have charged in suits. He places his Teamster power at the disposal of mob-ridden unions. Congressional investigators summed it up this way in a report last year: Unions under Hoffa's jurisdiction are riddled with "corruption, extortion and gangsterism." A dozen of Hoffa's subordinates have gone to jail or paid fines for extortion, bribe-taking, and violence against their own members.

Over the heated objection of his lawyer, Hoffa consented to an interview with me in Chicago. For two days I had a close-up

[2] From "The Riddle in the Middle of America's Most Powerful Union," by Lester Velie, roving editor, *Reader's Digest*. *Reader's Digest*. 67:91-6. December 1955. Reprinted by permission.

view of him. Face to face, the forty-two-year-old labor leader is open and engaging. He fixes you with earnest eyes. Only five feet five inches tall, he has the look of a bright and forthright boy.

The boyish candor vanishes when a reporter starts asking questions. Then Hoffa, talking at trip-hammer speed, has an answer for everything but an explanation for nothing. The smallest figure in a room, he's usually the biggest man in it. At a grievance session I watched union men state their cases and employers defend themselves; then all heads would turn respectfully to Jimmy. "Here's my decision," he would say—and, in his own phrase, "That would be it, brother!". . .

Hoffa introduced me to a member of his entourage [Paul Dorfman], a freckle-faced, redheaded man in his fifties, who drove him from the airport and hung about the hotel corridors while he was in conference. . . .

In an article last year I had described Dorfman as a central figure in shady welfare-fund deals. But Dorfman put out his hand. "You shouldn't of written that about me," he said cheerfully.

Dorfman holds one key to the riddle of Hoffa: his links to the underworld. A one-time associate of the Chicago Capone mob, Dorfman took over an AFL waste-handlers' union in 1940 after its leader was murdered. Hoodlums "on the lam" from Detroit get eating money from him in Chicago. He uses his mysterious power to get union charters for convicted extortionists and narcotics violators from New York, so testimony before the New York State Labor Relations Board has shown. . . .

It is to the insurance agency owned by the Dorfman family that Hoffa has channeled Teamster welfare-fund insurance that yielded well over a million dollars in commissions in three years.

When congressional investigators first tried to question Dorfman's wife and son they were missing. So were the insurance agency's books. When some of the records were found or reconstructed, they revealed that the Dorfmans cashed large commission checks but didn't deposit them in their agency's bank account.

Investigators wanted to know where a missing $100,000 had gone. Dorfman's son refused to tell, on the ground that "it might incriminate" him. Hoffa testified that none of the missing money had gone to him. . . .

Do the Capones have their hooks in the Teamsters? Is Paul Dorfman the conduit through which a piece of the regional Teamster welfare-fund insurance, controlled by Hoffa, flows to the Chicago underworld?

The underworld's assault on the midwest Teamsters is matched by the gangsters' designs on the union in the East. In New York, the hoodlum-ridden International Longshoremen's Association fights for a rich prize: control of the city's trucking lifelines. Hoffa supports them. [AFL President George Meany in 1957 forced the Teamsters, before they were expelled from the AFL, to cancel a loan to the ILA—Ed.]. . .

Hoffa . . . is battling to bring into the Teamsters the ILA, the union that was booted out of the AFL in 1953 as gangster-infested. As Teamsters, the longshoremen would wield the balance of power in New York City's Joint Teamster Council and throw control of the city's fifty-two trucking locals to the mobs.

I went to Joplin, Missouri, to see what Hoffa's kind of unionism means to Teamster card-holders. Several dozen brawny men in shirtsleeves crowded into their lawyer's office to tell of their ordeal under Hoffa, who is their local's trustee. . . . One man had sent his wife. She told how her husband had been beaten senseless for seeking to have his local investigated. . . .

"Why don't you throw your officers out?" I asked the men.

"Throw them out?" one driver hooted. "We haven't had any legal election in fifteen years. Last election should have been held in 1953. The officers just didn't show up for the meeting. They had the keys, and we couldn't get into the hall. There was no election. They just stayed on in office."

"And just try to find out how the dues money is spent," another driver volunteered.

The frustrated union men hired a Joplin lawyer, Stanley Clay, who got a court order to let members see the union's records. The lawyer showed me photostated checks and vouchers. One union check, signed by the local's president, Floyd C. Webb, was for furniture for his home. Others were for a lawn mower, ice-cream freezers, clothes washers, a bicycle for Webb's grandson.

The court ousted the local's boodling president and asked the Teamsters International to name a trustee to clean up the mess in Joplin. Who became trustee? Hoffa. How did he propose to clean up the mess? He urged the members to reelect the boss who had stolen their money.

When the members named their own slate, the rebels were ruled off the ballot. Hoffa told them they had failed to pay their dues regularly by the first of each month as required by the union's constitution. Since employers deduct dues before the first but do not send them to the union hall until several days later, almost any member can be barred from a union ballot on this technicality.

When rank-and-filers threatened to take the matter to court, Hoffa called off the election. That was about a year ago. It still hasn't been held. And the ousted president continues to run the local as business representative, a job to which trustee Hoffa's assistant named him. . . .

This disregard of members' rights, coupled with Hoffa's dealings with mobsters, distresses many labor leaders who see in his brand of unionism a threat to all labor. To understand why, let's see how Hoffa climbed to power.

At seventeen, while working as a platform loader in a Detroit bakery, he organized fellow employees into a union. This so impressed labor men that he was soon entrusted with a Teamster charter. At nineteen Hoffa reached for the second rung in the union power ladder. he ran for the presidency of the Detroit Joint Teamster Council and leadership of the city's three driver locals.

Young Hoffa got only four of the twenty council delegates' votes. But he made himself president anyway. "I just walked in and took over," he later boasted. Inside the Teamsters there was a more plausible explanation: the chunky, fist-swinging kid had support behind him which even the hard-bitten Teamsters in the Joint Council had to respect.

Next, Hoffa persuaded drivers to team up in a state-wide organization. He argued that his members in Detroit could refuse to unload nonunion trucks from out of town and so bring employers to book. He formed the first state-wide Teamster Conference, stepped up from city Teamster boss to state boss.

Hoffa tried to become an industry boss as well. He joined with businessmen to parcel out territory and dictate prices. At twenty-seven he was indicted on Federal charges of plotting with waste-paper collecting companies to set up a union-enforced monopoly. The indictment also charged that the home of a waste-paper executive was bombed. Hoffa pleaded *nolo contendere* (no contest), thus throwing himself on the mercy of the court. He was fined $1,000.

Undaunted, he tried to organize and regulate Detroit's little grocery shops. He demanded that the owners join the Teamsters and pay Teamster dues. They knew that if they didn't their deliveries would be cut off. The Detroit *News* observed in May 1946: "The aim is to exact dollars from persons whose only conceivable interest in the Teamsters is that of purchasing freedom from persecution."

The state called this extortion. Hoffa pleaded guilty to a labor-law violation—a lesser charge. He was fined $500 and placed on two years' probation. His union was ordered to return $7600 collected from the grocers. . . .

Over the years it became known that it was risky to cross Hoffa. His probation report in 1949 showed seventeen arrests: six were for brawls. (All but one of the assault charges were dismissed.). . .

Men "on the lam" from one section of the country got Teamster union jobs in another, so that Hoffa's bailiwick became riddled with underworld figures. When water front hoodlum Barney Baker left New York, Hoffa gave him a job as strong-arm man in Pontiac. Today Baker directs Teamster organizing in St. Louis. In Detroit Hoffa turned over a Teamster local to the nephew of one of the city's most notorious underworld characters.

By 1952 Hoffa wielded such political power inside the Teamsters that he could swing the presidency to Dave Beck. In return, Beck helped elect Hoffa vice president and named him head of two of the four regional conferences. From this summit Hoffa rules like a czar, destroys union records, spends union money as he pleases on political campaigns.

Just as congressmen were beginning their investigation of Hoffa last year, he made his biggest power play. Suddenly the hearings ground to a halt. Representative Wint Smith (Republican) of Kansas said: "Pressure came from so high that I can't even discuss it."

The Teamsters had approached key figures in the trucking industry to urge Republican Party leaders to end the hearings.

Hoffa once told reporters, "There's one thing you can't pin on me—communism." But racketeering is just as subversive to labor. Unchecked, it can destroy the unions.

WELFARE-PENSION FUND INVESTIGATION [3]

The subcommittee, on the basis of its studies and investigations, makes the following findings and conclusions:

1. Private employee welfare and pension programs have grown to such proportions in this country and involve the use of such large tax-exempt funds as to place upon the Government a grave responsibility for their sound operation and to protect the equities of the beneficiaries and the public interest.

(a) Over 75 million persons, employees and dependents, or about one half of the population of the nation, are covered in some measure by employee welfare and pension programs. This tremendous development has come about principally in the past ten years.

(b) Over $6.8 billion yearly are being contributed to such programs. Employers contribute approximately $4.5 billion and employees $2.3 billion. Between $20 and $25 billion have been amassed as reserves to meet the future contingencies of these programs, particularly future pension payments.

(c) The Government permits employers to deduct from taxable income their cost and contributions to these programs. The income from investment of reserves is also exempt from taxes.

(d) Since Congress has stated and the courts have held that employer contributions toward welfare and pension

[3] From final report of the Committee on Labor and Welfare, United States Senate, submitted by its Subcommittee on Welfare and Pension Funds, Senator Paul H. Douglas, Illinois, chairman, pursuant to S. Res. 225, 83d Congress, and S. Res. 40, as extended by S. Res. 200 and S. Res. 232, 84th Congress. 84th Congress, 2d session. Superintendent of Documents. Washington 25, D.C. 1956. p6-10.

benefits are in the nature of compensation to employees, it must be concluded that whether the funds for such programs are contributed by the employers, the employees, or both, the employees have a right to know the financial details of such plans as well as to have their interest in such plans protected.

2. The lack of standards and the inadequacies of state and Federal laws have permitted employee welfare and pension programs to operate in such manner as to give rise to many abuses, problems, weaknesses and unsound practices which could jeopardize the operation of this system and give insufficient protection to the rights and equities of the employee-beneficiaries.

(a) While the great majority of welfare and pension programs are being responsibly and honestly administered, the rights and equities of the beneficaries in many instances are being dangerously ignored. In other cases, the funds of the programs are being dissipated and at times become the hunting ground of the unscrupulous.

(b) There is no adequate legislation at either the Federal or state level to fully safeguard these welfare and pension funds or the rights of the employee-beneficiaries.

(c) Despite belief to the contrary, qualification by the Internal Revenue Service as to tax exemption for welfare and pension programs provides no real control over the operation of the plans and only minimum assurance of their actuarial soundness.

(d) A great many of these plans are sorely lacking in adequate accounting procedures. Auditing requirements in too many cases are nonexistent. It is the exception when welfare and pension programs provide for an accounting to or an audit on behalf of the beneficiaries.

(e) A serious problem at times in employer administered plans, particularly where the plan has been established or bargained for on a level-of-benefits basis, is that the employer takes the position that he is delivering or guaranteeing an end-product, i.e., the benefits under the program, and that the costs of these benefits are private and are therefore of no concern to the employees or others. If the employer's costs for these programs are a part of employees' compensation which he is permitted to deduct as such from taxable income, then he is not delivering a product from his own costs and his employees are entitled to information on the financial operation of the plan.

(f) Many of the worst abuses found in welfare plan operations involve certain insurance practices. These abuses include high commissions, excessive administrative fees, high insurance company retentions, unequal treatment of the policy-holders, activities of unscrupulous brokers and agents, including embezzlement of premiums, sometimes in collusion with union officials or management—mostly the result of inadequate control and nondisclosure to the interested parties.

(1) The insurance industry is entirely regulated by state law. Many state insurance authorities have been lax in cleaning up insurance practices. This is attributable in part to the fact that the problem of group insurance is interstate or national in scope and, perhaps in part, to the fact that some state regulatory agencies are too susceptible to the viewpoint of the industry;

(2) The insurance industry, which has long prided itself on maintaining high standards on a voluntary basis, has not yet set up a code of ethics to deter wrongdoing among its membership;

(3 Group insurance is a highly complex business, and serious impairment of beneficiaries' equities has at times occurred as a result of lack of knowledge of insurance practices on the part of those responsible for purchasing insurance;

(4) In many cases, group insurance is bought and not sold. The commissions paid by some insurance companies on group policies, frequently as high as 20 per cent of the first-year premium, give many a broker or agent an unearned commission. Such commission practices affect plans administered solely by a union or by an employer as well as those jointly administered;

(5) The beneficiaries of self-insured welfare and pension plans do not presently have adequate protection under state laws.

(g) Some of the worst instances of individual abuses were encountered in the jointly managed multiemployer and union administered welfare programs. The unilateral nature of employer and union administered plans affords less opportunity for disclosure of information as to abuses or maladministration.

(h) Lack of know-how, mismanagement, waste, extravagance, bad bookkeeping and indifference have caused a serious dissipation of the funds involved in these programs generally.

(i) Actuarial and investment soundness are the keystones to successful operation of pension programs. In many cases too little attention has been devoted to these factors.

(1) Corporate or bank trustees, while discharging their stewardships capably, cannot be held responsible for the financial and actuarial soundness of the plan. Often under the trust instrument they cannot control investments which impair the equities of the beneficiaries;

(2) A number of pension plans invest in substantial percentages of the securities and properties of the employing companies.

3. The subcommittee believes that the enactment of a Federal disclosure act would bring a great measure of order to the operation of private employee welfare and pension plans. The primary objective, the subcommittee has concluded, is one of assuring the immediate and long-range stability of private welfare and pension programs without impairing their voluntary or free-bargaining character. As shocking as the cases of dishonesty and fund looting have been and as great as the need is to bring this matter under control, the most important objective is to assure the maximum usefulness and safety of these programs in order that they may better meet the contingencies against which they were established.

(a) It cannot be assumed that the states will act uniformly or speedily, or that the problem can be met on a piecemeal basis. It is unrealistic to suppose that the forty-eight states will devise uniform procedures within a reasonable time to protect the interests and equities of the beneficiaries of these programs, lacking stimulus from the Federal level;

nor can it be anticipated that any one state is so influential in this area as to bring this about.

(b) Disclosure of the workings of welfare and pension plans to a Federal agency is a mild remedy, reserving to the states a wide area for additional control. There is much room, in fact, at the state level for enactment of legislation designed to more clearly fix the responsibilities of trustees and to strengthen insurance regulations.

Recommendations

1. The subcommittee recommends the enactment of a Federal registration, reporting, and disclosure act which would be effective for a three-year period and which should require—

(a) Registration of all types of employee welfare and pension benefit plans which cover twenty-five or more employees. This registration should include identifying information respecting the plan as prescribed by the act and the regulations of the agency. It should be made within ninety days of the effective date of the act or the establishment of plans subsequent thereto.

(b) An annual report, as prescribed by the act and regulations thereunder, by all employee welfare and pension benefit plans which (1) include one hundred or more employees and which (2) include less than one hundred employees but are in fact operated or administered on some common basis with other plans (namely, common officers or administrators, union bargaining representatives, or employers, etc.) and, together, include in the aggregate one hundred or more employees. The report should be attested to by the principal officer or officers thereof, and contain a detailed financial statement of the operations based upon an audit in accordance with accepted standards of auditing addressed to the beneficiaries and certified by an independent public accountant.

(1) The administrative agency should have discretion to require reporting and disclosure by a particular plan or plans covering between twenty-five and one hundred employees on an annual basis, or less frequently, and to require compliance with other provisions of the act when,

in the opinion of the agency, such action is deemed necessary to accomplish the objectives of the act.

(c) Disclosure of information contained in the annual report should be made to the beneficiaries of the plan and other interested parties by making copies available for examination at the principal offices of the plan and in the public documents room of the administrative agency and by providing the beneficiaries with information from the report in prescribed summary form by personal delivery or mail.

(1) The Federal agency should have authority to cause further distribution of annual reports to any other Federal or state agency.

(d) Criminal penalties should be imposed for willful violation or failure to comply with the act or willful false statements or misrepresentations or omission of a material fact, or for unlawful or willful conversion of the funds of any plan or program.

(e) Constitutional authority for such an act should rest upon jurisdiction over taxation, interstate commerce, and the general welfare.

(f) The agency should be given the usual administrative powers to carry out the functions of the act, compel the production of records, conduct investigations, and take any other measures necessary to administration and enforcement.

(g) Based upon its studies, and after two years' experience with the act, the administrative agency should make a comprehensive report to the Congress and include therein its recommendations as to the continuance, simplification, or modification of legislation. This report should be furnished in time to permit Congress to take appropriate action before the expiration of the act.

2. The subcommittee has no strong view as to which Federal agency should administer such an act. It is possible to use any one of several existing agencies—namely, the Department of Labor, the Department of Health, Education, and Welfare, the Internal Revenue Service, or the Securities and Exchange Commission—since the functions of each of these agencies have some relation to this field. It might also be feasible to create a new independent agency for this purpose. For the present, the sub-

committee is inclined to favor the Securities and Exchange Commission because of its organization setup and its established success in the administration of disclosure-type statutes.

3. The subcommittee also recommends the establishment of an advisory council to assist the Federal agency in the administration of such a disclosure act. The council should consist of thirteen members, including three employee representatives, two representatives of management, a representative of the insurance industry, a representative of the banking industry, and three representatives of the general public, with the Secretaries of Labor and of Health, Education and Welfare and the Commissioner of Internal Revenue ex-officio members.

LABOR'S VIEW ON "RACKETS" INQUIRY [4]

In a statement adopted at its meeting in Miami, Florida in January 1957, the executive council set forth the basic principles underlying the position of the American Federation of Labor and Congress of Industrial Organizations toward investigations of improper activities in the labor and management fields. . . . [See "Constitution of the Merged AFL-CIO," in Section II, above.—Ed.]

The forthright action of the AFL-CIO convention in expelling several of its largest affiliates [including the Bakers, Laundry Workers, and Teamsters] because of corruption is a clear and tangible demonstration of our determination to effectively implement this pledge. . . .

The executive council pledged:

It is the firm policy of the AFL-CIO to cooperate fully with all proper legislative committees, law enforcement agencies and other public bodies seeking fairly and objectively to keep the labor movement or any other segment of our society free from any and all corrupt influences.

After the issuance of this statement by the executive council, the United States Senate established the Senate Select Committee [McClellan committee] to Investigate Improper Activities in the

[4] From "Text of Labor's Views on Senate Rackets Inquiry," statement and resolutions presented by the AFL-CIO executive council to the second AFL-CIO biennial convention, Atlantic City, New Jersey, December 12, 1957. New York Times. p24. December 13, 1957. Reprinted by permission.

Labor and Management Field. This committee has held a number of hearings which have served to bring to light certain criminal and corrupt influences that have fastened themselves upon a segment of the labor movement and some sections of management in America. The existence of these criminal and corrupt influences in unions has brought damage to our movement. Where the committee has conducted its investigations with objectivity, the committee has served a useful purpose and has performed a necessary task.

In saying this, we do not of course, thereby endorse either the procedures of the committee or the apparent antilabor bias of some of its members. In order to perform its function properly, the committee must exercise a high degree of objectivity and fairness. The committee we regret, has not met this standard.

We view with concern the practice which the committee has indulged in of trying individuals in the press and by television; we deplore the practice of repeating questions for publicity purposes to which it is known that no answer will be made; we do not condone the issuance of announcements to the press, in advance of hearings, of the conclusions to be drawn from testimony not yet heard; we do not approve the publication of evidence obtained in violation of Federal law.

We believe that it is possible for a legislative committee to conduct an effective investigation without hunting for headlines. A striking demonstration of this was afforded by the methods and procedures followed by the subcommittee of the Senate Labor Committee to Investigate Welfare and Pension Funds, headed by Senator Paul H. Douglas, during the Eighty-fourth Congress. The operations of this committee were carried on in an atmosphere of objectivity and fairness. The acts the Douglas subcommittee brought to light have been the basis of actions taken by the AFL-CIO in four of its eight recent ethical practices cases. Its legislative proposals . . . have had and continue to have the full and wholehearted support of the AFL-CIO. [See preceding article, "Welfare-Pension Fund Investigation.—Ed.]

In addition to the defects in its procedures, the Senate Select Committee has permitted public faith and confidence in its fairness to be undermined by allowing several members to use the committee as a public platform to serve their own antilabor and political purposes. . . .

The committee has also tended to become a forum for committee members to expound and develop pet antilabor legislative proposals having little or nothing to do with the legitimate purposes or interests of the committee. For example, the chairman of the committee, Senator McClellan of Arkansas, has suggested a national right-to-work law. Other members have suggested consideration of proposals to subject unions to the antitrust laws or to impose further restrictions on political activities of labor unions.

Certain of these proposals raise questions of broad national policy having implications which relate to basic democratic rights of citizenship and free speech and which are therefore not properly withi.. the jurisdiction of this committee. These proposals are unrelated to the problem of labor or management corruption but are designed to weaken responsible unions and thereby render them less capable of keeping their own house in order.

Also, a disproportionately small amount of the committee's time and interest has been devoted to the study of improper practices in management. Serious instances of improper and corrupt influences in management by which management has sought to frustrate union organizations or to obtain "sweetheart contracts" [by bribing corrupt union officials] denying justice to the employees, have already been revealed. Other manifold instances of management corruption and improper practices have not even been explored. . . .

[Such] activities should be a matter of prime concern to the committee, therefore be it

RESOLVED: That the AFL-CIO reaffirms its adherence to the principles set forth in the executive council's resolution of Jannary 1957, and pledges to redouble its efforts to do everything possible to eliminate all forces of crime, racketeering and corruption within the trade union movement. We must, however, call attention to the public and to Congress that corruption within the American labor movement is but a small part of the over-all problem of corruption in the whole of our society.

While acknowledging the wrongdoings of a small minority in the leadership of a few unions, we believe that objectivity requires the recognition that in a society overemphasizing material wealth, more corruption will be found in business and in industry, and that as a free people we must be concerned with this problem as well as corruption in the labor movement.

The trade union movement is devoted to human services and must of necessity be motivated by higher ideals and moral standards. We are therefore determined to meet the challenge of corruption within the labor movement in order to keep the labor movement dedicated to the ideals of human service.

We pledge our full cooperation with all proper investigations of criminal and corrupt influences in labor or management which are pursued with objectivity and fairness. We express deep concern that the Senate Select Committee may allow itself to be used for political retaliation, and as a forum for the display of antiunion propaganda.

We deplore any effort by members of the committee to use its investigations as a basis for legislative proposals designed to weaken all unions, rather than eliminate corruption. We alert the committee against the lack of fairness and objectivity in its procedures.

EFFECT OF TEAMSTERS' OUSTER [5]

The merged labor movement is getting ready to oust the scandal-scarred International Brotherhood of Teamsters. [This was done by a 5-to-1 vote of delegates to the AFL-CIO Convention at Atlantic City, New Jersey, in December 1957.—Ed.] . . .

No union has a more pervasive role in the national economy.

The refusal of a handful of teamsters to make deliveries can shut down huge factories, cut off vital fuel supplies, deprive cities of bread or beer and force mass idleness among industrial or construction workers.

Whether the teamsters go through picket lines is often the make-or-break element in strikes or in attempts to unionize plants that have operated without union agreements. Dozens of now

[5] From "Ouster of Teamsters Now Appears Likely," by A. H. Raskin, labor reporter. New York Times. p2E. September 8, 1957. Reprinted by permission.

powerful organizations owe their present strength to aid they got from the teamsters in crucial labor-management battles.

Indeed, the number of unions indebted to the teamsters in the old American Federation of Labor was so great that Dave Beck's predecessor as president, the late Daniel J. Tobin, used to boast that a majority of the members of the federation's executive council owed their jobs—and their votes—to him.

In size and security the truck union is even more imposing today than it was before Tobin surrendered the steering wheel five years ago. It includes in its sprawling membership nearly 10 per cent of the total enrollment of the united labor movement. It contributes $1 million a year in dues to the federation and its auxiliary bodies. And it has been conducting successful raids on the membership of other unions even while it was inside the combined group. . . .

If George Meany, president of the AFL-CIO, gave any hint of wavering in his determination to make the truck union clean up or get out, many of his associates in the executive council would be ready to settle for a less draconian alternative to purity. . . .

The teamsters have demonstrated that, for all their independent power, they have no wish to face the moral obloquy of being forced into isolation. Their leaders have blustered that the federation needs them more than they need the federation. But they have lost no opportunity to try to persuade Mr. Meany and his colleagues that, whatever their derelictions in the past, they really mean to run an honest union from now on.

They have promised to overhaul their union constitution to make it more democratic and to adopt the federation's ethical practices mandates, except its call for the removal of union officials who invoke the Fifth Amendment to avoid answering questions in official inquiries into cases of labor racketeering.

The teamster high command also has let the word go out that it is about to jettison the six phony locals set up in . . . [New York] by such hoodlums as Johnny Dio and Tony (Ducks) Corallo. And the heir apparent to the teamster presidency, James R. Hoffa, has given assurance that he will stop being a businessman and that he will no longer place his lush welfare accounts through the insurance agent whose past record evoked criticism from Senate racket investigators.

No one in AFL-CIO headquarters doubts that the teamsters will make a good many more clean-up moves. . . . But almost the only way they could satisfy Mr. Meany that a real purge was on would be to eliminate four of their top leaders all under Senatorial and court fire—Beck, Hoffa, Frank W. Brewster of Seattle and Sidney L. Brennan of Minneapolis. [Hoffa was elected president at the Teamsters' annual convention at Miami in December 1957, but was delayed in assuming that office by an injunction which was obtained by a group of dissident rank-and-file union members. Hoffa took office in January 1958 when the injunction proceeding was ended by a compromise settlement calling for a court-appointed board of three monitors to supervise Teamsters' affairs for one year. In December Beck was convicted in Seattle of stealing $1900 belonging to the Western Conference of Teamsters. He faces a prison term of fifteen years on this conviction but the sentence has been deferred pending a new trial. Beck, named president emeritus of the Teamsters at full salary, also faces trial for Federal income tax evasion.—Ed.] . . .

That [ouster] does not mean the teamsters will automatically drop dead. On the contrary, they are much surer of retaining their membership and bargaining strength than the International Longshoremen's Association was when it was expelled from the AFL four years ago.

In the first place, the teamsters are unlikely to have to contend against a rival union or a significant bolt of locals out of their ranks. The revelations of corruption touch so many of the power centers in the truck union that the federation nurtures little expectation of a major split within its ranks.

In contrast to the bankrupt ILA, the teamsters can count on an international treasury of nearly $40 million, with at least as much more in the treasuries of its locals and joint councils. In some areas the teamsters will be so strong that they might take the offensive in conducting membership raids against other unions. In general, however, local working arrangements are so cordial and well-established that they would probably not be much changed, despite the compulsory exclusion of teamsters units from state and city central bodies.

Whether an independent teamster movement became the focus of a new labor federation would depend in large measure on how much sympathy John L. Lewis displayed for an alliance with the outcast truck union. The seventy-seven-year-old president of the United Mine Workers has walked alone for ten years and his age has not dimmed his enjoyment of a brawling place in the spotlight. The ILA would be happy to flock to the new banner. So would unions dropped from the old Congress of Industrial Organizations for Communist domination. Then appeals would be made to unhappy craft unionists still inside the merged union.

A PLEA FOR MORE DEMOCRACY IN UNIONS [6]

I hope I won't be considered an advocate of class warfare if I suggest that in too many instances we carry our deification of stability in industrial relations to a point that stifles the free choice of workers and eventually provokes such discontent that we wind up with chaos as the fruit of our prized stability. . . .

The splendid series of monographs issued some years ago by the National Planning Association on the causes of industrial peace . . . [had as] one of its cardinal themes . . . that a strong, secure union is one of the requisites for a productive, harmonious relationship. This is a virtuous notion, one that has given rise to many, many constructive associations of great benefit to workers, to owners and to the community. But on occasion the application of this maxim becomes the vehicle for keeping workers chained to a union that has lost or is . . . losing their confidence.

When that happens, the catalog of evil perpetrated in the name of stability can become terrifying. We have recently had a sample of that in our own [New York City] subway system. The practitioners were men of intelligence and good will, schooled in the best tenets of liberal-labor philosophy and actuated by a sincere belief that the way to efficient, strike-free operation of the city's underground lifeline lay in the extension to the dominant union of Transit Workers of the maximum sense of security.

[6] From address by A. H. Raskin, labor reporter, New York *Times,* at 382d meeting of the National Industrial Conference Board, Hotel Commodore, New York, January 17, 1958. The Board, 470 Park Avenue, New York 22. Reprinted by permission from unpublished transcript of proceedings.

Yet in the application of this wholesome philosophy, these well-intentioned administrators found themselves descending from one noisome device to a worse, and still a worse one, in an attempt to stifle employee uprising against the union to which they had accorded exclusive representation on the strength of a showing four years ago that it had the backing of an overwhelming majority of all subway employees. . . .

These actions, aimed at rebels against an established union, drew no protest from the official agencies of organized labor. On the contrary, the full force of these agencies was concentrated on shoring up the established union, even though a new election raised substantial doubt that a majority of the workers still wanted it as their spokesman.

It is not my purpose to argue the rights or wrongs of the entire episode from the standpoint of the pubic interest, or even the material welfare of the subway workers. What concerns me is whether we are not getting away from the concept that George Meany stresses so often and so well: namely, that the unions are workers' organizations. They belong to the workers, not the workers to them.

The merger of the AFL-CIO itself was in one rather fundamental sense founded on a negation of that principle. The essence of the no-raiding pact—the key instrument in bringing about unity two years ago, and a very necessary instrument—was the idea that no union could take members from another without its consent, no matter how eager the members themselves might be to secede. In so far as this meant there would be no interunion piracy, it was of course wholesome. But to the extent that it meant there was no way out for workers dissatisfied with the kind of representation they were getting, it was a full turn from the old Wagner Act principle that workers were entitled to be represented by organizations of their own selection.

George Meany, whose adherence to the free-choice principle is both genuine and profound, has made it clear that he is no worshiper of per capita income or monumental membership totals. He took the lead in forcing out of the Federation the biggest of all its affiliates, the Teamsters, along with the Bakers and Laundry Workers, on charges of racket control. He has made it equally emphatic that the ban on raiding does not prevent AFL-CIO unions from affording sanctuary to workers seeking to escape sell-out contracts by exploiters still operating under Federation charters.

But this, as we have seen, is only part of the answer. Some excellent agreements cover a rank and file in open rebellion against their officials. Indeed, the more signs there are that a favored union is in trouble, the better contract the employer may feel obliged to give. This is a case of membership weakness becoming an instrument of bargaining strength, but it is hardly a matter of democracy.

I think the greatest need of our unions today is an imaginative crusade to reorganize the organized. With million-member unions, highly centralized leadership, union shop requirements, the dues checkoff and long-term wage contracts, the remoteness of the worker from any sense of ownership of his organization is bound to be substantial. This is true even where the union administration tries energetically to build up a sense of meaningful participation, a belief by the member that what he thinks and what he wants are important.

I am not unaware of the difficulty of getting the rank and file to exercise the privileges of industrial democracy, nor am I insensitive to the fear of many union leaders and many industrialists that too active interest by the membership may bring forward demagogues and factionalists to upset the orderly processes of industrial democracy. I think these dangers, however, are far less than those involved in a worsening of the trend toward bureaucratic collusion with all its antipublic and antiworker overtones.

Unless unions can do a better job of demonstrating that they possess the enthusiastic support of their members, it may become necessary to require by law that they undergo a periodic test of their right to retain exclusive bargaining rights through new certification elections under government auspices.

Too many unions are doing their organizing these days solely by organizing employers. If a reemphasis on democracy means some temporary and limted upsurge in labor's strife, it is a price that we can afford, however regretfully, to pay as an alternative to drifting into the cynical and ingrown relations that characterize many top-level relations today. . . .

Without any strikes, we are blacking out almost half of our potential steel production now through the voluntary closing down of furnaces and the lack of demand at current prices; and many other basic industries are running at 15, 25 and even 35 per cent below their capacity. . . . If we can lose this flow of finished goods and raw materials with scarcely an outcry as part of an economic readjustment, a transitory rise in strikes won't cripple us, painful as it will prove to those immediately involved.

In the end, a democratic understanding and support by workers for their unions and for the decisions their unions make is a much better foundation for responsibility and stability than an entrenched position built on unwholesome relations at the upper levels of union and management. The creation of a sound internal democracy is a task no less urgent than the uprooting of corruption, the combating of inflation, or the restoration of full employment.

IN DEFENSE OF UNION ETHICS [7]

The problem of democracy in a union is no different from the problem of democracy in our society at large, and the problem of determining majority versus minority rules is a problem in unions no different from in our democracy at large. We could not function in any aspect in our political economy if we so pushed minority rights that the rights of the majority were subverted.

If you had a labor relations situation such as Mr. Raskin portrayed, where every minority group in a unit that we once determined is a sound one would be permitted to divest itself, secede, go out, I would venture the prediction that we could have no type of labor relations that would be worthy of the name. . . .

This year is also, in addition to being a collective bargaining year [with several long-term major-industry contracts expiring], a legislative year. As you see in the papers, there are all sorts

[7] From an address by Arthur J. Goldberg, special counsel, AFL-CIO, at the 382d meeting of the National Industrial Conference Board, Hotel Commodore, New York, January 17, 1957. The Board, 470 Park Avenue, New York 22. Reprinted by permission from unpublished transcript of proceedings.

of proposals in the legislative area relating to labor. This is, of course, not entirely due to, but very largely an outgrowth of, the McClellan hearings. . . .

I have no reservations in saying that to the extent that they have exposed corruption, racketeering, underworld connections within the labor movement, they have done a very valuable service, indeed. At the same time I have no hesitancy in saying that I do not think it is any of the business of the Committee, for the reasons that have now openly prompted it to do so, to investigate the United Auto Workers and the Kohler situation. [See "A Strike Pattern," in Section III, above.—Ed.] . . .

No member of that Committee, including the Republican members who proposed the resolution to investigate the Kohler strike, charges that the UAW is a corrupt union or that Walter Reuther is a corrupt trade unionist.

What they are saying is that "we ought to look into that"— that is, a strike situation—and that "it's about time we got around to Walter Reuther." They have overlooked the fact that the Kohler strike has been investigated by the Labor Board. There is a trial examiner's report . . . and the whole thing is a matter of public record.

Now, having said that, however, I want to make these observations: Corruption in the labor movement has been a difficult problem for the labor movement. Notwithstanding that the corruption that has been revealed has been corruption of the few, proving the integrity of the many who direct the labor movement, I personally am very proud of the vigorous reaction of the labor movement to this matter. I am proud of the leadership George Meany has given in this situation, and I think the record of the labor movement in this area is second to none.

When we get into the legislative area, I notice something very peculiar. While some proposals have been advanced dealing with the problem of corruption, the major proposals that have been advanced have nothing to do with the problem of corruption. These are the proposals that have now been thrown into the hopper relating to secondary boycotts, relating to organizational picketing, relating to "right-to-work" laws, and relating to antitrust laws. . . .

I want to suggest just one [legislative proposal] because it relates in a sense to this problem of union democracy. The essential problem in the field of boycotts and organizational picketing is—and I want to put it to you as business men and from the standpoint of labor interested in its own welfare and in the welfare of employers with whom it has collective bargaining relations: If you have the great bulk of an industry organized, the economic conditions in the unorganized plants very often will prejudice the organized employers and, as a result, the organized workers.

The question involved in this type of legislation, both in boycotts and in organizational picketing, is: Does the union have enough of an economic interest in these other unorganized areas so as to use its economic power to attempt to eliminate from its standpoint the unfair competition of those unorganized plants? . . .

I suppose that on dozens of occasions in collective bargaining I have had employers come to me and say: "Look, we cannot continue to do this if you fellows do not go out and organize the plants. It is too rough on us to continue to do this."

And they are right. Now I haven't got the time to explain . . . why you can't just go in and pass out cards because these plants may have so-called independent unions. There are all kinds of complications, . . . helped by some of the Taft-Hartley provisions, which make that type of organization difficult, if not impossible.

A last word about the "right-to-work" and the antitrust laws. . . . "Right-to-work" laws have nothing to do with corruption. . . The question of policy there is: Should you permit labor and management to negotiate union security clauses, or should you by law prevent it? That is the whole question involved there. . . .

The same is true about the antitrust laws. There is no possible connection [with corruption]. . . .

[In response to a question from his audience about what labor has done, before being prodded by the Senate investigation, to combat corruption in its unions, Mr. Goldberg made the comments which follow.—Ed.]

Long before there was a McClellan committee, in the old CIO before the merger, we established a Committee on Ethical Practices. . . .

Also long before the McClellan disclosures, the AFL moved in the ILA situation and took action in that area. [The AFL expelled the International Longshoremen's Association in 1955—Ed.]

When the merger came about, again before the McClellan Committee, . . . after a very fine and dispassionate study by a congressional committee headed by Senator Douglas in the welfare fund field [see "Welfare-Pension Fund Investigation," in this section, above.—Ed.], the labor movement decided that one of the bases of the merger would be machinery to police this particular area. There have been a variety of actions taken in this field. . . .

George Meany was very frank about it when he said he never in a million years dreamed about some of the problems that exist in this area. I think the labor movement has been shocked by what has happened. I do not think we have come to the end of the road, I am sorry to say, in that there will be other shocks in the situation.

But I want to say to you that we have had the Ten Commandments for a long time, and we still have quite a few sinners among us. I suspect we will have them in the labor movement as we have them in other walks of society. The important thing in this area, I think, the thing that gives me a great deal of comfort and satisfaction, is that there is recognition by constitution, by by-law and by action that . . . [corruption] has no place in the labor movement.

BIBLIOGRAPHY

An asterisk (*) preceding a reference indicates that the article or a part of it has been reprinted in this book.

Books, Pamphlets, and Documents

AFL-CIO. Codes of ethical practices. (Publication no50) 31p. AFL-CIO. 815 16th St. Washington 6, D.C. '57.

*AFL-CIO. Constitution. (Publication no 1) 55p. AFL-CIO. Division of Publications. 815 16th St. Washington 6, D.C. '55.

AFL-CIO. COPE's position on political expenditures; excerpts from statement by J. L. McDevitt and Jack Kroll, co-directors of AFL-CIO Committee on Political Education, before Special Committee to Investigate Campaign Expenditures, December 17, 1956. 11p. AFL-CIO Committee on Political Education. 815 16th St. Washington 6, D.C. '57.

AFL-CIO. Industrial unions and Taft-Hartley. 27p. AFL-CIO. Industrial Union Department. 815 16th St. Washington 6, D.C. n.d.

AFL-CIO. Labor looks at automation. (Publication no21) 24p. AFL-CIO. Department of Education. 815 16th St. Washington 6, D.C. '56.

AFL-CIO. "Labor monopoly" myth. 11p. AFL-CIO. Department of Research. 815 16th St. Washington 6, D.C. '56.

*AFL-CIO. 25 questions about wages, prices, profits. (Publication no58) 17p. AFL-CIO. 815 16th St. Washington 6, D.C. '57.

AFL-CIO. Unions must be secure. G. M. Leader. 2p. AFL-CIO. Department of Education. 815 16th St. Washington 6, D.C. '57.

AFL-CIO. What is COPE? 4p. AFL-CIO. Committee on Political Education. 815 16th St. Washington 6, D.C. '56.

American Civil Liberties Union. Democracy in labor unions; a report and statement of policy. 16p. The union. 7 Fifth Ave. New York 10. '52.

Barbash, Jack. Labor movement in the United States. (Public Affairs Pamphlet no262) 28p. Public Affairs Committee. 22 E. 38th St. New York 16. '58.

Barbash, Jack. Practice of unionism. 465p. Harper & Bros. New York. '56.

*Barbash, Jack. Taft-Hartley act in action. 51p. League for Industrial Democracy. 112 E. 19th St. New York 3. '56.

Chamber of Commerce of the United States. Constitutional freedom of association; address by Donald R. Richberg at annual meeting of Chamber, Washington, D.C., April 30, May 1-2, 1956. 6p. mimeo. The Chamber. 1615 H St. Washington 6, D.C. '56.

Dunlop, J. T. Public interest in internal affairs of labor unions; address before American Bar Association, Washington, D.C. July 12, 1957. 18p. mimeo. The Author. Littauer 226. Harvard University. Cambridge 38, Mass.

Evans, J. E. Guaranteed security. 4p. Foundation for Economic Education. Irvington-on-Hudson, N.Y. n.d.
  Reprinted from Wall Street Journal, Ap. 20, 21, 22, 1957.

Faulkner, H. W. and Starr, Mark. Labor in America. 330p. new rev. ed. Oxford Book Co. New York. '57.

Fitch, J. A. Social responsibilities of organized labor. 237p. Harper & Bros. New York. '57.

General Motors Corporation. Text of reply of General Motors president Harlow H. Curtice to Walter P. Reuther, president, UAW. 4p. The Corporation. 3044 W. Grand Blvd. Detroit 2. '57.

Gompers, Samuel. Seventy years of life and labor. rev. ed. 334p. E. P. Dutton & Co. New York. '57.

*Harrison, W. T. Forced union membership steals your freedom. 16p. National Right to Work Committee. 125-B Cafritz Building, Washington 5, D.C. n.d.

*Indiana University. Bureau of Public Discussion. How free should the individual be to earn and to own? (Package Library Briefs. v 13, no3) 27p. mimeo. The University. Bloomington. '56.

International Association of Machinists. "Right-to-work" laws; three moral studies. 53p. The Association. 9th St. and Mt. Vernon Place. Washington 1, D.C. '55.

Keller, E. A. Case for right-to-work laws. 128p. Heritage Foundation. 121 W. Wacker Drive. Chicago 1. '56.

Kerr, Clark. Unions and union leaders of their own choosing. 24p. Fund for the Republic. 60 E. 42d St. New York 17. '57.

League for Industrial Democracy. Forward march of American labor: a brief history of the American labor movement. (LID pamphlet series) 32p. The League. 112 E. 19th St. New York 3. '56.

Lipset, S. M. and others. Union democracy. 455p. Free Press. Chicago. '57.

Marx, Herbert L. Jr. American labor unions. (Reference Shelf. v21, no5) 240p. H. W. Wilson Co. New York. '50.

Millis, H. A. and Montgomery, R. E. Economics of labor. 3v. McGraw-Hill Book Co. New York. '38-'45.

Myers, James and Laidler, H. W. What do you know about labor? 301p. John Day Co. New York. '56.

*National Association of Manufacturers. Monograph discussing the major aspects of the intercollegiate debate issue, "Resolved: that the requirement of membership in a labor organization as a condition of employment should be illegal." The Association. 2 East 48th St. New York 17. '57.

*National Association of Manufacturers. Monopoly power as exercised by labor unions. 31p. The Association. 2 E. 48th St. New York 17. '57.

National Association of Manufacturers. Organized labor's program to organize the legislative halls. 15p. The Association. 2 E. 48th St. New York 17. '56.

*National Association of Manufacturers. Union monopoly power; challenge to freedom; address by Cola G. Parker. 10p. The Association. 2 E. 48th St. New York 17. '57.

National Association of Manufacturers. Union shop amendment; compulsory "freedom" to join a union. J. A. McClain Jr. 10p. The Association. 2 E. 48th St. New York 17. '56.

*National Association of Manufacturers. Wages . . . prices . . . profits . . . and inflation. 10p. The Association. 2 E. 48th St. New York 17. '57.

*National Association of Manufacturers. What management expects of organized labor; address by C. R. Sligh, Jr., at the Congress of American Industry, New York, December 1955. 19p. The Association. 2 E. 48th St. New York 17. n.d.

National Council of the Churches of Christ in the U.S.A. Department of the Church and Economic Life. Division of Christian Life and Work. Union membership as a condition of employment. 11p. The Council. 297 Fourth Ave. New York 10. '56.

*National Industrial Conference Board. Addresses by Arthur J. Goldberg and A. H. Raskin, January 17, 1958, at 382d meeting of the Board. The Board. 470 Park Ave. New York 22. '58.
  Texts from unpublished transcript of proceedings.

Pound, Roscoe. Legal immunities of labor unions. 58p. American Enterprise Association. 1012 14th St. Washington 5, D.C. '57.

Reuther, W. P. Impact of automation. 33p. International Union, United Automobile, Aircraft, and Agricultural Implement Workers of America. Public Relations Department. 8000 E. Jefferson Ave. Detroit 14. '55.

Richberg, D. R. Labor union monopoly. 175p. Henry Regnery Co. Chicago. '57.

Sufrin, S. C. and Sedgwick, R. C. Labor economics and problems at mid-century. 385p. Alfred A. Knopf. New York. '56.

Tagliacozzo, D. L. Trade-union government, its nature and its problems. 29p. University of Chicago. Industrial Relations Center. 975 E. 60th St. Chicago 37. '56.

Tyler, Poyntz. Social welfare in the United States. (Reference Shelf. v27, no3) 209p. H. W. Wilson Co. New York. '55.

United Automobile Workers. Historic new contracts. UAW. Department of Education. 8000 E. Jefferson Ave. Detroit 14. n.d.

*United States. Department of Labor. Address by James P. Mitchell, Secretary of Labor, before 16th convention, Congress of Industrial Organizations, Los Angeles, California, December 7, 1954. 11p. mimeo. The Department. Washington 25, D.C. '54.

United States. Department of Labor. American workers' fact book, 1956. 433p. Supt. of Docs. Washington 25, D.C. ['56]

*United States. Department of Labor. Directory of national and international unions in the United States, 1955. (Bulletin no 1185) 64p. Supt. of Docs. Washington 25, D.C. '55.

*United States. Department of Labor. Federal provisions affecting union security. 3p. mimeo. The Department. Washington 25, D.C. n.d.

*United States. Department of Labor. United States Department of Labor . . . and what it does. 20p. Supt. of Docs. Washington 25, D.C. '56.

*United States. Department of Labor. Bureau of Labor Standards. State "right-to-work" laws. 8p. The Department. Washington 25, D.C. '57.

*United States. Department of Labor. Bureau of Labor Statistics. Analysis of work stoppages, 1956. A. J. Herlihy and H. H. Moede. (BLS Bulletin 1218) 35p. The Bureau. Washington 25, D.C. '57.

United States. Department of Labor. Bureau of Labor Statistics. Brief history of the American labor movement. (BLS Bulletin 1000) (1957 edition) 85p. Supt. of Docs. Washington 25, D.C. '57.

*United States. Department of Labor. Bureau of Labor Statistics. Union-security provisions in agreements, 1954. Rose Theodore. 10p. The Bureau. Washington 25, D.C. '55.

*United States. Federal Mediation and Conciliation Service. Facts behind the headlines in labor-management disputes. 7p. Supt. of Docs. Washington 25, D.C. '57.

United States. House of Representatives. Committee on Education and Labor. Interim report of a special subcommittee on investigation of welfare and pension funds, pursuant to H.Res. 115. 23p. 84th Congress, 1st Session. Supt. of Docs. Washington 25, D.C. '54.

*United States. Senate. Committee on Labor and Public Welfare. Final report of the Committee on Labor and Public Welfare, submitted by its Subcommittee on Welfare and Pension Funds, pursuant to S.Res. 225, 83d Congress, and S.Res. 40, as extended by S.Res. 200 and S.Res. 232, 84th Congress. 84th Congress, 2d session. Supt. of Docs. Washington 25, D.C. '56.

United States. Senate. Select Committee on Improper Activities in the Labor or Management Field. Investigation of improper activities in the labor or management field; hearings, February 26-August 19, 1957. 4926p. 85th Congress, 1st session. Supt. of Docs. Washington 25, D.C. '57.

*University of Mississippi. Department of Conferences and Institutes. Proceedings of the Taft-Hartley forum, March 5-6, 1954. 115p. The Department. University, Miss. '54.

    Reprinted in this book: Provisions of the Taft-Hartley law. W. P. Murphy. p2-29.

Wilensky, H. L. Intellectuals in labor unions. 336p. Free Press. Chicago. '56.

*Witte, E. E. Development of labor legislation and its effect upon the welfare of the American workman; address at Conference on Government and Public Affairs, University of Illinois and Twin City Federation of Labor, Urbana, Illinois, October 31, 1954. (Lecture Series no 11) 24p. mimeo. Institute of Labor and Industrial Relations. 704 S. 6th St. Champaign, Ill. '54.

PERIODICALS

AFL-CIO American Federationist. 64:4-7+. Ja. '57. This is how we licked 198: the "right to work" forces tried to sell their poison in Washington state. W. T. Holloman.

*AFL-CIO American Federationist. 64:8-9. F. '57. "Right to work" laws are a fraud. Averell Harriman.
		Also separate. 2p. AFL-CIO. Department of Education. 815 16th St. Washington 6, D.C. '57.

AFL-CIO American Federationist. 64:3-7. Mr. '57. Crooks must go. H. C. Fleisher.

America. 98:104-7. O. 26, '57. Reflections on union leadership. C. W. Anrod.

America. 98:188-9. N. 16, '57. States' rights, states' duties.

America. 98:270-2+. N. 30, '57. Amending Taft-Hartley. B. L. Masse.

America. 98:370-1. D. 21, '57. Unions, corporations and politics. B. L. Masse.

*Annals of the American Academy of Political and Social Science. 274: 118-22. Mr. '51. Labor's political role. Jack Kroll.

*Annals of the American Academy of Political and Social Science. 274: 145-51. Mr. '51. Labor in industrial society. P. F. Drucker.

*Atlantic Monthly. 196:63-6. S. '55. Labor's new victory: threat or promise? S. H. Slichter.

Business Week. p159-60+. F. 9, '57. AFL-CIO is grouping around two rivals [Reuther, Hoffa].

Business Week. p50+. Ap. 6, '57. Labor's crisis: a perspective.

Business Week. p46-8. Jl. 6, '57. Union officials: who they are, how much they are paid, how they are elected.

*Business Week. p76-90. Ag. 31, '57. Labor violence and corruption.
		Also separate. 18p. Reprint Department. Business Week. 330 W. 42d St. New York 36. '57.

*Business Week. p 174. S. 7, '57. Third man grows in importance.

Business Week. p40. Ja. 4, '58. Probers take off on a new tack; Kohler strike.

Christian Century. 74:1500. D. 18, '57. Union labor acts responsibly.

Commentary. 25:68-74. Ja. '58. Union democracy and the public good. Paul Jacobs.

Commonweal. 67:404-7. Ja. 17, '58. Expulsion of the teamsters. J. C. Cort.

*Current History. 27:1-6. Jl. '54. Brief labor history. H. W. Laidler.

*Economic Intelligence (Chamber of Commerce of the United States). no 107:1-2. Je. '57. Labor union immunities.

Editorial Research Reports. 2, no 17:751-68. O. 31, '56. Union organizing. H. B. Shaffer.

*Fortune. 51:92-3+. Mr. '55. What labor means by "more." George Meany.

*Fortune. 56:235-6+. S. '57. Right-to-work laws.

Fortune. 56:241-2. N. '57. New labor law?

Fortune. 56:152-5+. D. '57. Where does labor go from here? Daniel Bell.

Free Labour World. p 15-20. S. '56. Women in the labour movement of the United States. P. M. Newman.

Free Labour World. p7-10+. N. '56. Automation and collective bargaining. V. G. Reuther.

IUD Digest. (AFL-CIO Industrial Union Department). p 19-26. Spring '56. Labor's two-way fight. Albert Whitehouse.

International Labour Review. 74:303-13. S. '56. Bibliography [selected list of publications on economic, social and labor conditions].

*Labor's Economic Review (AFL-CIO). 1:1-8. Ja. '56. "Right-to-work" controversy.

Monthly Labor Review. 78:519-23. My. '55. Implications of automation. W. S. Buckingham, Jr.

*Monthly Labor Review. 79:647-53. Je. '56. Labor status and collective bargaining. H. M. Douty.

    Also separate. Reprint no 2212. 7p. United States Department of Labor. Bureau of Labor Statistics. Washington 25, D.C. '56.

Monthly Labor Review. 79:1068-9. S. '56. Chronology of recent labor events [July 1956].

Monthly Labor Review. 79:1077-85. S. '56. Book reviews and notes [publications of labor interest].

*Monthly Labor Review. 80:151-4. F. '57. Observations on the changing nature of American unions; excerpts from a paper read at the annual meeting of the Industrial Relations Research Association, Cleveland, Ohio, December 28-29, 1956. G. W. Brooks.

*Monthly Labor Review. 80:157-60. F. '57. Management's attitudes toward employes and unions; excerpts from a paper read at the annual meeting of the Industrial Relations Research Association, Cleveland, Ohio, December 28-29, 1956. D. V. Brown and C. A. Myers.

Monthly Labor Review. 80:855-8. Jl. '57. Union affairs.

Monthly Labor Review. 80:1186-8. O. '57. Contemporary structural changes in organized labor. M. L. Kahn.

Nation. 185:387-9. N. 23, '57. Right-to-work laws. Frederic Meyers.

*Nation's Business. 45:36-7+. F. '57. Experts who guide labor's leaders.

*Nation's Business. 45:38-9+. Ag. '57. What the labor board is saying; interview with Boyd Leedom.

Nation's Business. 45:41+. D. '57. Senator McClelland weighs labor probe impact; interview.

Nation's Business. 46:38-9. Ja. '58. 1958: new labor problems, new ways to meet them.

Nation's Business. 46:68-9. Ja. '58. Labor law changes coming.

*New York Herald Tribune. p 14. O. 11, '57. Kohler Co. ruled unfair to labor.

New York Times. p80. Ag. 18, '57. Reuther's letters proposing that big three companies cut prices on 1958 cars.

*New York Times. 2E. S. 8, '57. Ouster of teamsters now appears likely. A. H. Raskin.

New York Times. p20. D. 6, '57. Text of Secretary Mitchell's address on legislation to AFL-CIO convention.
    Same: New York Herald Tribune. sec2, p8. D. 6, '57.

New York Times. p 1+. D. 11, '58. Meany skeptical on labor curbs.

New York Times. p24. D. 11, '57. Text of labor resolution on new laws.

*New York Times. p24. D. 13, '57. Text of labor's views on Senate rackets inquiry.

New York Times. p9. Ja. 18, '58. Peril is foreseen in curbing unions. Will Lissner.

New York Times. p 16. Ja. 27, '58. Economist scores union pay theory. J. A. Loftus.

*New York Times. p 16. Ja. 27, '58. Recession testing jobless aid plans. A. H. Raskin.

New York Times. p 1+. Mr. 25, '58. Senate unit asks reform of laws in labor, business. J. A. Loftus.

New York Times. p20. Mr. 25, '58. Excerpts from the Senate committee's labor report and two opposing views.

New York Times Magazine. p 17-18+. Mr. 31, '57. Moral issue that confronts labor. A. H. Raskin.

*New York Times Magazine. p 19+. O. 20, '57. Crusader for clean unionism. A. H. Raskin.

*New York World Telegram & Sun. p 1. O. 8-16, '57. Big labor—a giant on a tightrope [series of eight articles]. Charles Lucey.
    Reprinted in this book: Labor a lusty force in politics [article 4]. O. 11, '57.

Newsweek. 50:132. N. 25, '57. Is T-H a dead letter? Raymond Moley.

Newsweek. 50:20. D. 23, '57. 10,000 questions [conviction of Beck].

*Reader's Digest. 67:91-6. D. '55. Riddle in the middle of America's most powerful union. Lester Velie.

Reader's Digest. 70:37-42. Je. '57. Labor's two-front war against the rackets. Lester Velie.

Reader's Digest. 71:131-6. S. '57. How to steal a union. Lester Velie.

*Reader's Digest. 71:91-8. O. '57. Strike without end—the Kohler story. W. L. White.

Reader's Digest. 71:74-8. N. '57. How a labor leader went wrong. Lester Velie.

Reporter. 17:2. D. 26, '57. In the house of labor.

Rotarian. 91:10-11+. O. '57. Should there be right-to-work laws? J. C. Gibson; A. W. Brussell.
　　　　Discussion. 91:1-2+. D. '57.

Saturday Evening Post. 230:31+. Ag. 24, '57. Can labor live down Dave Beck? B. Pearse, C. S. Ching, eds.

Senior Scholastic. 70:15-17. Ap. 12, '57. Labor takes the spotlight.

Senior Scholastic. 71:14-16. S. 20, '57. Operation big sweep in the house of labor.

Social Studies. 47:260-2. N. '56. Right-to-work laws: a changing attitude toward labor. T. J. Hailstones.

*Time. 65:20-2. Je. 20, '55. G.A.W. man.

Town Meeting (Bulletin of America's Town Meeting of the Air) 21, no33:1-12. What will be the effect of the labor merger? M. S. Pitzele and others. D. 11, '55.

U.S. News & World Report. 41:116-19. Ag. 24, '56. Where you don't need to join a union to work.

U.S. News & World Report. 41:66-70+. S. 7, '56. Should labor unions be partisan? interview with James P. Mitchell, secretary of labor.

U.S. News & World Report. 42:124-33. Mr. 8, '57. Story of a union and underworld ties.

U.S. News & World Report. 42:54-6+. Ap. 5, '57. How unions can avoid rackets.

U.S. News & World Report. 43:110+. S. 20, '57. Strike threats of '58.

U.S. News & World Report. 44:103-5. Ja. 17, '58. Why senators are taking a look at Reuther's union.

Vital Speeches of the Day. 21:1314-18. Jl. 1, '55. Industry can afford guaranteed annual wage. W. P. Reuther.

Vital Speeches of the Day. 23:328-30. Mr. 15, '57. Labor racketeering. J. P. Mitchell.

Vital Speeches of the Day. 23:629-35. Ag. 1, '57. Industrial relations, 1975; future role of management and unions in our economy. J. S. Bugas.

Vital Speeches of the Day. 24:77-82. N. 15, '57. Nation's number one problem. George Romney.

Vital Speeches of the Day. 24:174-7. Ja. 1, '58. Protection of individual workers; address, December 5, 1957. J. P. Mitchell.

Vital Speeches of the Day. 24:177-9. Ja. 1, '58. Can labor clean its own house? S. J. Petro.

THIS BOOK MAY BE KEPT

14 Days

and may be renewed if not called for by
someone else.
A fine of 2¢ per day is charged if the book
is kept after the last date stamped below.

DUE	DUE	DUE
DEC 3 '58		
MAR 20 59		
MAR 16 '63		
DEC 15 '72		
APR 19 '84		
APR 11 1987		
APR 07 1988		
MAR 25 1994		
APR 2 4 2005		